SACRED TIME, SACRED PLACE

Sacred Time, Sacred Place

Archaeology and the Religion of Israel

edited by

BARRY M. GITTLEN

Winona Lake, Indiana
EISENBRAUNS
2002

Cataloging-in-Publication Data

Sacred time, sacred place : archaeology and the religion of Israel / edited
by Barry M. Gittlen.
    p. cm.
   Includes bibliographical references.
   ISBN 1-57506-054-X (cloth : alk. paper)
    1. Bible. O.T.—Evidences, authority, etc. 2. Bible. O.T.—
Antiquities. 3. Archaeology and religion. 4. Middle East—
Religion. 5. Judaism—History—To 70 A.D. 6. Jews—History—To
70 A.D. 7. Middle East—Antiquities. I. Gittlen, Barry M.

BS1180.S16 2001
221.9′3—dc21

                2001033724
                CIP

Contents

PART IV
Death in the Life of Israel

INDEXES

Abbreviations

General

EB	Early Bronze Age
GHD	Genealogy of the Hammurapi Dynasty
LB	Late Bronze Age
LXX	Septuagint
MB	Middle Bronze Age
MT	Masoretic Text
NJPSV	New Jewish Publication Society Version
NRSV	New Revised Standard Version
NT	New Testament
OB	Old Babylonian
OT	Old Testament
RS	Field numbers of objects excavated at Ras Shamra
RSV	Revised Standard Version

Reference Works

AASOR	Annual of the American Schools of Oriental Research
AB	Anchor Bible
ABD	*The Anchor Bible Dictionary*. Edited by D. N. Freedman. 6 vols. Garden City, N.Y.: Doubleday, 1992
AfO Beiheft	Archiv für Orientforschung Beiheft
ALASP	Abhandlungen zur Literatur Alt-Syrien-Palästinas
ANEP	Pritchard, J. B. (editor). *The Ancient Near East in Pictures Relating to the Old Testament*. 2d ed. Princeton: Princeton University Press, 1969
ANET	Pritchard, J. B. (editor). *Ancient Near Eastern Texts Relating to the Old Testament*. 3d ed. Princeton: Princeton University Press, 1969
AOAT	Alter Orient und Altes Testament
ARMT	Archives royales de Mari (texts in transliteration and translation)
ASOR Dissertation Series	American Schools of Oriental Research Dissertation Series
ATD	Das Alte Testament Deutsch
BA	*Biblical Archaeologist*
BARev	*Biblical Archaeology Review*
BASOR	*Bulletin of the American Schools of Oriental Research*
BBB	Bonner biblische Beiträge
BDB	Brown, F., S. R. Driver, and C. A. Briggs. *Hebrew and English Lexicon of the Old Testament*. Oxford: Clarendon, 1907
BeO	*Bibbia e oriente*

Bib	*Biblica*
BMB	*Bulletin du Musée de Byrouth*
BN	*Biblische Notizen*
BO	*Bibliotheca Orientalis*
BRL	Galling, K.. *Biblisches Reallexikon*. Tübingen, 1937; 2d ed., 1977
BWANT	Beiträge zur Wissenschaft vom Alten und Neuen Testament
BZ	*Biblische Zeitschrift*
CAD	Oppenheim, A. L., et al. (editors). *The Assyrian Dictionary of the Oriental Institute of the University of Chicago*. Chicago: The Oriental Institute of the University of Chicago, 1956–
CahRB	Cahiers de la Revue biblique
CBQ	*Catholic Biblical Quarterly*
CTM	*Concordia Theological Monthly*
ErIsr	*Eretz-Israel*
HALAT	Koehler, L., and W. Baumgartner, et al. (editors). *Hebräisches und aramäisches Lexikon zum Alten Testament*. 4 Vols. Leiden: Brill, 1967–90
HSM	Harvard Semitic Monographs
HSS	Harvard Semitic Studies
HUCA	*Hebrew Union College Annual*
IEJ	*Israel Exploration Journal*
JANES(CU)	*Journal of the Ancient Near Eastern Society (of Columbia University)*
JAOS	*Journal of the American Oriental Society*
JBL	*Journal of Biblical Literature*
JCS	*Journal of Cuneiform Studies*
JJS	*Journal of Jewish Studies*
JNES	*Journal of Near Eastern Studies*
JNSL	*Journal of Northwest Semitic Languages*
JQR	*Jewish Quarterly Review*
JSOTSup	Journal for the Study of the Old Testament Supplement Series
JTS	*Journal of Theological Studies*
KAI	Donner, H., and W. Röllig. *Kanaanäische und aramäische Inschriften*. Wiesbaden: Harrassowitz, 1962–64
KTU	Dietrich, M., O. Loretz, and J. Sanmartín. *Die Keilalphabetischen Texte aus Ugarit*. Alter Orient und Altes Testament 24. Kevelaer: Butzon & Bercker / Neukirchen-Vluyn: Neukirchener Verlag, 1976
MARI	*Mari: Annales de recherches interdisciplinaires*
MDOG	Mitteilungen der deutschen Orient-Gesellschaft
NABU	*Nouvelles assyriologiques brèves et utilitaires*
NEA	*Near Eastern Archaeology*
OBO	Orbis biblicus et orientalis
OIP	Oriental Institute Publications
OrAnt	*Oriens antiquus*
OTL	Old Testament Library
OTS	*Oudtestamentische Studiën*
PEQ	*Palestine Exploration Quarterly*
PTMS	Pittsburgh Theological Monograph Series

RB	*Revue biblique*
RHPR	*Revue d'histoire et de philosophie religieuses*
RlA	Ebeling, E., et al. (editors). *Reallexikon der Assyriologie*. Berlin: de Gruyter, 1932–
SAHL	Studies in the Archaeology and History of the Levant
SEL	*Studi epigrafici et linguistici*
Sem	*Semitica*
SJOT	*Scandinavian Journal of Old Testament*
StudOr	*Studia Orientalia*
TA	*Tel Aviv*
TCL	Textes cunéiformes du Louvre. Paris: Geuthner, 1910–
TLZ	*Theologische Literaturzeitung*
TynBul	*Tyndale Bulletin*
UBL	Ugaritisch-Biblische Literatur
UF	*Ugarit-Forschungen*
VT	*Vetus Testamentum*
VTSup	Vetus Testamentum Supplements
WZKM	*Wiener Zeitschrift für die Kunde des Morgenlandes*
YO(S)R	Yale Oriental Series, Researches
ZA	*Zeitschrift für Assyriologie*
ZAH	*Zeitschrift für Althebräistik*
ZAW	*Zeitschrift für die Alttestamentliche Wissenschaft*
ZDMG	*Zeitschrift der deutschen morgenländischen Gesellschaft*
ZDPV	*Zeitschrift des deutschen Palästina-Vereins*

Archaeology and the Religion of Israel

BARRY M. GITTLEN

Baltimore Hebrew University

William F. Albright's *Archaeology and the Religion of Israel* long ago established foundations for the multidisciplinary scientific study of Israelite religion. Since that publication, biblicists, archaeologists, and other scholars have made important contributions to the elucidation of Israelite religion. Nevertheless, a concentrated coordinated effort by a variety of scholars of differing specializations must be orchestrated to achieve a new synthesis; that is, to clearly assess and understand the problems, chart new approaches to the issues, and reach possibly new conclusions.

Archaeologists and biblicists have not always clearly and fully communicated with one another. This unfortunate situation has led to the methodologies and goals of each becoming masked by misunderstanding. The biblical text, like the archaeological data, has contexts, associations, and stratigraphy that denote particular sets of behaviors that we want to understand. Our inability to be as sure of the archaeological or of the biblical evidence as we would like to be is matched by the inability of the biblicist and of the archaeologist to keep abreast of developments in each other's field and to competently utilize the most appropriate methodologies of the other field in assessing the relevance of that field's data.

As archaeological inquiry grew more sophisticated, it discovered its inability to answer many of the questions emanating from analysis of the biblical text. This was not necessarily because the knowledge was unattainable; rather, the problem partly resides in our ability to formulate proper questions and appropriate research strategies. Indeed, the problem also results from our own scholarly misconceptions and faulty presuppositions. As biblical research has become literarily as well as historically more sophisticated, these same questions, being posed in different terms, may approach the realm of the answerable. Nevertheless, one's attempt to explain one's conception of the biblical text will continue to be influenced by one's conception of the archaeological evidence and vice versa. This interface of archaeological remains with text and with analogy is basic to the reconstruction of ancient societies in any time and place and is critical in the case of ancient Israelite religion.

The ASOR program unit, Archaeology and the Religion of Israel, was constructed to draw the disciplines of archaeology and biblical studies together; to encourage and enhance the quality of the dialogue; to produce the beginnings of a fundamental study of Israelite religion based not only on the results of new methods of examining textual data but also on the latest archaeological data—a new synthesis.

My 1992 graduate seminar on the archaeology of Israelite religion motivated organizing the ASOR program unit that convened during the Annual Meetings of 1993–1996 and whose results form this book. Conversations with David Noel Freedman, Baruch Halpern, and Bill Dever strengthened my resolve to propose the idea to ASOR. Bill Dever, Ziony Zevit, Mark Smith, and Beth Alpert-Nakhai formed the coordinating committee, which met with me to select each year's topic, speakers, and respondents. This book contains most of the content of those four yearly sessions. Each section, Parts I–IV, consists of the papers and responses of a single year, in the order presented.

I wish to thank all of the participants for their contributions and my committee members for their help, advice, and ideas (Ziony Zevit devised the title "Prayers in Clay"). My secretary, Elise Baron, expertly retyped the manuscripts onto diskettes, which went to Eisenbrauns. Thanks to our editor at Eisenbrauns, Beverly Fields, and to Jim Eisenbraun for moving the project along. Finally, thanks to my students' questions, the pages that follow represent another step toward mutual understanding between the "two cultures" of archaeology and biblical studies.

Part I

Charting the Course:
The Relationship between Text and Artifact

Religion Up and Down, Out and In

JONATHAN Z. SMITH

University of Chicago

I

Perhaps not since that short-lived, all but mythical moment—just how mythical, the on-going work of David A. Trall continues to reveal—when Schliemann "in the name of the divine Homer," "rechristened" and "baptized" his dig "Troy," noting that its situation "correspond[ed] perfectly with all the statements of the Iliad," have archaeology and philology, site and text (or, in the witty title of one of ASOR's programs several years ago, Tell and Tale) seemed so utterly congruent. The Trojan moment established an expectation, still strong in the public domain, that, like some illustration in a book, the novelties of archaeological discovery would confirm and/or supplement familiar old texts. While many examples of the latter could be offered, one only needs to think of the *New York Times*, which in its coverage of Meso-American archaeology always emphasizes the problematic nature of the evidence and its effect on rival theories, while in its coverage of biblical archaeology always emphasizes the confirmatory quality of the data and rarely suggests the presence of theory, let alone theoretical discord. (The *Times*'s reporting of the challenge of Norman Golb to the consensual understanding of the Qumran site remains a notable exception.)

At the level of theory, there is no principled reason to expect congruency between the two disciplines. Indeed, there is every reason to both predict and celebrate their incongruency. At the simplest level, what counts as data for each (using this term in its proper sense as a fact taken for granted for purposes of an argument) is different, and complex rules of translation would have to be proposed to compare, to translate one into the terms of the other or to reduce one to the other. Simple juxtaposition will not do. The general absence of such rules in the literature precludes further discussion. (Colin Renfrew's *Archaeology and Language* [1987] constitutes an important beginning attempt at this enterprise.)

It is a familiar chestnut that no matter how many white swans one observes they do not justify the utterance that all swans are white, but the observation of one black swan is sufficient to invalidate the utterance. For our

3

purposes, this means that multiple instances of the same carry no more gravity than a single exemplum. It is difference that generates thought, whether at the level of data or of theory. Thus, a model gains its cognitive power by not according in all respects to that which it models. "Map is not territory" and is, therefore, of intellectual value. In the words of one scholar, the intrinsic value of a small-scale model is that it compensates "for the renunciation of sensible dimensions by the acquisition of intelligible dimensions" (Lévi-Strauss 1966: 24). Hence, depending on one's philosophical orientation, the common employment of terminology for models such as "simplicity" or "approximation," as well as the on-going debate on the relationship of models to both theories and analogies, witness to the intellectual necessity for incongruency, most especially in interdisciplinary discourse such as that proposed between text-based studies and archaeology. Interdisciplinary research and theory may be formalized as a Venn diagram. The relatively small domain in which two disciplines overlap or intersect is, to no small degree, a function of the larger spheres in which they remain different with respect to both data and theoretical interests. Interdisciplinary research is necessarily narrower than the total disciplinary domains that it brings into mutual intellectual relationship.

Within biblical archaeological/literary discourse, the non-event of the "Conquest," with its attendant negative implications for both the "Exodus" and the so-called "Settlement" of Canaan, has played the exemplary role of the black swan in making plain the essential differences between the models employed by the two fields of study. It is a difference that no amount of prattle about "faith and history" can paper over. Of more significance, it is a difference that has given rise to provocative (that is to say, to interesting) theories in both fields in answer to new questions—especially, in this case, to matters of "continuity/discontinuity" and "ethnic identity," which have strong analogues in other fields of study as yet scarcely deployed because of the continued prevalence of notions of absolute uniqueness rather than of the ordinary, reciprocal kind ("if Israel is unique with respect to Canaan, then Canaan is unique with respect to Israel"). It is one thing to observe distinctiveness, difference, and individuality; these are all categories that invite comparison and explanatory efforts. It is quite another matter to assert uniqueness, which prevents, indeed forbids, such efforts.

To no small degree, the tension between textual scholars and archaeologists hinges on this issue of comparability. Much literary theory (including current ones) insists that a literary text, at some basic level, is incomparable; much archaeological theory (as well as practice) is fundamentally comparative. More than 60 years ago, Leonard Woolley gave a BBC series on archaeology for lay folk. As his central thesis, he insisted that "the historical value of an object depends not so much on the nature of the object itself as on its associations." While he was thinking primarily in terms of gold versus clay, the distinction he drew remains cogent: for the biblical scholar, the text of the Bible has incomparable worth in and of itself (whether expressed in a theological or secular idiom). For the archaeologist, a datum has interest only when placed in a systemic frame; it has no intrinsic worth. (I think here, among others, of the 1972 response of Charles Redman to a paper by G. Ernest Wright, in which Wright insisted on the uniqueness of the Near Eastern tell. Redman rejoined: "It would be more useful to analyze the tell as the center of a region which is itself the unit of reconstruction and analysis. . . . The city takes on characteristics not inherent in itself, but are values given to it by the way it functions within an on-going system" [Redman 1972: 133].)

The discontinuity between the archaeological and the textual has become, in the hands of many literary scholars, an occasion for the jettisoning of any historicistic approach to the text that is understood, through an appeal to an ill-assorted group of literary theories, as autonomous and, therefore, essentially open to modes of intrinsic interpretation, the latest secular version of a well-known model of inspiration. But, one must observe, in a manner all too typical of the appropriation of methods from the human sciences by religious studies, these methods are never accepted in their strong form and hence tend to be inconsequential. For example, there was a brief flurry of structuralist interpretations of biblical texts capitalizing on the requirement to take the text "as it is," without postulating a prehistory. But the same scholars ignore the strong structuralist insistence that the codes are universal and that, therefore, no privilege can be conferred on any particular text as well as the concomitant, equally strong, methodological requirement that "a text consists of all of its versions," which would prevent any focus on the valued canon as normative.

By contrast, because of its focus on relations, it has been possible for many forms of archaeological research, especially those influenced by American systematics, to be genuinely multidisciplinary, cutting across even the traditional divide between the human and natural sciences. (In the absence of a reigning paradigm, or in the present state of unease with respect to the desirability of a paradigm, interdisciplinarity, in the sense of a Venn diagram, has yet to be achieved.) Among many implications, this means that the basic archaeological dossier of potential data is that much greater, so that certain analytic techniques (especially those featuring statistical or quasi-statistical procedures such as clustering or diffusion) become possible. There is theoretical interest in proposing a diffusion thesis; there is no theoretical interest in the literary penchant for genealogies, "backgrounds," and "influences." The only field within literary studies that approaches the archaeological with respect to the generation of "thick" dossiers is text criticism, but even here the presuppositions of autograph/original and of archetype and variations preclude its results from having theoretical interest.

It may well be that the sort of nominalism, effectively argued for recently by Philip R. Davies, is an accurate description, though scarcely a prescription, for our present situation. Davies writes that we must learn to think in terms of

> three Israels: one is literary (the biblical), one is historical (the inhabitants of the northern Palestinian highlands during part of the Iron Age [as recovered archaeologically]) and the third, "ancient Israel," is what [contemporary] scholars have constructed out of an amalgamation of the two others. (Davies 1992: 11)

This sort of disjunctive model seems parallel to another dichotomy. As confidence in the "fit" between the archaeological and the literary dims, the relatively early dating of much biblical tradition increasingly yields to an exilic and postexilic dating which, among other things, renders the "fit" implausible. While there are good reasons to applaud this shift, it presents its own theoretical problems. It is even more wedded than the "settlement" controversy to a crisis/response model of history. As debates in other areas of historical studies have persistently demonstrated, the definition of "crisis" has proved to be more difficult of specification than many of its supporters suppose.

II

Thus far I have made several observations congruent with my understanding of the disciplinary agendum as formulated by our conveners. But the protocol of this program unit went on to raise a substantive topic: that of "the religion of Israel." Therefore it seems appropriate to shift lenses and adopt my more usual point of view as that of a student of religion who is a consumer of both literary and archaeological studies but a practioner of neither. This is a different sort of discourse in that neither of the two fields under review has proposed much of interest. That is to say, there is little explicit meditation on the subject of religion. It is generally assumed to be a collection, an inventory, of discrete items or topics, most of which are capable of being interpreted by some highly generalized functionalist approach. The construal of religion above the ground in literary studies joins with the construction of religion below the ground in archaeological studies to produce a weak modeling of religion "on the ground."

Let me begin with a statement that will seem at first to be utterly paradoxical: the Bible in its prebiblical form, that is to say in the period under discussion, is not a religious document. I mean this in two quite ordinary senses and not in any ambitious Barthian fashion.

First, despite much scholarly ingenuity, there are no clear social loci in ancient Israel for the various sorts of materials and traditions that became biblical. (For that matter, despite recent interest in the question, there is no convincing historical or social locus for the origin of the collection, most likely beginning in the third century B.C.E., which later came to be associated with the canon of the Hebrew Bible.) Some of the historical materials may well have been situated in royal courts (though surely not Solomon's!); some of the narrative and legal traditions seem to have been housed in late, learned circles; the prophetic materials may have come from small groups of devotees—but, for example, no biblical materials can be convincingly related to what would seem to be the most dominant religious and political institution, the Temple. I take the fantasy of "covenant renewal festivals," the diversity of inconclusive attempts to assign cultic functions to the individual components of the Psalter, and other similar stratagems to be, at the very least, indirect testimony to this fact. For the later period of Bible-formation we can go further, along the lines suggested by Gary Porton, and see Temple(s) and Bible(s) as oppositional authorities (Porton 1981: 64–65).

The second sense in which the Bible in its prebiblical form is not a religious document stems from its nature as a second-order text, a nature already grasped by Hubert and Mauss in their classic essay on sacrifice (1898) when they term the priestly sacrificial materials an "arbitrary . . . simplification . . . of the system of sacrifices. . . . In reality, these four typical forms are not . . . real types of sacrifice, but kinds of abstract component elements" (Hubert and Mauss 1964: 16). This abstraction results in the fact, among other consequences, that no ritual, so described, can be performed on the basis of the literature by either priest or lay person. Whatever else they are, the biblical materials correspond neither to official praxis nor to lay cultic activity.

This latter point is worth emphasizing because it has consequences for the most perduring formulation of the relationship between archaeological and literary studies with respect to Israelitic religion(s)—the notion that the literary data constitute an "official" or "elitist" religion while archaeological data open a window to "popular" or "folk" belief and practice, suggesting, thereby, that the two data bases can be "complimentary," Venn diagram-like.

The positive, correlative possibilities inherent in this sort of formulation are further strained by the choice of a tertiary notion as most characteristic of the second-order biblical texts, the concept of "monotheism" (even when apparently softened in expressions such as "Yahwism"), which does not occur within the texts but is rather the result of one sort of reflection upon them.

The preoccupation with the overdetermined issue of monotheism (along with apparently concomitant constructs such as "centralization") has skewed the discussion of archaeological data by focusing too much attention on efforts at explaining the presence of Canaanite deities (which, by sheer virtue of their presence are, of course, Israelitic deities) and the varied phenomena of locality, resulting among other consequences in the widespread use of inadequate interpretive categories ("fertility deities," "nature gods/goddesses," and the like) that have been subject to searching criticism in the wider fields of religious studies.

Indeed, it may be argued, the deities' presence should have occasioned no surprise. At the level of the particular, I would have thought that Morton Smith's model of "functional monotheism" in the ancient Near East would have disposed of the question (M. Smith 1952: 137–40). At the general level, as magnificently illustrated by the work of Mel Spiro on the alleged atheism of Theravada Buddhism, the fact that there is a discrepancy between what some folks say they (religiously) do or believe and what they actually do is a ubiquitous phenomenon in religion that does not require the postulation of ethnic- or class-based dichotomies for its explanation (Spiro 1967: 247–53). For contemporary societies, it is consciousness of this very gap that makes field work necessary and that, ultimately, strongly privileges the anthropologist's interpretation over the interpretation of the native.

What ought to be welcomed in the archaeological challenge to literary data is not the discovery that the literature represents a theory of Israelitic religion that ignores diversities, but a closer accounting of the cost of that archaic theoretical enterprise and an occasion to undertake an attempt to account for its interests.

It is remarkable what is not taken up in the biblical text, except occasionally in narrative asides. Some of these lacunae can be met by archaeological findings. We know almost nothing about birth (whether medical or cultic), little about marriage, less about death and funerary observances, let along anything concerning a cult of the dead. We know a great deal about forbidden animal foods that no one would have eaten in any case but little about people's ordinary diet, let alone any rituals attending daily meals. In short, we know almost nothing about that wide class of central rituals called "life-crisis" rites, let alone the wider sphere of domestic religion. It is the latter that archaeology provides the richest evidence for, although we lack firm conceptual tools for its interpretation (see now van der Toorn 1996).

It is not that the horizon of the texts is overwhelmingly focused on public, institutionalized models of religion; after all, the strand of tradition that we label "priestly" is preoccupied with some rituals that have clearly domestic loci: circumcision, sabbath observance, and, to some degree, Passover. It is rather that the biblical texts are curiously and selectively silent on the public sphere of religion as well. We learn much from the biblical texts concerning the ideology of that central religious actor, the king, but almost nothing of his coronation (or funeral) rites. Considering the space devoted to the topic, we have remarkably little performative information about sacrifices of any sort. In what hand is the knife held? How are the animals slaughtered? Are there any verbal formulas of dedication? What are the rituals for consecrating altars? In short, the logic of the texts' economy has yet to be deciphered. This is an urgent task for literary studies if it is to take up the question of religion; it is a task made more urgent by the expansion of the items of religion as disclosed through archaeological discovery.

In short, I welcome the call for conversation between archaeological and literary scholars, while cautioning that much theoretical work needs to be done: a theory of discourse and translation to govern the conversation and a more adequate theory of religion to govern interpretation. The latter will have to display far less concern for issues of "borrowing" and genealogy and give more attention to matters of semantics, syntactics, and pragmatics. Nevertheless, I applaud the effort. It is high time a Bible dictionary had an entry under "Religion," precisely because it is *not* a native term.

Bibliography

Achinstein, Peter
  1964   Models, Analogies and Theories. *Philosophy of Science* 31: 328–50.
Davies, Philip R.
  1992   *In Search of "Ancient Israel."* JSOTSup 148. Sheffield: Sheffield Academic Press.
Dever, William G.
  1990   *Recent Archaeological Discoveries and Biblical Research.* Seattle: University of Washington Press.
  1992   Archaeology, Syro-Palestinian and Biblical. Pp. 354–67 in vol. 1 of *Anchor Bible Dictionary.* New York: Doubleday.
Dunnell, Robert C.
  1971   *Systematics in Prehistory.* New York: Free Press.
Hubert, Henri, and Mauss, Marcel
  1899   Essai sur la nature et la fonction du sacrifice. *Année sociologique* 2: 29–138.
  1964   *Sacrifice: Its Nature and Function,* trans. W. D. Halls. Chicago: University of Chicago Press.
Lévi-Strauss, Claude
  1966   *The Savage Mind.* Chicago: University of Chicago Press.
Moore, C. B.
  1974   P. 139 in *Reconstructing Complex Societies: An Archaeological Colloquium,* ed. Charlotte B. Moore. Bulletin of the American Schools of Oriental Research Supplement Series 20. N.p.: American Schools of Oriental Research.
Porton, Gary G.
  1981   Defining Midrash. Pp. 55–92 in vol. 1 of *The Study of Ancient Judaism,* ed. Jacob Neusner. New York: KTAV.

Redman, Charles L.
    1974   Comments on Professor Wright's Paper. Pp. 130–39 in *Reconstructing Complex Societies: An Archaeological Colloquium*, ed. Charlotte B. Moore. Bulletin of the American Schools of Oriental Research Supplement 20. N.p.: American Schools of Oriental Research.

Renfrew, Colin
    1987   *Archaeology and Language: The Puzzle of Indo-European Origins*. London: Jonathan Cape..

Smith, Jonathan Z.
    1987   *To Take Place: Toward Theory in Ritual*. Chicago Studies in the History of Judaism. Chicago: University of Chicago Press.

    1990   *Drudgery Divine: On the Comparison of Early Christianities and the Religions of Late Antiquity*. Jordan Lectures in Comparative Religion 14. London: University of London School of Oriental Studies / Chicago: University of Chicago Press.

Smith, Morton
    1952   The Common Theology of the Ancient Near East. *JBL* 71: 135–48.

Spiro, Melford E.
    1967   *Burmese Supernaturalism: A Study in the Explanation and Reduction of Suffering*. Prentice-Hall College Anthropology Series. Englewood Cliffs, N.J.: Prentice-Hall.

Toorn, Karel van der
    1996   *Family Religion in Babylonia, Syria and Israel: Continuity and Change in the Forms of Religious Life*. Studies in the History and Culture of the Ancient Near East 7. Leiden: Brill.

Watson, Patty J.; LeBlanc, Steven A.; and Redman, Charles L.
    1971   *Explanation in Archaeology: An Explicitly Scientific Approach*. New York: Columbia University Press.

Woolley, (Charles) Leonard
    1937   *Digging Up The Past*. London: Penguin.

Theology, Philology, and Archaeology: In the Pursuit of Ancient Israelite Religion

WILLIAM G. DEVER

University of Arizona

Introduction

Modern critical biblical scholarship since Wellhausen has made a reconstruction of ancient Israelite religion a primary objective. Indeed, it has assumed that the application of philological and, later, theological methods to the biblical literature would enable us to reach this goal. Then, beginning in this century, it was thought that our understanding of Israelite religion would be enhanced immeasurably by adding archaeology to the basic disciplines of philology and theology, and thus "biblical archaeology" grew apace with the "biblical theology" movement (often in the hands of the same practitioners, as with G. E. Wright).

In the past fifteen years or so, there has been a hopeful revival of interest in Israelite religion and cult in several scholarly fields, including archaeology (as I had predicted in the Freedman Festschrift; see Dever 1983), and even the beginning of the interdisciplinary *dialogue* that I believe is crucial. Yet, as I shall show, the pursuit has been largely in vain: the quarry still eludes us. Nor shall I run it to ground in this essay; I can only attempt a critique of the faulty *methodology* of all three subdisciplines—which in my opinion has led us astray—and point anew to the common goal to which we should aspire.

The Philological Approach to Israelite Religion

In many ways, philology has been the basic tool of modern critical biblical scholarship. Insofar as the philological revolution of the 18th and 19th centuries was a child of the Enlightenment and thus a reaction against the dogmatic theology that had stifled any but an orthodox understanding of the Hebrew Bible for centuries, it was refreshing. It was also promising, because its emphases on empirical data and on comparative methods made it compatible with other modern approaches to Israelite religion, such as *Religionsgeschichte*, ethnography, folklore, and anthropology. All this seemed to move the study of ancient religions from the realm of fascination with primitive superstition and the occult to documenting respectable cultural-historical phenomena. In method, the newer approaches, especially philology, substituted *reason* for orthodox belief, personal piety, or any other motivation (Jewish, Christian, or secular) for identifying with a particular religious tradition. Thus by the early 20th century there emerged the notion of an objective, academic, ecumenical "science of religion." Philology would become the queen of this science.[1]

In my view, this ambition rested not on a defensible concept of religion but on a conceit. The fundamental flaw in the philological approach lay in its unexamined positivist presuppositions. It is simply *assumed* (1) that the texts of the Hebrew Bible as they have come down to us, despite the seemingly intractable nature of some passages, constitute overall an accurate witness to the actual phenomenon of ancient Israelite religious belief and practice; and (2) that the rapid progress of comparative Semitic philology would enable us to read these texts correctly and comprehend their meaning. As Morton Smith put it in his 1968 presidential address to the Society of Biblical Literature,

> for a correct history of the Israelites we must have the archaeological facts determined quite objectively and independently by competent archaeologists, and the biblical facts likewise determined by competent philologies, and then we can begin to compare them. (Smith 1968: 34)

In other words, philologians were confident that they really could penetrate behind the obfuscation of centuries of theological interpretations to *das Ding an Sich*—if not to religious truth then at least to an "exegetical truth" based not on correct belief but on a correct reading of the *texts*. Much of the vaunted optimism of classic Protestant Liberalism in its heyday regarding the task of reconstructing Israelite religion rested on the assumed superiority of such an "objective approach," largely philological.

Today this seems naive, wistful, and rather sad. Already in the late 19th century, as Baruch Halpern (1988: 23) points out, the Greek philologian Burckhardt had castigated then-burgeoning classical philology for its "spiritual bankruptcy." It is not simply that the texts—Greek, Latin, Hebrew, or ancient Near Eastern—are not truly representative of the whole gamut of ancient society and culture; or even that such texts are highly symbolic, cryptic "encoded messages" about past human thought and behavior that can never be fully deciphered.

---

1. For orientation to the history of *Religionsgeschichte* and related approaches, see Hahn 1956; Kraeling 1955; and McKenzie and Haynes 1993.

The more intransigent problem with mere philology is that such an excessively rationalistic, and ultimately literalistic, approach to any religion can never grasp its spiritual reality, if I may phrase it thus. Or to put it another, less impressionistic way: *literature is not life* but, rather, the product of the intellectual and literary imagination of a creative few. Thus the study of texts of the Great Tradition alone, no matter how fanatically pursued or capable of precision in detail, can never enlighten us fully on matters as esoteric and complex as religious belief and practice. In short, in this post-modern, post-positivist era, we ought to acknowledge at least that, even in possession of abundant textual data, we cannot really "reconstruct the past." The past is gone irretrievably; and, whatever our data, as Binford reminds us, we can only draw inferences about "what it was like in the past." All these inferences are indirect and partial; most are untestable; and many are simply modern notions, not derived at all from that past but imposed upon it. What we think we "know" reveals more about us and our ignorance than about the past we are proposing to investigate. To counter von Ranke's familiar phrase, we can never really know "wie es eigentlich gewesen war," historically or archaeologically. But, unlike the current "revisionists," we can know *something*.

These methodological observations may be commonplace; but I should like to apply them specifically to the pursuit of Israelite religion through the medium of texts. As a basic methodological tenet, I would hold that the historical texts of the Hebrew Bible regarding Israelite religion in their present form, as compiled and finally edited by the Deuteronomistic and Priestly schools in the exilic and postexilic periods, are severely limited as sources for understanding the actual nature and development of Israelite religion. This is because the textual tradition is: (1) much later than the events it purports to describe contemporaneously; (2) highly selective, sometimes quite arbitrary, in what it chooses to include; (3) elitist and patriarchal throughout, biased in favor of what the editors thought of as the religious and political Establishment (though that was more ideal than reality); and (4) almost exclusively representative of the extremist views of the orthodox religious parties and scribal schools that produced the final version of the Hebrew Bible after the fall of Judah.

The Bible, as one of my staunch Baptist friends likes to say, is "a minority report." It is revisionist history, written in this case not as usual by winners but by the "losers," those who were never really in favor during the monarchy, but who became by default bearers of the *literary tradition* after ancient Israel's history was over. The Hebrew Bible is thus not history but is largely propaganda (even if in what most of us believe to be a good cause). By its own admission, the Bible is not the story of what really happened but of what the writers and editors *wished* had happened—and might have, had they only been in charge. The fact that we judge these latest redactors of the tradition to have been right in the long run (that is, to our liking) is beside the point.

A recent work of "revisionist" biblical scholarship, Philip R. Davies' *In Search of "Ancient Israel"* (1992), illustrates the ultimate absurdity to which the exclusive use of the philological method leads. Davies contends that there was no "ancient Israel." It is simply a literary construct that has been invented by later Rabbinic Judaism (perpetuated by Christianity as well), in other words, by a postexilic community seeking an identity to vindicate itself in the aftermath of national tragedy. Davies' real villains are those of the "scribal class" who finally shaped the literary tradition, who he thinks were Temple personnel. But they were not consciously producing Scripture, or even a "Bible," just propaganda. Even the language of these "scribal schools" is artificial—not a Hebrew that was ever spoken during the monarchy but an archaizing *Bildungssprache*. In short, *all* the literature of the Hebrew Bible, based on Davies' *philological analysis* (certainly not his amateurish theology or historiography), is Hellenistic, even the prophetic books; a Hasmonean fantasmagoria; worthless as sources of history for any other period. There is no "ancient Israel"; but Davies is its chronicler.[2]

Davies' nihilism is echoed in both of the most recent, comprehensive attempts to write a history of ancient Israel: T. L. Thompson, *Early History of the Israelite People from the Written and Archaeological Sources* (1992); and the late Gösta Ahlström, *The History of Ancient Palestine from the Paleolithic Period to Alexander's Conquest* (1993). These recent works do not in my opinion signal a new approach, much less a breakthrough in writing the history of Israel. Rather, they mark a return full-circle to Wellhausen; they simply confirm the intellectual exhaustion, after a century and a half, of the philological method and the classic literary-critical apparatus that accompanied it (Dever 1995). In this pessimistic view, I as an archaeologist am neither beyond the pale nor alone. Rolf Rentdorff, in the inaugural issue of the new journal *Biblical Interpretation*, in an article entitled "The Paradigm is Changing: Hopes—and Fears," points out that the classic documentary hypothesis is dead. The question is, rather, whether the texts are preexilic or postexilic; and the consensus is for the latter dating. "We will have to redesign our image of Israel's history and the history of its religion" (Rendtorff 1993). But on what basis?

This leads me to a few final observations on the attempts of biblical scholars to reconstruct ancient Israelite religion from texts alone. They seem to think that texts are the only "primary data"; that the study of texts is "objective"; and that archaeology, because it typically does not produce texts, is "mute." As I have remarked elsewhere, archaeology is not mute, but perhaps

2. For orientation to biblical "revisionism," as well as my own sharp critique, see Dever 1995a; 1998; forthcoming; and references there. For the quotations from Davies, see Davies 1992.

the historian is deaf. The bias of many biblical scholars against material culture remains is often due, I am sorry to say, to a combination of arrogance,
parochialism, and ignorance—yes, ignorance of the potential of anything but
epigraphic remains to illuminate Israelite religion.

The literary bias of biblical scholarship is nowhere better illustrated than
in the fact that virtually all "histories of the religion of Israel" end up being
simply histories of the *literature about* that religion. Clearly, such efforts remain
"hung up in the prolegomenon," far short of the goal. Yet in this category I
would place most treatments of Israelite religion, from Sellin's *Israelitische-
Jüdische Religionsgeschichte* (1933); to Kaufmann's monumental *History of
Israelite Religion* (1937–56); Pfeiffer's *Religion in the Old Testament* (1961);
Krauss's *Worship in Israel* (1966); Ringgren's *Israelite Religion* (1966); and Fohrer's *History of Israelite Religion* (1972). Rainer Albertz's two-volume *A History
of Israelite Religion in the Old Testament Period* (1994) is a refreshing exception
(Dever 1995; 1996).

It is commendable, of course, that one of the main thrusts of biblical
scholarship since the rise of form and tradition criticism two generations ago
has been to seek to understand individual texts and larger pericopes concerning both Israelite history and religion in their original *Sitz im Leben*. I would
argue, however, that in practice biblical scholars have settled merely for a *Sitz
im Literatur*. And as we noted above, literature does not necessarily mirror
"real life"—at least not the life of the majority. At best, we might obtain from
the biblical and other texts a picture of "official" religion or the state cult but
not of "folk" religion, except in the caricature of the biblical writers. At
worst, the portrait drawn from the texts is so misinterpreted that it ends up
being simply a modern theological construct read back into the texts.

As a cautionary tale, I point out that recent analyses of Buddhology
have suggested that the discipline is predominantly a modern, Western,
male-dominated, exclusively textually-based enterprise. (Does this sound familiar? It is characteristic of much of biblical scholarship.) Such a discipline
focuses, not surprisingly, on intellectual issues that are perceived by the
scholars involved as crucial in classical Buddhist theology—*not* on actual
Buddhist practice in its larger, mostly Oriental context and especially in the
more remote past. By contrast, departing momentarily from the Classical
texts, from *Scripture* with its inherent limitations, and looking instead at
other sources of data—such as folk shrines, ruined monasteries, tombs, and
burial inscriptions and graffiti—produces a rather different picture. Which
portrait is the most reliable? Which religion, if either, is "normative"? If
canonical texts reflect mostly orthodox theology, do we not need complimentary *material cultures remains* to inform us about nonconformist ideology,
popular religion, and the actual religious practices of the majority? Canonical texts alone will not suffice. This is what Karel van der Toorn has deni-
grated as "book religion."

The Theological Approach to Israelite Religion

A second traditional approach to the religion of ancient Israel has been through theology, either so-called "biblical" theology, or systematic and dogmatic theology.[3] Whatever the merits of this approach, I shall argue that it is ill-suited to a productive investigation of ancient Israelite religion.

Since Johann Philip Gabler's famous inaugural address at Altdorft in 1787, there have been innumerable attempts to distinguish "biblical theology" from systematic or dogmatic theology by separating it as a descriptive-historical discipline that forms the basis of the latter, resting largely on rational methods and philological analysis. This "historical" school of biblical theology is represented in modern times by Wrede, Jacob, Wright, Wernberg-Møller, and others. It has found its most forceful and persuasive contemporary support in Krister Stendahl's (1962) now-famous insistence on separating the historical, exegetical, and theological tasks into two questions: "What *did* it mean?" and "What *does* it mean?" To this, I would add somewhat hopefully a third dimension to our inquiry: "What really *happened* in the past that gave rise to the tradition?"

Despite a historical thrust of some sort or another, the fact is that the vast majority of Old Testament theologies in the last two centuries have had a frankly confessional character—that is, their goal has been to reconstruct a "normative" religion of ancient Israel as a foundation for modern belief and morality within the religious community. That category would certainly include the works of influential 20th-century Old Testament theologians such as Eichrodt, Sellin, Procksch, von Rad, Wright, Knight, Vriezen, Fohrer, Westermann, Clements, Zimmerli, Kaiser, and Hasel, among others.

Robert Dentan's useful survey, *Preface to Old Testament Theology* (1963), defines biblical theology as "the study of the religious ideas of the Bible in their historical context," arguing that this is the only definition that does justice to the discipline's history. Yet, four pages later Dentan proceeds to define the branch of biblical theology that we are considering here, Old Testament theology, as "that Christian discipline which treats of the religious ideas of the Old Testament *systematically*, i.e., not from the point of view of historical development, but from that of the structural unity of Old Testament religion, and which gives due regard to the historical and ideological relationship of that religion to the religion of the New Testament" (Dentan 1963: 94–95).

As for the scope of this discipline in the Old Testament period, Dentan contends that (1) it should be limited to the canonical books; (2) it should deal only with "distinctive and characteristic religious ideas" or "normative re-

---

3. The literature on "biblical theology" is vast; but for orientation, see Hasel 1991; and many of the essays in Ollenburger, Martens, and Hasel 1992.

ligion," not "history or institutions"; (3) it should exclude "mere archaeological information," since "there is no need to go into such matters as the details of the sacrificial cultus or the pre-Hebrew origins of cultic objects and acts"; and (4) it should include a discussion of "Hebrew piety" and ethical principles (Dentan 1963: 96–112). This hardly sounds like a "historical" discipline.

When it comes to method, Old Testament theology becomes even more problematic for the historian of Israelite religion. A number of leading Old Testament scholars and theologians candidly (or is it naïvely?) propose the New Testament—and thus Christian faith—as the starting point for investigating the Old Testament (that is, the religious traditions of ancient Israel). Thus Wolff states: "the OT can be properly understood only in the light of the New," which he then extends to mean that "more essential help can accrue to OT science from the NT than from the ancient Orient" (Wolff 1963: 187, 183). Even Noth announced in his introduction to the *Biblischer Kommentar* that he was editing that the exegetical treatments in these volumes would stress above all that "the NT preaches Christ as the end of the OT acts of God" (quoted in Anderson 1963: 50). Von Rad states: "Often the best 'historical' exegesis is achieved from a theological point of view—that is to say, in the final analysis, from the side of the Christian faith" (von Rad 1963: 38). The extreme of "spiritualizing exegesis" (really *eisegesis*) is surely seen in Wilhelm Vischer's approval of Luther's dictum: *Universa scriptura de solo Christo est ubique*, 'Everywhere the Scripture is about Christ alone' (cited in Anderson 1963: 90).

Such a "pneumatic" approach leads, on the one hand, to the sophisticated but somewhat contradictory position of Bultmann, for whom, as an existentialist living in the last days, the Old Testament is simply irrelevant to the believing Christian community: whoever undertakes to examine the Old Testament as a reflection of the religious mentality of the Israelites (or later Jews) "is stuck in the procedure of a romantic historical view, which is worthless to the present" (Bultmann 1963: 21). Nevertheless, Bultmann's basic antihistoricist tendency drives him to try to understand the Old Testament before dismissing it. And the essential method, not surprisingly, is the *Vorverständnis* or "pre-understanding" that the interpreter derives from the NT. This methodology is fully developed in *Glauben and Verstehen I* (1933) and in many subsequent works.

One may note in passing that Baumgärtel—even more a "Marcionite" than Bultmann—cuts the Gordion knot of Old Testament hermeneutics by declaring simply that the Old Testament is a witness to "a *non-Christian religion*," which "in its self-understanding has *nothing* at all *to do with the gospel*"; or again, "the OT facts are not facts at all, and thus the OT history of salvation (*Heilsgeschichte*) is not a history of salvation at all" (quoted in Wolff 1963: 195; see also Eichrodt 1963: 236).

Pneumatic exegesis leads, at its extreme, to typology, which although vigorously opposed by Bultmann, Baumgärtel, Wright, Barr, and others, is a methodology with which numerous Old Testament theologians have flirted, either coyly or overtly. Among them are Eichrodt, von Rad, Vischer, and others. Typology may take the more benign form of simply seeing the Old Testament as the "prophecy" (*Verheissung*) of which the New Testament is the "fulfillment" (the familiar Pauline and Lutheran dichotomy of Law versus Gospel). Or it may become truly pernicious in the form of allegorical interpretation, which denies to the literary tradition—and thus to the experience and faith of ancient Israel—any historical reality at all. Even as sober a scholar as Zimmerli can declare: "In (Christ's) cross, the impossibility (which the prophets had proclaimed) of a righteousness of Israel's own, and the end of the covenant conceived in the law, emerges radically. . . . In the Resurrection of Christ, however, *the remnant-event of Israel occurs*," an event "made visible" in the new creation (Zimmerli 1963: 113). In short, not only were the interpretations of events on which the writers of the Hebrew Bible based their faith wrong, but the "events" themselves are called into question. That is, they had no intrinsic "reality" but were merely "prototypes"—foreshadowings of the Gospel. Secular or "profane" history, since it is not *Heilsgeschichte*, is not a "true" history, is in fact no history at all. In this apocalyptic perspective, the *eschaton* in which we are living reduces all that precedes it to meaninglessness; *Urzeit* is swallowed up in *Endzeit*. The "Christ-event" becomes the only "authentic" event, because it alone is relevatory.

A final way in which Christian Old Testament theology devalues the history of ancient Israel and its religion is an outgrowth of the salvation-history approach, namely, the appropriation of the Old Testament as simply the starting point of a *Vergegenwärtigung*. The term is difficult to translate precisely, and the concept is rather esoteric. But what is involved is the attempt, not merely to "retell" the story (*nacherzählen*), and thus to contemporize God's savings acts on behalf of Israel, but to "actualize" these events in the proclamation so as to recreate the (supposedly) biblical faith that was originally inspired by the events. This method, *Vergegenwärtigung*, as the most appropriate form of theological discourse, was pioneered by von Rad, followed by Westermann, Porteous, Ackroyd, Anderson, Sanders, and many others. The concept is perhaps most accessible in Wright's popular *God Who Acts: Biblical Theology as Recital* (1952). (I still remember the surge of excitement I felt upon discovering that little book as a seminarian nearly fifty years ago.)

Sometimes regarded as an aspect of the traditio-historical method, this approach actually begs the question of historicity, as Barr (1976) has pointed out trenchantly of Wright's work. The "story" eclipses the "facts." "What really may have happened" in ancient Israel is subverted by the question "What should I *do*?" History is less significant than repetition of the biblical

writers' interpretations (and ours) of the supposed events. Confessional recital may be effective theology; but can it claim to be *history*? Is it even interested in the mundane event? It seems to me that seeing history only *sub specie
aeternitatis* may depreciate it to the point that history is not worth seeing at
all (allegory, again.)

Now the reader may object that this portrait of Old Testament theology
is unfair because it is drawn largely from outdated works. If so, I suggest that
he refer to Gerhard Hasel's very thorough 1991 résumé, *Old Testament Theology: Basic Issues in the Current Debate*. Things have changed very little since
Eichrodt and von Rad. Despite Childs's incisive but premature obituary of
the movement in 1970, in *Biblical Theology in Crisis*, or Barr's frequent, devas-
tating critiques and his somewhat pessimistic view of biblical theology's
chances for survival presented at the ASOR meetings in 1989, biblical theology demonstrates an amazing longevity and vitality—not only in Europe,
and not just in conservative or evangelical circles in America.

Yet in my opinion, Old Testament theology, even in its best guise, represents a dead end (or, better, a closed circle) when it comes to the task of ap-
preciating the religion of ancient Israel *in its own context and on its own terms*.
There are many reasons for its impotence, of which I summarize only a few.

(1) It is obvious that Old Testament theology, as an almost exclusively
Christian enterprise (and largely Protestant at that), proceeds from a Christian stance, from the vantage-point of the Christian community and tradition. Such a bias, in my mind, hopelessly compromises the investigation,
indeed precludes any honest historical scholarship. The last books of the Hebrew Bible were written two centuries before the Christian era and cannot
have anything to do directly with it. This literature is regarded as the "Old"
Testament only by an incredible *tour de force* that violates its integrity as Hebrew Scripture.

(2) The methodological dilemma of Old Testament theology from the
beginning has been that it must impose an ideological unity on the Hebrew
Bible that is simply not there, one that is artificial, if not arbitrary. Above all,
one must seek *die Mitte*, the center that determines all, or Eichrodt's "cross-
section" (*Querschnitt*) at a particular point in time. If theology does not find
such a unity, it lacks the systematic character that "theology" requires; but if
it supposes that it has found a thematic unity, it is not then genuinely "historical" (that is, true to the facts we know regarding the diversity and complex evolution of Israelite religion). I doubt that the problem can be resolved
without undermining the very foundations of biblical theology as a *separate
discipline*. Some would simply say that there is no "theology" in the Hebrew
Bible, at least not in the modern sense (below).

(3) Even when it is willing to grapple with diversity, Old Testament theology is forced to try to isolate what it calls "normative" religion. That is, it

cannot escape the familiar "faith and history" issue or the issue of "the authority of Scripture" (both Old and New Testaments, of course). This is simply because the discipline cannot be content with being merely descriptive-historical, as most practitioners have concluded de facto, but must assay to be a part of theology. Yet in always seeking "normative" religion (one may ask, whose norm?), Old Testament theology blinds itself to the reality, the *authentic* religion of ancient Israel, "warts and all."

(4) Whatever and however a selection is made from the many strands of literary traditions regarding Israel's religion, the results tend to say more about a given scholar's predilections than the reality. Christian Old Testament theology, for instance, has overwhelmingly preferred the prophetic tradition—despite the fact that it clearly presents a late and minor tradition within ancient Israel and the Hebrew Bible—and has pointedly ignored or rejected the Priestly tradition, with its emphasis on ritual and cult. The Deuteronomistic tradition has been favored by Old Testament theologians secondarily, in my opinion largely because its theological program, masked by quasi-historiographical intentions, suits the "political history" orientation stemming from the Reformation heritage of the Protestant scholars who have dominated Old Testament theology. Indeed, I would argue that the characteristically Protestant mode of Old Testament theology explains many things: its excessively rationalistic preoccupation with ideology, theology, and systematics; its philological penchant in exegesis, stemming from the doctrine of *sola scriptura*; a verbal *Gestalt* that results in a bias against ritual and cult and in favor of the proclamation of the Word; a disproportionate emphasis on faith that stems from Pauline and Lutheran antinomianism, rejects Law out of a false dichotomy with Gospel, and tends to justify faith by appeals to history and historical proofs; its obsession with what Jon Levenson calls "repristinization," which must always find its "biblical" origins, its continuity with an earlier and thus presumably more "authentic" religion. *Why* this compulsion to "baptize" the religion of ancient Israel and the Hebrew Bible, to make Moses (and Paul) a proper Lutheran? Is it not mostly wishful thinking—a "nostalgia for a biblical past that never was"—and perhaps also a chronic crisis of faith, despite the slogan-prevalent doctrine of *sola fide?* An observation of Jon Levenson is eloquent: "In part, biblical theology results from the fact that Christians read the Hebrew Bible through a logic of displacement. It draws much of its energy from the anxieties of the younger sibling" (Levenson 1987: 296).

(5) This leads me to the next objection. Christocentric Old Testament theology, having rejected Judaism as the legitimate heir to the traditions of the Hebrew Bible, tends to go a step further to anti-Semitism. What else can we make of such statements as Bultmann's that the Old Testament is a "miscarriage (*Scheitern*) of history," which is only saved by the fact that its promise

is fulfilled in Christianity (quoted in Hasel 1991: 173)? What of Eichrodt's declaration that Rabbinic Judaism has "only a torso-like appearance in separation from Christianity" (quoted in Levenson 1987: 287)? Or consider Garbini's statement that Judaism as it developed in the postexilic period was a sort of "pious religious fraud" (Garbini 1988: 16). This typically Protestant contempt for Judaism (based, if I may say so, on ignorance of Jewish tradition and literature, especially biblical commentaries, and sometimes simply on the incompetence of would-be Hebraists) goes all the way back to Wellhausen. He found the "center" of Old Testament religion not at the point from which later Judaism drew its very existence—the Law as Torah—but rather in the "ethical monotheism" of the 8th–7th century prophets. This he believed to have been the loftiest stage in the evolution of Israelite religion, after which all was decadence. (Admiration for the prophets, or appreciation of their contemporary relevance, need not carry us that far.)

The other side of this appropriation of the Hebrew Bible as Christian Scripture—as grist for the theological mill—is the curious fact that *Jews*, meanwhile, as Levenson has shown, have never even been interested in biblical theology. This disaffection of Jewish biblical scholars is due not simply to the latent anti-Semitism of some of Old Testament theology or to its Christocentric character and context. It is due to the fundamental *differences* in Judaism, which has traditionally focused not on theology but on practice, which "lacks the apocalyptic urgency of apostolic Christianity" (Levenson 1993: 46–51). Even orthodox Judaism has deliberately and self-consciously separated itself from the religion of ancient Israel and "biblical faith." Judaism has little interest in restoring the Temple and none in reviving the sacrificial system. It accepts the later Talmud and Mishnah almost on a par with Scripture and feels no need to "historicize" biblical studies. Levenson compares Judaism's typical stance with Protestantism's quest for historical certitude and for the systematization of religious beliefs in theology, concluding that Jews today approach the past, even the biblical past, partly in imitation of non-Jews. They do so, however, "not because of faith, but because of the lack of it, not in hopes of defining a theology, but of finding a replacement for theology" (Levenson 1987: 290). To be sure, the late Moshe Goshen-Gottstein, a brilliant and seminal Jewish thinker, has proposed a "Tanakh theology" alongside Christian Old Testament theology (Goshen-Gottstein 1987). But he conceives this quite frankly as a confessional enterprise, like most Old Testament theology, with no pretensions to descriptive-historical "objectivity," more typically Jewish philosophy than theology. And he acknowledges that in this enterprise he is entirely alone among Jewish scholars, a maverick. The near-total absence of "biblical theologies" among Jewish scholars—the community that surely represents the mainstream of continuity with the various tributaries of the Hebrew Bible—should at least give us pause. Even in its most benign manifestation, Christian Old Testament theology is an enormous piece of *hutzpah*.

In concluding this brief summary of Old Testament theology, I hold that this discipline, by definition, is better conceived as a branch of theology than of biblical studies, at least in the historical sense—that is, it employs philology and exegesis but is largely an aspect of the use of the Bible by the church. Old Testament theology, however legitimate and useful, in my opinion belongs in the realm of Christian apologetics and is inimical to a genuinely historical investigation of Israelite religion. Where historical investigation is concerned, Old Testament theology is parochial, elitist, excessively rationalistic, dogmatic, ultimately sterile when it comes to grasping the actual variety and vitality of religious belief and practice in ancient Israel. It produces only a chimera, a dangerous illusion.

The Archaeological Approach to
Ancient Israelite Religion

Thus far, we have looked at the attempt to understand Israelite religion through its ideology, by the philological and theological analyses of the canonical texts of the Hebrew Bible. Now we turn to archaeology and its ability to reveal religious *practice*, as reflected in the material remains of the cult. First, however, we must offer a definition of religion that differs from the definition presupposed by most investigators, proceeding as they do almost exclusively on the basis of texts. For these scholars, the texts of the Hebrew Bible are preferred—indeed considered the only "primary" data—because they reflect: (1) what should have been normative beliefs; (2) official or state religion; and (3) the orthodox literary tradition in its final, frozen form. Now the biblical texts may indeed reflect these aspects of Israelite religion; but if so, there is an obvious bias that is elitist, establishment-oriented, heavily theological, interested in the cult as liturgy, and dominated by the overriding concept of "political history." The bias of the biblical texts is evidently *shared* by most commentators, who operate as though analysis of these texts is the proper path to reconstructing the "authentic" religion of ancient Israel. Such a bias, however, stems from the conception of religion as (1) ideology and (2) institutional power. Without necessarily offering a critique of this notion of religion, I simply ask whether it is a coincidence that all of the writers and editors of the Hebrew Bible and the vast majority of its later interpreters up to the present day have been literati, officials of the religious establishment in one way or another, authoritarian in outlook, and male. Here, then, is one tradition, a tradition that has been regnant.

By contrast, archaeology is biased toward (1) artifactual remains as data; (2) the ways in which material objects mirror human individual and social behavior; (3) the diversity of religious manifestations and their evolution over time; (4) the cult in all its forms, official and popular; and (5) the larger socio-economic context of religion. With archaeology, the investigation focuses not on ideology but on religious *practice*; not on theoretical conformity but on the actual variety of religious expressions, that is, on "popular religion."[4]

Such a phenomenological or functionalist approach to religion through archaeological remains cannot, of course, do justice to all dimensions of religion, which always has something to do with ideology and power. But if religion, as a sociocultural and historical phenomenon, is what the majority of people *actually* believe and do in the name of that religion—not simply what theologians and clerics say they *ought* to believe and do—then we have a practical working definition.

I shall argue that this definition is one in which both textual and artifactual studies can cooperate, with the expectation of significant results. Moreover, such a joint enterprise is likely to provide more detailed, better-balanced, and ultimately more satisfying portraits of ancient Israelite religion. But the interdisciplinary inquiry and the dialogue that I envision can obviously be fruitful *only* if archaeology can become an equal partner, that is, can actually produce "primary data" that parallel the data of the biblical texts. I am confident that it can, and I am not alone.

One of the ironies of the current impasse (shall we say "crisis"?) in Israelite historiography is that at the very time when biblical scholars have almost despaired of writing a satisfactory history of ancient Israel and its religion, some archaeologists are thinking of taking up the challenge. This is no surprise to me. Indeed, even during the virulently antihistorical phase of the early New Archaeology, I assumed that the maturation of a *genuinely* socio-anthropological approach would bring Syro-Palestinian archaeology back to history—this time with adequate tools for the task. And this is just what is happening in today's "post-processual" archaeology, as seen in the work of Ian Hodder and a growing number of other archaeologists. We are beginning to move away from more extreme materialist and determinist paradigms that sought to explain cultural adaptation and change only in terms of ecological and technological factors. We are moving instead toward an "archaeology of society," in which ideology, including religion—the ancients', and ours—is seen to play a major role (one thrust of the new Critical Archaeology). There has also been a focus recently in structuralist archaeology on symbols meaning and "deep structure" that have created almost a subbranch of archaeology and cult. Now there is even an "archaeology of mind" in the wind, of which

4. There has been growing interest in "popular religion" in recent years. Cf. Dever 1987; 1990; 1995b; 1996; 1997a; Holladay 1987; Ackerman 1992; Berlin-erblau 1993; van der Toorn 1997; Zevit forthcoming.

many are very skeptical, although I think without good cause.[5] (We *need* to recapture the vision of the people behind the pots.)

Based on these and other trends in the larger discipline of archaeology, of which biblical scholars are generally unaware, I have been speaking and writing optimistically for the past decade on the potential of a mature, autonomous, academic, and professional discipline of Syro-Palestinian archaeology for illuminating the Israelite cult. This is because, in my view, archaeological data are *not* "mute," as an astonishingly large number of biblical scholars still seem to think, parroting Noth in the 1950s. As I have suggested elsewhere, some historians are simply deaf—or, shall we say, illiterate. Ernst Axel Knauf (1991: 41) has pointed out cogently that the Hebrew Bible is mute for those who do not know Hebrew. In exactly the same way, the "archaeological record," however eloquent a commentary it may be on human thought and behavior, is a text that cannot be read by those who do not know the vocabulary, grammar, and syntax of material culture and the modern discipline of archaeology (Dever 1997b).

This is precisely why Syro-Palestinian archaeology today is a separate, highly specialized, professional discipline, no longer simply "the handmaiden of biblical history" (an unfortunate metaphor). And it is also why as an archaeologist I am appalled by the spate of recent attempts by biblical scholars to "play archaeologist." I refer to several works of Flanagan, Thompson, Ahlström, Davies, and others (Dever 1995a). To give them credit, these scholars are reacting against traditional, narrowly theological views of Israel's history, as I am; and they do attempt to take archaeological data seriously. But so-called "archaeological syntheses" by textual scholars are usually presumptuous; ill-informed; lacking in critical judgement and balance; full of dreadful jargon, so idiosyncratic that they are amusing; without an independent value. Not only are they amateurish and incompetent, but they are *monologues*—not the dialogue between specialists that I have been advocating for twenty years. As an example or two of what I mean, the reconstruction of the Iron Age in Flanagan's *David's Social Drama: A Hologram of Israel's Early Iron Age* (1988) is such a caricature that it would not even be recognized by a single Palestinian archaeologist. Or again, to which archaeological "authority" does Davies' *In Search of "Ancient Israel"* (1992) appeal for its nihilist treatment of the Iron Age in Palestine? Tom Thompson! If Syro-Palestinian archaeologists perpetrated such frauds, they would be laughed out of the profession. A fruitful dialogue depends not only on scholarly expertise in one's own field but the honesty, integrity, and humility (yes) to submit one's opinions to the rigid

5. For an orientation to post-processual archaeology, see Whitley 1998 and full references there. For possible applications to Syro-Palestinian archaeology, see Dever 1993.

scrutiny of specialists in allied disciplines. Better recent works of biblical scholars attempting to use archaeological data would be those of Gottwald, Coote and Whitelam, Hopkins, and Dearman—better in the sense of being less pretentious and more balanced. But these are still monologues (cf. Halpern 1997). I hope that a more serious dialogue will be inaugurated in the forthcoming work by myself and others, tentatively entitled A *Social History of Iron Age Palestine and Biblical Israel.*

Assuming that a dialogue is the ideal, what constitutes its archaeological data-base, and what are its distinctive contributions where Israelite religion is concerned? (1) The data-base obviously comprises material culture remains, not in the usual sense of "mere objects" (probably the misconception that prompted Noth's comment about "mute archaeology"); but, rather, in the sense of what is now widely termed "the archaeological record." This record consists of all of the architectural and artifactual remains that can be recovered by sophisticated modern methods: environmental, paleobotanical and zoological, and other data that help to reconstruct the ancient ecological setting, technology, and economy; inferences from these data on socioeconomic, political, and even ideological systems; and, finally, the modern intellectual and social framework within which these miscellaneous bits of information about the past are interpreted to become data relevant to our quest.

Thus the archaeological record consists of highly complex, "encoded messages" about past human thought, intent, and behavior in their broad natural and cultural setting, over long timespans. In theory, it is all there; and, to use Wright's phrase, "We can get back there." But of course in practice, we can never retrieve all of the potential information or satisfactorily interpret some of the enigmatic material. In short, we can never know the past *fully,* but with modern sophisticated methods we can know much more than previous generations assumed. To this end, I would argue that parallels between the archaeological record and the textual record are extremely close, and the problems of "reading" both are similar. One source of data for history-writing is no more "objective" or informative or "primary" than the other. The new archaeological hermeneutic looks surprisingly like the hermeneutic now taking shape in biblical and historical studies, a fact that bodes well, at last, for a proper interdisciplinary dialogue (Dever 1997b).

Let me now comment more specifically on the nature of archaeological data compared to textual data. The textual data in the Hebrew Bible do give us reliable portraits of some aspects of Israelite religion—mostly when we "read between the lines" of the polemics against the popular cults that were tolerated earlier but became anathema to the later editors. By and large, however, the texts of the Hebrew Bible in its present form tend to be: (1) late; (2) highly selective and heavily edited; (3) elitist and idealistic; (4) concerned largely with theocratic ideology; and (5) static in their final edited form, with no more such texts to be expected. Archaeological data, on the other hand, are: (1) contemporary; (2) random, not edited at all (until we begin to edit), and thus more representative of a broad spectrum of society; (3) populist, reflecting the majority and actual belief and practice; (4) indicative more of social behavior than any particular ideology; and (5) dynamic, potentially almost unlimited, and barely beginning to be exploited.

It would be no great exaggeration to say that the biblical texts deal with the "sacred," archaeology with the "secular" (although this is, of course, a modern distinction); texts with literature, archaeology with "real life." (Again, not *Sitz im Literatur*, but *Sitz im Leben*). On which plane should history-writing move? Obviously, on *both*. That is, our two disciplines need to be writing parallel, complementary histories of ancient Israel, histories that ideally would finally converge. With these two histories possible, I believe that a separate, comprehensive "natural history" of Palestine, based primarily on archaeological data and on nonbiblical texts, should be the prolegomenon to any projected *Heilsgeschichte* (although I leave the latter to others).

Are there any examples of how recent archaeological discoveries of the type that I have described have *changed* our concept of Israelite religion? Absolutely! Among many examples, I would single out (1) the 10th–8th century cultic installations at Dan, Taʿanach, Tell el-Farʿah/Tirzah, Lachish, Arad, and other sites, which in my judgment are full-fledged examples of *bāmôt*, which for the first time illustrate what the biblical writers had in mind in using that term. (2) The hundreds of terracotta female figurines—more from Jerusalem than anywhere else—are what Ziony Zevit calls aptly "prayers in clay" and provide a powerful commentary on rites of popular fertility cults only dimly hinted at in the Hebrew Bible. (3) Above all, the 8th-century inscriptions from my el-Qôm tombs and from the Israelite-Judean sanctuary at Kuntillet ʿAjrûd, in their full archaeological context, have *alone* revolutionized our appreciation of monotheism, polytheism, and the prevalence of the cult of Asherah. If you doubt that scholarly views of Israelites are changing and that archaeology and noncanonical texts are often the catalysts, simply compare the literature of the 1970s with more recent treatments, such as many of the essays in the Cross Festschrift, *Ancient Israelite Religion* (1987); Saul Olyan's *Asherah and the Cult of Yahweh in Israel* (1988); Mark Smith's *The Early History of God* (1990); Susan Ackerman's *Under Every Green Tree* (1992); the works of the "Freibourg school," such as Othmar Keel and his students; or the forthcoming volume of the Bern symposium that I mentioned earlier, *JHWH unter Göttinnen und Göttern des Altes Orients* (Dietrich and Klopfenstein 1994).

Yet these long-overdue changes in our conception of Israelite religion are slow, often reluctant, and cautious in the extreme. And the sophistry, the intellectual contortions, in which some biblical scholars engage to avoid confronting the obvious are amazing. For instance, in the Cross Festschrift, Kyle McCarter wants to have it both ways. Thus, at Kuntillet ʿAjrûd, the Hebrew texts do indeed suggest that "Asherah" was Yahweh's consort; but she/it was not the Canaanite Asherah, and not really a separate deity, only a hypostatization of Yahweh (McCarter 1987: 139–49). Jeffrey Tigay confronts these same texts (and also those at el-Qôm) but concludes that they are "Phoenician," not Israelite/Judean Hebrew; that they are not typical and only "point in the direction of paganism"; that early Israel was overwhelmingly monotheistic, with only some "superficial, fetishistic polytheism" (Tigay 1987: 173–93).

A distinguished Jewish biblical scholar remarked to me in a recent public debate on monotheism in monarchical Israel that he simply could not bring himself to believe that his ancestors were polytheists. What we can "bring ourselves to believe" is beside the point. Traditional views die hard, especially when not only ego and professional reputation are invested in them but matters of religious conviction are involved. But archaeology, not to mention scholarship, requires that we *separate* fact and faith, knowledge and wishful thinking, professional obligations as scholars and personal commitments to religious or other institutions. Whether Christians, Jews, or secular historians, it is only when we concede that Israel's religion and morality are not ours—perhaps not even necessarily the foundation—that we can begin to see Israel's religion clearly and see it whole.

Does this sound radical? Not if we grasp the reality that archaeology brings to light; that is, if we recognize that the portrait of Israelite religion in the final literary tradition of the Hebrew Bible—especially in the P and Dtr redactions—is hopelessly idealistic and can never have been part of more than a tiny minority. Thus the prevailing biblical notions of a formative, pre-Israelite "Mosaic age" that saw Yahwism, Covenant, and Law fully formed; of an elaborate Priestly establishment and ritual in the period of the judges; or a national monotheistic cult centralized in the Jerusalem Temple during the Monarchy—all of these notions must simply be given up. They are late literary constructs and have little historical validity, any more than traditional portraits of "Israelite religion" based on these texts have.

What then *was* the religion (or better, the religions) of Israel and Judah by and large? We must distinguish between the minority, orthodox, state cult enshrined in the canonical literature and what a number of scholars are now beginning to isolate as "folk religion," "popular religion," "nonconformist cults," or "local and family religion," or "book religion." It will no longer do to dismiss these as "syncretistic," "pagan," "due to foreign influence," or "non-Yahwistic." This popular religion (sic), in its many manifestations, *was* "Yahwism" as it actually existed throughout the monarchy. This amalgam is what Albertz characterizes as "practical henolatry," or "poly-Yahwism." It was

especially evident in the widespread local cults and family cults in the rural
areas, but also in Jerusalem itself. I would say that the major elements of this
truly "normative" Israelite-Judean religion in ancient Israel included: fre-
quenting *bāmôt* and other local shrines; the making of images; veneration of
ʾašērîm (whether sacred trees or iconographic images), and the worship of
Asherah the Great Lady herself; rituals having to do with childbirth and
children; pilgrimages and saints' festivals; *mārzēʾaḥ* feasts; various funerary
rites, such as libations for the dead; baking cakes for the "Queen of Heaven,"
probably Astarte); wailing over Tammuz; various aspects of solar and astral
worship; divination and sorcery; and perhaps child sacrifice. These and other
elements of "folk" religion are often assumed to have characterized the religion of "hearth and home" and thus to have been almost the exclusive prov-
ince of women. This assumption, typically made by male scholars, inevitably
carries with it a note of condescension. After all, women in ancient Israel
were largely illiterate and marginalized; they played an insignificant role in
the sociopolitical processes that shaped Israelite life and institutions.

Recently, however, several female scholars have challenged the conven-
tion—for instance, Phyllis Bird in her "Israelite Religion and the Faith of Israel's Daughters." She acknowledges that "visits to local shrines, pilgrimages,
and individual acts of petition and dedication related to particular needs were
favored by women and better suited to the general rhythms and the exigen-
cies of their lives than were the major communal rites and celebrations" (Bird
1991: 102, 103). I agree with Bird that it is wrong to regard these concerns of
women as "marginal," much less as somehow not properly religious (that is,
merely "superstition"). What *is* the ultimate reality with which religion
should be concerned? Surely a *broader* concept of religion, as Bird says, would
include "a wider area of practice, feeling, and cognition characterized by understanding of social obligation and welfare, of duty to family, community,
nation, or people, of 'right' action or conduct pleasing to God" (Bird 1991:
104). Carol Meyers (1991) has also explored the neglected role of women in
ancient Israelite religion by focusing on the "household mode of production"
that characterized ancient Israel's economy and society, which was, of course
influenced by women to a considerable degree. Her book *Discovering Eve: Ancient Israelite Women in Context* (1988) is an excellent prolegomenon to a
fuller discussion of women's cults and their relevance.

Conclusion

With this study, I am registering a passionate plea for a renewed commitment to history, not theology, in pursuing ancient Israelite religion; for a return of the basic evolutionary, comparative, and ecumenical approach of
Religionsgeschichte—coupled with the rich supplementary and corrective data

that archaeology alone can supply, and with the potent socioanthropological models and orientation toward a broader social and economic history that characterize recent scholarship. We must embrace *better* histories, using improved methods, including philology, not putting all our hopes in trendy new approaches such as canonical criticism, rhetorical criticism, semiotics, "new literary criticism," structuralist and poststructuralist paradigms, liberation theology, feminist critiques, or what have you. Nevertheless, it is in *interdisciplinary dialogue* that our best hope lies. And if this dialogue is to be truly scholarly and not simply faith-centered, it must be willing to see faith as just that: belief, not knowledge; risk, not certainty. With Paul, "we see through a glass darkly," and with another saint, Kirkegaard, we must be willing to leap into the abyss, to undertake the "teleological suspension of the ethical." Such an approach to the religion of ancient Israel liberates us, both as scholars and as private persons responsible to ourselves and our various communities.

Von Rad at one point suggested that in their enthrallment to the biblical tradition, both Christians and Jews must live with "the double witness of the choir of those who await and those who remember" (von Rad 1960: 39). I want to give this choir a new song—perhaps even an anthem.[6]

6. Portions of this essay were previously published in Dever 1997c.

Bibliography

Ackerman, S.
 1992 *"Under Every Green Tree": Popular Religion in Sixth-Century Judah.* Atlanta: Scholars Press.
Ahlström, G. E.
 1993 *The History of Ancient Palestine from the Paleolithic Period to Alexander's Conquest.* Sheffield: Sheffield Academic Press.
Albertz, R.
 1994 *A History of Israelite Religion in the Old Testament Period,* Volume 1: *From the Beginnings to the End of the Monarchy.* Louisville: Westminster/John Knox.
Anderson, B. W., ed.
 1963 *The Old Testament and Christian Faith: A Theological Discussion.* New York: Harper & Row.
Barr, J.
 1976 Story and History in Biblical Theology. *Journal of Religion* 56: 1–17.
Berlinerblau, J.
 1996 *The Vow and the "Popular Religious Groups" of Ancient Israel: A Philological and Sociological Inquiry.* Sheffield: Sheffield Academic Press.
Bird, P. A.
 1991 Israelite Religion and the Faith of Israel's Daughters: Reflections on Gender and Religious Definition. Pp. 97–108 in *The Bible and the Politics*

    *of Exegesis: Essays in Honor of Norman K. Gottwald on His Sixty-Fifth
    Birthday,* ed. D. Jobling, P. L. Day, and G. T. Sheppard. Cleveland:
    Pilgrim.
Bultmann, R.
    1963   Prophecy and Fulfillment. Pp. 50–75 in *Essays on Old Testament Herme-
              neutics,* ed. C. Westerman. Richmond: John Knox.
Childs, B. S.
    1970   *Biblical Theology in Crisis.* Philadelphia: Westminster.
Collins, J. J.
    1990   Is a Critical Biblical Theology Possible? Pp. 1–17 in *The Hebrew Bible
              and Its Interpreters,* ed. W. Propp, B. Halpern, and D. N. Freedman.
              Winona Lake, Ind.: Eisenbrauns.
Davies, P. R.
    1992   *In Search of "Ancient Israel."* Sheffield: Sheffield Academic Press.
Dentan, R. C.
    1963   *Preface to Old Testament Theology.* New Haven: Yale University Press.
Dietrich, W., and M. A. Klopfenstein, M. A.
    1994   *Ein Gott allein? JHWH-verehrung und biblischer Monotheismus im Kontext
              der israelitischen und altorientalischen Religionsgeschichte.* Freiburg: Univer-
              sitätsverlag Freiburg.
Dever, W. G.
    1981   Biblical Theology and Biblical Archaeology: An Appreciation of G. Er-
              nest Wright. *Harvard Theological Review* 73: 1–15.
    1983   Material Remains and the Cult in Ancient Israel: An Essay in Archaeo-
              logical Systematics. Pp. 571–87 in *The Word of the Lord Shall Go Forth:
              Essays in Honor of David Noel Freedman on His Sixty-Fifth Birthday,* ed.
              C. L. Meyers and M. O'Connor. Winona Lake, Ind.: Eisenbrauns.
    1987   The Contribution of Archaeology to the Study of Canaanite and Early
              Israelite Religion. Pp. 209–47 in *Ancient Israelite Religion: Essays in
              Honor of Frank Moore Cross,* ed. P. D. Miller, Jr., P. D. Hanson, and S. D.
              McBride. Philadelphia: Fortress.
    1990   *Recent Archaeological Discoveries and Biblical Research.* Seattle: University
              of Washington Press.
    1993   Biblical Archaeology: Death and Rebirth? Pp. 706–22 in *Biblical Ar-
              chaeology Today, 1990: Proceedings of the Second International Congress on
              Biblical Archaeology, Jerusalem, June 1990,* ed. A. Biran and J. Aviram.
              Jerusalem: Israel Exploration Society.
    1994   Ancient Israelite Religion: How to Reconcile the Differing Textual and
              Artifactural Portraits? Pp. 105–25 in *Ein Got allein? JHWH-Verehrung
              und biblischer Monotheismus im Kontext der israelitischen und altoriental-
              ischen Religionsgeschichte,* ed. W. Dietrich and M. A. Klopfenstein. Frei-
              burg: Universitätsverlag Freiburg.
    1995a   Will the Real Israel Please Stand Up? Archaeology and Israelite Histori-
              ography: Part 1. *Bulletin of the American Schools of Oriental Research* 297:
              61–80.

1995b   Will the Real Israel Please Stand Up? Archaeology and Israelite Histori-
         ography: Part II. *Bulletin of the American Schools of Oriental Research* 198:
         37–58.
1996   Archaeology and the Religions of Israel. *Bulletin of the American Schools
         of Oriental Research* 301: 83–90.
1997a   Folk Religion in Early Israel: Did Yahweh Have a Consort? Pp. 27–56 in
         Aspects of Monotheism: How God is One, ed. H. Shanks. Washington:
         Biblical Archaeology Society.
1997b   On Listening to the Texts and the Artifacts. Pp. 1–23 in *The Echoes of
         Many Texts: Reflections on Jewish and Christian Traditions: Essays in Honor
         of Lou H. Silberman*, ed. W. G. Dever and J. E. Wright. Atlanta: Scholars
         Press.
1997c   Philology, Theology, and Archaeology: What Kind of History Do We
         Want, and What Is Possible? Pp. 290–310 in *The Archaeology of Israel:
         Constructing the Past, Interpreting the Present*, ed. N. A. Silberman and
         D. Small. Sheffield: Sheffield Academic Press.
1998   Archaeology, Ideology, and the Quest for an "Ancient" or "Biblical Is-
         rael." *Near Eastern Archaeology* 61: 39–52.
2001   *What Did the Biblical Writers Know, and When Did They Know It? Archae-
         ology and the Realia of Ancient Israel*. Grand Rapids: Eerdmans.

Eichrodt, W.
1963   Is Typological Exegesis an Appropriate Method? Pp. 224–45 in *Essays in
         Old Testament Hermeneutics*, ed. C. Westermann. Richmond: John Knox.

Flanagan, J. W.
1988   *David's Social Drama: A Hologram of Israel's Early Iron Age*. Sheffield:
         JSOT Press.

Garbini, G.
1988   *History and Ideology in Ancient Israel*. New York: Crossroads.

Goshen-Gottstein, M.
1987   Tanakh Theology: The Religion of the Old Testament and the Place of
         Jewish Biblical Theology. Pp. 617–44 in *Ancient Israelite Religion: Essays
         in Honor of Frank Moore Cross*, ed. P. D. Miller Jr., P. D. Hanson, and
         S. D. McBride. Philadelphia: Fortress.

Gottwald, N. K.
1979   *The Tribes of Yahweh: A Sociology of the Religion of Liberated Israel, ca.
         1250–1050 B.C.E.* Maryknoll, NY: Orbis.

Hahn, H. F.
1956   *The Old Testament in Modern Research*. London: SCM.

Halpern, B.
1988   *The First Historians: The Hebrew Bible and History*. New York: Harper &
         Row.
1997   Text and Artifact: Two Monologues? Pp. 311–41 in *The Archaeology of
         Israel: Constructing the Past, Interpreting the Present*, ed. N. A. Silberman
         and D. Small. Sheffield: Sheffield Academic Press.

Hasel, G.
    1991   *Old Testament Theology: Basic Issues in the Current Debate.* 3d edition.
            Grand Rapids: Eerdmans.
Holladay, J. S.
    1987   Religion in Israel and Judah under the Monarchy: An Explicitly Archae-
            ological Approach. Pp. 249–99 in *Ancient Israelite Religion: Essays in
            Honor of Frank Moore Cross,* ed. P. D. Miller, Jr., P. D. Hanson, and S. D.
            McBride. Philadelphia: Fortress.
Knauf, E. A.
    1991   From History to Interpretation. Pp. 26–64 in *The Fabric of History, Text,
            Artifact, and Israel's Past,* ed. D. V. Edelman. Sheffield: JSOT Press.
Kraeling, E. G.
    1955   *The Old Testament Since the Reformation.* London: Lutterworth Press.
Kraus, H. J.
    1966   *Worship in Israel.* Richmond: John Knox.
Levenson, J. D.
    1993   Why Jews Are Not Interested in Biblical Theology. Pp 33–61 in *The He-
            brew Bible, The Old Testament, and Historical Criticism,* ed. J. D. Leven-
            son. Louisville: Westminster/John Knox.
McCarter, P. K.
    1987   Aspects of the Religion of the Israelite Monarchy: Biblical and Epi-
            graphic Data. Pp. 137–55 in *Ancient Israelite Religion Essays in Honor of
            Frank Moore Cross,* ed. P. D. Miller, P. D. Hanson, and S. D. McBride.
            Philadelphia: Fortress.
McKenzie, S. L., and S. R. Haynes, eds.
    1993   *To Each Its Own Meaning: An Introduction to Biblical Criticisms and Their
            Application.* Louisville: Westminster/John Knox.
Meyers, C.
    1988   *Discovering Eve: Ancient Israelite Women in Context.* New York: Oxford
            University Press.
    1991   "To Her Mother's House": Considering a Counterpart to the Israelite *bêt
            ʾāb.* Pp. 39–51 in *The Bible and the Politics of Exegesis: Essays in Honor of
            Norman K. Gottwald on His Sixty-Fifth Birthday,* ed. D. Jobling, P. L. Day,
            and G. T. Sheppard. Cleveland: Pilgrim.
Miller, P. D., P. D. Hanson, and S. D. McBride, eds.
    1987   *Ancient Israelite Religion: Essays in Honor of Frank Moore Cross.* Philadel-
            phia: Fortress.
Noth, M.
    1960   *The History of Israel.* New York: Harper & Row.
Ollenburger, B.C., E. A. Martens, and G. F. Hasel, eds.
    1992   *The Flowering of Old Testament Theology: A Reader in Twentieth-Century
            Old Testament Theology, 1930–1990.* Winona Lake, Ind.: Eisenbrauns.
Olyan, S. M.
    1988   *Asherah and the Cult of Yahweh in Israel.* Atlanta: Scholars Press.
Pfeiffer, R. H.
    1961   *Religion in the Old Testament.* New York: Harper & Row.

Rad, G. von
   1963   Typological Interpretation of the Old Testament, Pp. 17–39 in *Essays on Old Testament Hermeneutics*, ed. C. Westermann. Richmond: John Knox.
Rendtorff, R.
   1993   The Paradigm is Changing: Hopes—and Fears. *Biblical Interpretation* 1: 34–53.
Ringgren, H.
   1966   *Israelite Religion*. Philadelphia: Fortress.
Smith, M. E.
   1968   The Present Status of Old Testament Studies. *Journal of Biblical Literature* 88: 19–35.
Smith, M. S.
   1990   *The Early History of God: Yahweh and Other Deities in Ancient Israel*. San Francisco: Harper & Row.
Stendahl, K.
   1962   Biblical Theology, Contemporary. Pp. 418–32 in volume 4 of *Interpreters Bible Dictionary*, ed. G. A. Buttrick. Nashville: Abingdon.
Thompson, T. L.
   1992   *Early History of the Israelite People from the Written and Archaeological Sources*. Leiden: Brill.
Tigay, J.
   1987   Israelite Religion: The Onomastic and Epigraphic Evidence. Pp. 157–94 in *Ancient Israelite Religion: Essays in Honor of Frank Moore Cross*, ed. P. D. Miller Jr., P. D. Hanson, and S. D. McBride. Philadelphia: Fortress.
Toorn, K. van der
   1997   *The Image and the Book: Iconic Cults, Aniconism, and the Rise of Book Religion in Israel and the Ancient Near East*. Leuven: Peeters.
Wolff, H. W.
   1963   The Understanding of History in the OT. Prophets. Pp. 336–55 in *Essays on Old Testament Hermeneutics*, ed. C. Westermann. Richmond: John Knox.
Whitley, D. S., ed.
   1998   *A Reader in Archaeological Theory: Post-processual and Cognitive Approaches*. London: Routledge.
Wright, G. E.
   1952   *God Who Acts: Biblical Theology as Recital*. London: SCM.
Zimmerli, W.
              Promise and Fulfillment. Pp. 89–122 in *Essays on Old Testament Hermeneutics*, ed. C. Westermann. Richmond: John Knox.
Zevit, Z.
   2001   *The Religions of Ancient Israel: A Synthesis of Parallelactic Approaches*. London: Cassell.

Philology and Archaeology: Imagining New Questions, Begetting New Ideas

ZIONY ZEVIT

University of Judaism, Los Angeles

A story is told by cuneiform scholars about the late Sumerologist of the Oriental Institute, Benno Landsberger. Despite the fact that he was a Jew, had trained a number of Jewish and Israeli scholars, and was known to be a Zionist, the government of Iraq invited him to visit the sites of ancient Sumer, the focus of his life's work. He refused the invitation. When his students asked him, "Don't you want to see all the places about which you have written?" he is said to have replied: "I don't have to see how they look; I know how they looked."

The great philologist was acknowledging his debt to scholarly imagining in a way that scholars rarely do, lest they be accused of being romantics, undisciplined, or even unscientific.

Imagination, however, is to be welcomed because it enlivens our various disciplines and fructifies them. Had Albert Einstein not tried to imagine what the world would look like were he riding on a beam of light, he would not have asked the questions that led to his great discoveries about light, energy, and time; had Picasso not imagined what it would be like to represent visible realities located in real time and space from multiple perspectives, he would not have broken single perspective reality into visual fragments of front and back and up and down and presented them to us simultaneously—cubism would not have been conceived; and had Schliemann not imagined that it was possible to see parts of the past in the present, many archaeologists might be unemployed. Einstein, Picasso, and Schliemann—all three manipulated time and space.

Imagining—first wild, fun imagining, and then disciplined imagining— is no less a part of what scholarship is about than is disciplined inquiry. "What if" and "Why not" questions are the midwives of "Why? When? and How?"

*   *   *

The size of the group that gathered at the 1993 session on Archaeology and the Religion of Israel under the aegis of the American Schools of Oriental Research, about 300 people, was an indication of the continuing interest in the topic under discussion. The size cannot be explained by a lack of sessions bearing on Israelite religion in the parallel meetings of the SBL. Most of us assembled there, not only because we anticipated sparkling and illuminating lectures by Bill Dever and Jonathan Smith, but also because we thought that ASOR had something significant to contribute to the study of Israelite religion, something that remained undeveloped in most of the ongoing research—the use of data discovered and processed by archaeologists, and hence the name of the section: Archaeology and the Religion of Israel. Certainly, this was the optimistic sentiment of the steering committee that organized the session.

Implicit in the convening of the session was a statement to other sessions in other societies, to wit: we think that something is amiss with your work. (After all, do we really need another session on Israelite religion at these interminal meetings?) And part of what is amiss in much contemporary study is the heavy intellectualism that overrides comprehensions of what Israelite religion was.

Dever's critique of historical intellectualizing study pointed to its lack of imagination. It sees its subject in terms of ethics not ethos, in terms of creeds and catechisms, not in terms of pageantry and processions. From one of Jonathan Smith's astute remarks I infer that the lack of imagining about these topics originates in the silence of the Bible itself about them and the willingness of scholars to accept the biblical silences as parameters for their critical inquiry. The understanding of much contemporary study is that religion is something of the mind cut off from our five senses, our limbs, and our organs. It is a religion of some fourth dimension, not of any three-dimensional world. I still concur with the general thrust of this criticism. These comprehensions may be modern or medieval, but they certainly are not ancient.

Dever and I are interested in a different approach to religion and have different questions than the ones asked by earlier generations of scholars. All of us who participated in the 1993 session were aware that we could ask new questions about Israelite religion that may be answered in the light of new discoveries. Our awareness is in part due to familiarity with new types of data, but most important, to the fact that we live in an academic environment where the buzz-word *interdisciplinary* encourages new ways of thinking about Israelite religion and of teasing new information out of old data.

Earlier generations of scholars are not to be faulted for trying their best. I cannot fault scholars of another generation for lacking the wisdom, insights, and the methodological sophistication that we claim for ourselves; nor can I fault scholars of the past for failing to ask questions that interest me. The universe of knowledge that we occupy is constructed out of the hypotheses of our predecessors, the discarded hypotheses along with those that have been verified. Its newer levels are shaped by the questions that we find interesting and worthy of asking.

It is my contention that there are three types of data to be considered in producing a historical, three-dimensional comprehension of Israelite religion: (1) literary-intellectual data that derive from the historical-philological study of biblical texts in their ancient Near Eastern contexts, more or less according to the classical agenda; (2) artifactual data from archaeological study; and (3) religiological data from various specialized approaches to the non-apologetic, academic study of religion. The questions that we may wish to ask about Israelite religion can come from any of these disciplines, but all three must be considered in providing answers.

Dever has outlined clearly, albeit with a pen dipped in smoking polemicism, his perception of some of the major problems in the ways that various disciplines aside from archaeology study Israelite Religion. Unfortunately, my first type of data, "literary-intellectual," puts me at odds with some of his comments.

He lambasts the philological approach to Israelite religion as "naïve, wistful, and rather sad," criticizing its "unexamined positivistic presuppositions. It simply assumed (1) that the texts of the Hebrew Bible as they have come down to us, despite the seemingly intractable nature of some passages, constitute overall an accurate witness to the actual phenomenon of ancient Israelite religious belief and practice; and (2) that the rapid progress of comparative Semitic philology would enable us to read these texts correctly and comprehend their meaning" (p. 12 above).

I respond to these particular criticisms because, if perceived valid, they undermine the interdisciplinary dialogue before it begins.

First, all disciplines have presuppositions, be they explicit or implicit, and often they are not particularly well articulated. One can do science well and produce significant, concrete, and useful results without being well versed in the philosophical presuppositions of the disciplines. (A biologist friend who is constantly badgered by a mutual acquaintance, a philosopher of science, once commented about him: "He always can tell me why something is wrong. He may be a great philosopher of science but he's useless in a lab and he knows nothing about doing science.") So I am not particularly concerned with the problem of ill-defined presuppositions; but I am concerned with the implication that the positivistic approach to research should be swept into the deconstructionist dust-bin. Dever did not go quite that far. He is too good an archaeologist, and archaeology is a discipline characterized by a positivistic approach to knowledge.

Second, the philological approach has resulted in significantly more sophisticated lexicography and grammar than was available one hundred years
ago, which in turn has made many intractable passages clear, perhaps for the
first time since the Iron Age (or the Neo-Babylonian period), when they were
written. It has provided us with many insights into the nature of the Israelite
cult as described and prescribed officially in the P source of the Torah and referred to casually in various historical and prophetic texts. Furthermore, it
has partially located them within the matrix of ancient Near Eastern cultic
practices and beliefs. One has only to think of the points of agreement between the works of Jacob Milgrom, Baruch Levine. and David Wright, each
of whom has written extensively on this material.[1] Note that I emphasize
points of agreement.

Of course, not everything is perfectly neat and clear, and of course philological fisticuffs will continue. But without the critical philological studies
of such texts and of similar texts in Akkadian, Hittite, Punic, Sumerian, and
Ugaritic, how would we interpret archaeological finds, clarify their functions,
and discern their "meaning" in the cult? Philological research brakes free-
wheeling imagination, and it helps keep us honest.

Concerning Dever's statements that the Bible is "revisionist history,"
"propaganda," I am willing to grant him his predications only for the sake of
argument, but then I have to ask, "So what?"

"Content Analysis," a particularly focused type of critical reading of Nazi
propaganda and censored publications by allied military intelligence during
World War II, provided much significant true information to military analysts
that was verified after the war. It was not, however, developed for intelligence
analysis. Critical historians since the Renaissance have being doing "Content
Analysis" when reading historical documents. Dever referred to this as "reading between the lines." This is exactly how Graf, Kuenen, and Wellhausen
and hundreds of others were reading biblical texts; this is how they were able
to distinguish and characterize the distinctive documents in the Torah, and
this is what a whole new generation of scholars was undertaking in the
1990s—new source analyses of the Pentateuch as well as of the historical
books with their often casual references to cult.

It is not the method that Dever faults but what he considers the erroneous conception of who was responsible for the texts and their *Sitz im Leben*.

---

1. B. Levine, *In the Presence of the Lord: A Study of Cult and Some Cultic Terms in
Ancient Israel* (Leiden: Brill, 1974); idem, *Leviticus* (Philadelphia: Jewish Publication
Society, 1989); J. Milgrom, *Studies in Levitical Terminology I* (Berkeley: University of
California Press, 1970); idem, *Leviticus 1–16* (AB 3; New York: Doubleday, 1991);
D. P. Wright, *The Disposal of Impurity: Elimination Rites in the Bible and in Hittite and
Mesopotamian Literature* (Atlanta: Scholars Press, 1987).

Dever concedes this when he says: "At best we might obtain from the biblical and other texts a picture of 'official' religion . . . but not of 'folk' religion, except in the caricature of the biblical writers" (p. 15 above). Indeed, if we obtain a picture "at best," it will be no mean accomplishment, since this form of religion was certainly a significant component of the complex of cults that we call Israelite Religion.

If—and note that I say "if"—if we recognize such a thing as Israelite civilization, civilization ipso facto implies some sort of centralization. Martin Noth's hypothesis of an amphictyony is discredited as ever having been the institution that he thought it was; but the answer that it supplied for the vexing question of centralization in Israelite religious civilization has not yet been replaced.[2] Smith alluded to this problem when he said that "there are no clear social loci in ancient Israel for the various sorts of materials and traditions that became biblical" (p. 6 above). No one has looked to archaeology for an answer. (I will return to this below.) No one has looked to religiology for parallel situations or for possible ways of rephrasing the question or reconceptualizing the situation.

Third, in contrast to my disagreement with Dever's negative assessment of the role of philological research in the study of Israelite region, I am almost in complete agreement with his estimation of the contribution that biblical theology has to make—namely—zilch.

I believe, however, that he underestimates Brevard Childs's contribution to the venture that interests us. In his still very important volume, *Biblical Theology in Crisis*, Childs inoculates anybody who reads his book against mistaking biblical theology for a disciplined historical study of Israelite thought and cautions against the imposition of anachronistic categories of thinking on the theological ruminations of ancient Israelite authors.[3] If the influence of this book has diminished, it is because we have stopped assigning it to our students.

Yet it is clear that Israelite authors made explicit and implicit statements about subjects that we recognize as being of a religious nature, such as deity, death, cult, covenant, the structure of the cosmos, human nature and life; and theoretically, we should be able to process them into groups of attitudes

2. M. Noth, *Gesammelte Studien zum Alten Testament* (2d ed.; Munich: Chr. Kaiser, 1960). See his discussion of "der sakrale Verband der zwölf israelitischen Stämme," pp. 42–53; idem, *The History of Israel* (rev. ed.; New York: Harper & Row, 1958) 97–109.

The main articles precipitating the demise of the amphyctionic hypothesis were the following: H. M. Orlinsky, "The Tribal System of Israel and Related Groups in the Period of the Judges," *OrAnt* 1 (1962) 11–20; B. D. Rathjen, "Philistine and Hebrew Amphictyonies," *JBL* 24 (1965) 101–4.

3. B. Childs, *Biblical Theology in Crisis* (Philadelphia: Westminster, 1970).

and trace their development over various periods. Their predications should be grist for our academic mill. In order to work with this material, is it not possible to cull a methodology appropriate to the limited biblical data from scholars specializing in intellectual history or the history of ideas à la Hayden White, Carlo Ginsberg, and Dominique La Capra, rather than from theologians and philosophers?

But even in this somewhat rarefied area of inquiry, a body of important work exists. Norbert Lohfink and Moshe Weinfeld have done intellectual history instinctively in their studies of Deuteronomic and Deuteronomistic thinking for more than twenty-five years and, more recently, so have Marjo Christina Korpel and Marc Brettler in their comparative studies of metaphors applied to the divine, and so too Mark Smith in his *Early History of God*. In a different field, this is certainly what Thorkild Jacobsen did in *Treasures of Darkness*, his masterful study of Mesopotamian religion.[4]

What I suggest is that we, producers and consumers, self-consciously move the study of Israelite "religious thought" out of the discipline of "theology," which is always apologetic, into the discipline of "intellectual history," with its presuppositional self-consciousness, methodological openness, and its tradition of critical revisionism. Then it may be examined in the same way that the religious thought of the Qumran sectarians or of the communities that produced what we call the extracanonical literature is examined. These were communities in whose thought no extant group or church has a stake, so the only things involved are the pursuit of knowledge and the bruisable egos of individual scholars. Through this kind of study we may, or we may not, be able to trace patterns of Israelite thinking and the various, perhaps changing, concerns of their speculations. We may or we may not, if data do not suffice, gain access to various Israelite conceptions of their ecosphere, which enveloped all perceived and experienced physical and metaphysical realities: social, political, economic, cultic, and numinous.

This enterprise may achieve what Dever referred to as "the archaeology of the mind" (a phrase echoing Michel Foucault's *Archaeology of Knowledge*). It may help supply what he calls the "vision of the people behind the pots." Note, however, the subjunctive nature of the preceding agenda.

---

4. T. Jacobsen, *The Treasures of Darkness: A History of Mesopotamian Religion* (New Haven: Yale University Press, 1976); M. C. A. Korpel, *A Rift in the Clouds: Ugaritic and Hebrew Descriptions of the Divine* (Münster: Ugarit-Verlag, 1990); N. Lohfink, *Theology of the Pentateuch: Themes of the Priestly Narrative and Deuteronomy* (Minneapolis: Fortress, 1994) 227–89; M. S. Smith, *The Early History of God: Yahweh and the Other Deities of Ancient Israel* (San Francisco: Harper & Row, 1990); M. Weinfeld, *Deuteronomy and the Deuteronomic School* (Oxford: Oxford University Press, 1972; repr. Winona Lake, Ind.: Eisenbrauns, 1992).

But what has all this to do with nitty-gritty, dirt archaeology? Just this: *to the extent that the artifactual world of cult sites in Iron Age Israel is a semiotic expression of the religio-intellectual world view of a given society in a given time, as is the world of transmitted texts, there is meaning in the way cult places are arranged; there is meaning in realistic or nonrealistic representational art and in graffiti.*

For example, let me present three questions stimulated by archaeological discoveries alone that have major bearing on various aspects of Israelite religion:

(1) The layout of the Iron II cities with integrated city walls, ring roads, and a patterned layout of structures at Tel Beit Mirsim, Beer-sheba, and Tel en-Nasbeh attests to centralized, organized town-planning in Judah 450 years before Hippodamus of Miletus introduced it in Piraeus for the Athenians (ca. 450 B.C.E.). It is reasonable to think that military engineers and the army were involved in these building projects.

In a study of Levitical cities published many years ago, Benjamin Mazar hypothesized that the Levites were part of the standing army and public work force of the centralized Davidic-Solomonic state.[5] Do these planned sites have any implications for the notion of a controlled, centralized, organized religious cult imposed or influenced by a political-cultic and economic center? Can they have any implications for the development of a hierarchically organized, logically systematized concept of cosmos such as that underlying the creation story in Genesis chapter 1?

(2) The industrial area of Ekron has produced a rich harvest of small altars of various types, shapes, and sizes found in different oil press installations. These were described by Seymour Gitin in the Avraham Biran volume of *Eretz Israel.*[6]

Now, as a general rule, it is generally accepted in the sociology of religion that once societies become complex, they become stratified and specialized, and the right to sacrifice becomes restricted. What then are the religio-cultic implications of these altars? Do the altars attest to cultic generalism? the privatization of cult? or to cultic anarchy?

(3) Hundreds of scarabs inscribed with Egyptian motifs and with hieroglyphs have been found in Iron Age Israelite sites. Given the large number and their pattern of dispersal, it is quite possible that these were of local manufacture and that Israelite artisans worked from set models and motifs, carving hieroglyphs that they could not read. Can these be sorted by deity represented, epithets cited chronologically? Did the religious content of the scarabs express anything relevant to Israelites? What myths did they evoke? What might this imply about Israelite religion?

5. B. Mazar, "The Cities of Priests and Levites," *VT* 7 (1960) 193–205.
6. S. Gitin, "Incense Altars from Ekron, Israel, and Judah," *ErIsr* 20 (Avraham Biran Volume; 1989) 52–67.

There is no reason why an archaeological report could not broach questions like these in a special chapter. There is no reason why archaeologists interested in Israelite religion should not consider these questions that are natural outgrowths of their own processed data, even though in the end the answers will also involve philological, historical, and religiological considerations.

And if the archaeological data do not jibe well with what the analyzed texts contain, *then we must understand that there is meaning in the nonconfirmatory dialectics of the archaeological and the textual.*

If the dialogue that the 1993 ASOR session encouraged will not be one of the uninformed, some reeducation is in our stars. Just as biblicists dealing with Israelite religion must become familiar with archaeology, far beyond what is available in *Biblical Archaeology Review,* so too archaeologists wishing to deal with the topic responsibly must become familiar with biblical data— that is, literary references in Iron Age II texts. Their bibliography must include, minimally, sizable chunks of the Bible including, unfortunately, some of the boring parts, Leviticus and Numbers, read with critical, philological commentaries; it must include the major "golden oldie" essays of scholars such as Albrecht Alt, Martin Noth, W. F. Albright, and Yehezkel Kaufmann, as well as recent critical analyses of their work. In addition, many studies in the monumental Anchor Bible projects edited by David Noel Freedman are significant.

The reason for this crash course in Israelite civilization is that knowledge is based on knowledge, and new understandings derive from old understandings. Archaeologists who demand that biblicists meet them at the tell must be prepared to meet biblicists on their own turf. The shared insights from different disciplines must be drawn and comprehended in terms of the current state of each field in what Jonathan Z. Smith described as "a mutual intellectual relationship." The philologically competent biblicist who is an archaeological naïf and the archaeology *maven* who takes his Bible either literally or not at all are hardly going to engage in sophisticated discussions about Israelite religion. The conversations must be between those who are competent professionals in one field and informed amateurs in another, between confident individuals who are sometimes teachers but always, always students. Only then will we be able to responsibly imagine Israelite religion, not as Einstein viewed time or as Picasso viewed space, but as Schliemann viewed the past—only, for us, it will have to be Schliemann without the schmaltz. Only then will discussants be able to grasp the bridging implications of new knowledge and to apply them creatively in new syntheses; and only then will we be able to possess the integral awareness that is the progenitor of new ideas.

Part II

Prayers in Clay:
A Multidisciplinary Approach to Figurines

Israelite Figurines:
A View from the Texts

KAREL VAN DER TOORN
University of Amsterdam

The study of Israelite figurines has as long a history as that of Israelite archaeology itself. In recent years, however, the subject has aroused an interest amounting to fascination. Three reasons combine to account for the popularity of our theme: the realization that religion addresses the senses as much as the mind; the sentiment that the popular religion of ancient Israel may have been vastly different from the official cult; and, since many of the figurines represent women, the awareness that the religious experience of Israelite women has been neglected by generations of scholars.

It is my task here to interpret the evidence in the light of the texts. Some may object that this is a "mission impossible" because explanations of popular religious phenomena (and figurines fall into this category) based on official texts (and the Hebrew Scriptures fall into that category) are bound to fail. Is not the Bible, biased and late as it is, unreliable as a source on early Israelite religion? In illustration of this opinion, let me quote from a review of a recent historical survey of Israelite iconography.[1] The reviewer hails this book as "the first true history of Israelite religion," because it is based on authentic evidence contemporary with the period described; in the same breath, he disqualifies the latest *History of Israelite Religion* as merely interesting for the history of Old Testament theology, since its author is unfamiliar with the iconographic evidence.[2] This argument is expressed by other writers on Israelite religion as well.[3] Yet, though the insistence on the necessity of using

---

1. E. A. Knauf, "Review of O. Keel and C. Uehlinger, *Göttinnen, Götter and Gottessymbole*," *Bib* 75 (1994) 298–302.

2. Ibid., 299, referring to R. Albertz's *Religionsgeschichte Israels in alttestamentlicher Zeit*, vols. 1–2 (ATD Ergänzungsreihe 8/1–2; Göttingen: Vandenhoeck & Ruprecht, 1992).

3. Thus W. G. Dever in a number of contributions, for example: "Material Remains and the Cult in Ancient Israel: An Essay in Archeological Systematics," in

45

Israel's material remains for the reconstruction of the history of religion can only be applauded, the wholesale disqualification of the Hebrew Bible seems misplaced. The fact that the Bible, in its final shape, is the product of rivaling schools and currents, most of them postexilic, does not disqualify the Bible as a source of information on the monarchical period. The data must be used with discrimination, it is true, but they should not be simply dismissed.

I hasten to add that recourse to the texts in an attempt at interpretation of the figurines should not be restricted to the Bible. The small but steadily increasing number of extrabiblical Hebrew inscriptions must be fully exploited, since they provide the possibility of a view from the other side. In practice, however, the epigraphic material does not take the place of the Bible but orients its interpretation. A prime example, to which we shall have occasion to return, is that of the inscriptions speaking of Yahweh "and his Asherah." These have allowed us to appreciate biblical data that were largely discarded before. A similar effect may be produced by the study of comparative evidence from other Near Eastern civilizations. Israel did not exist in a cultural void; it was surrounded by various civilizations with which it was in contact. Together they shared some fundamental concepts, values, and practices, all of which reflected on their material culture. The scarcity of written data on ordinary life in early Israel can be palliated, to some degree, by the use of the comparative approach.[4]

These preliminary matters having at least been mentioned, let me explain what I set out to do in this contribution. I will present a view from the texts on Israelite figurines. The statistics show that, among the figurines, animal forms predominate over human; the most common animal representa-

---

The Word of the Lord Shall Go Forth: Essays in Honor of David Noel Freedman in Celebration of His Sixtieth Birthday (ed. C. L. Meyers and M. O'Connor; Winona Lake, Ind.: Eisenbrauns, 1983) 571–87; idem, "The Contribution of Archaeology to the Study of Canaanite and Early Israelite Religion," *Ancient Israelite Religion: Essays in Honor of Frank Moore Cross* (ed. P. D. Miller, P. D. Hanson, and S. D. McBride; Philadelphia: Fortress, 1987) 209–47. The approach advocated by Dever, or one much like it, has been followed by G. W. Ahlström, *Royal Administration and National Religion in Ancient Palestine* (Leiden: Brill, 1982); idem, *An Archaeological Picture of Iron Age Religions in Ancient Palestine* (Studia Orientalia 55/3; Helsinki, 1984). See also J. S. Holladay, "Religion in Israel and Judah under the Monarchy: An Explicitly Archaeological Approach," in *Ancient Israelite Religion: Essays in Honor of Frank Moore Cross* (ed. P. D. Miller, P. D. Hanson, and S. D. McBride; Philadelphia: Fortress, 1987) 249–99.

4. On the methodological issues involved in the comparative approach in Old Testament studies, see my "Parallels in Biblical Research: Purpose of Comparison," in *Proceedings of the Eighth World Congress of Jewish Studies*, Division A: *The Bible and Its World* (Jerusalem: World Union of Jewish Studies, 1994) 1–8.

tions include horses (often with rider), birds, and bovines. Among the human figurines, the great majority consists of pillar figurines, usually classified as "Mother-Goddess" figures and "Astarte" plaques.[5] What I intend to do is to provide a context, constructed on the basis of the texts, in which these figurines may be interpreted. I will not give a lexical study of the various terms for "image" and "figurine," nor will it be my aim to establish one-to-one correspondences between figurine types and figures known from the texts. I merely wish to narrow down the field of possible interpretations and suggest the milieu in which the figurines were at home. A question I will be especially concerned with is the relation between figurines and the official cult.

The Presumed Aniconism of the Official Cult

Many authors who have studied the Israelite figurines have argued that they belong to the realm of Israel's popular religion.[6] They base their conclusion not only on the domestic context in which many of the figurines were found, but more importantly on the aniconic nature of the official cult. They will admit that the temples of both Bethel and Dan harbored an image of a young bull; this bull, however, they interpret either as a theriomorphic throne for an invisible god or as a heathen intrusion in Israelite religion. In Jerusalem, at any rate, there was no image of God, they reason: In Zion, God was an invisible presence above the ark with the cherubim that served as his throne: is not God said to be 'seated upon the cherubim' (*yōšēb hakkĕrūbîm*)?[7] If aniconism was the hallmark of the official religion, however, the Israelite figurines—particularly if gods or goddesses—belong to the unofficial, the popular, religion. Variants of this view are mainly terminological; they may use such words as *Establishment* instead of *official cult* and *noncomformism* for *popular religion*; whatever the terms, though, the pair is always a contrast.

---

5. Based on T. A. Holland, "A Study of Palestinian Iron Age Baked Clay Figurines with Special Reference to Jerusalem: Cave 1," *Levant* 9 (1977) 121–55, esp. 124–25.

6. See, for example, M. Rose, *Der Ausschliesslichkeitsanspruch Jahwes: Deuteronomische Schultheologie und die Volksfrömmigkeit in der späten Königszeit* (BWANT 106; Stuttgart: Kohlhammer, 1975) 186 (the Asherah-statuettes served as house goddesses once the deity had been banned from the official cult); Holland, "A Study of Palestinian Iron Age Baked Clay Figurines," 134 ("the outward expression of popular 'Israelite' religion"); U. Hübner, "Das Fragment einer Tonfigurine vom *Tell el Milḥ*: Überlegungen zur Funktion der sog. Pfeiler-figurinen in der israelitischen Volksreligion," *ZDPV* 105 (1989) 47–55.

7. So, for example, T. N. D. Mettinger, "The Veto on Images and the Aniconic God in Ancient Israel," in *Religious Symbols and Their Functions* (ed. H. Biezais; Stockholm: Almqvist & Wiksell, 1979) 15–29.

For the identification of the social and religious setting of the figurines, it is necessary to reassess the thesis of Israel's aniconism.[8] Let me say, in anticipation of my arguments, that the Israelite cult, until the Deuteronomic reform, was not aniconic, neither in Bethel and Dan nor in Jerusalem. I have been led to this conclusion by five considerations, which I will here summarize.

(1) The first consideration concerns the date of the prohibition of cult images. According to the Hebrew Bible, the rejection of divine images goes back to Moses. The formal ban on images, however, is found for the first time in Deut 5:8: "You shall not make for yourself a graven image, or any likeness of anything that is in heaven above, or that is on the earth beneath, or that is in the water under the earth." Though the prohibition has antecedents in polemics against the cult of images, the interdiction does not precede the late 7th century B.C.E.[9] The vehemence of the Deuteronomic combat against the images ("beware lest you act corruptly by making a graven image for yourselves, in the form of any figure, the likeness of male or female," Deut 4:16) is testimony to their popularity in the late 7th century.[10]

(2) The fact that the cult of Yahweh was conducted in temples (called 'house' בית or 'palace' היכל) implies that he was believed to inhabit these places in some way. Though this need not imply that this presence took the form of an image, the latter is the rule in the temples known from the surrounding cultures. To the Babylonians, Canaanites, and Egyptians, a temple without a divine image was an abandoned house.[11] It is true that not all Near

---

8. The literature on the subject is staggering and ever-increasing. For an orientation see S. Mowinckel, "A quel moment le culte de Yahvé à Jerusalem est-il officiellement devenu un culte sans images?" *RHPR* 9 (1929) 197–216; Holladay, "Religion in Israel and Judah under the Monarchy," 295–99.

9. See F.-L. Hossfeld, *Der Dekalog: Seine späten Fassungen, die originale Komposition und seine Vorstufen* (OBO 45; Fribourg/Göttingen, 1982) esp. 270–73; C. Dohmen, *Das Bilderverbot: Seine Entstehung und seine Entwicklung im Alten Testament* (BBB 62; Königstein/St.-Bonn: Hanstein, 1985) 262–73; Sylvia Schroer, *In Israel gab es Bilder* (OBO 74; Fribourg: Universitätsverlag / Göttingen: Vandenhoeck & Ruprecht, 1987) 11–13.

10. There is no unanimity on the date of the aniconic requirement. Various authors hold that in its earliest form it goes back to the time (and possibly the person) of Moses. Thus K.-H. Bernhardt (*Gott und Bild* [Berlin: Evangelische, 1956] 113) argues that the formulation *lōʾ taʿăśeh lĕkā pesel* goes back to Moses.

11. For the theology of the divine image in Egypt and Mesopotamia, see J. Assmann, *Ägypten: Theologie und Frömmigkeit einer frühen Hochkultur* (Stuttgart: Kohlhammer, 1984) 50–58; idem, "Semiosis and Interpretation in Ancient Egyptian Ritual," in *Interpretation in Religion* (ed. S. Biderman and B. A. Scharf; Leiden: Brill, 1992) 87–109; T. Jacobsen, "The Graven Image," in *Ancient Israelite Religion: Essays in Honor of Frank Moore Cross* (ed. P. D. Miller, Paul D. Hanson, and S. D. McBride; Philadelphia: Fortress, 1987) 15–32.

Eastern peoples shared the cult of divine images; the Nabateans, for instance, are regularly quoted as an example of a nomadic people with an aversion for divine images.[12] Yet such aniconism is normally coupled with a simple cult, conducted not in temples but in open-air sanctuaries; the coexistence of a temple cult and a strict aniconism is highly unusual—and therefore suspect.

(3) There is positive evidence in the Bible of the worship of theriomorphic images representing deities. Nehushtan, the bronze serpent, is an example: Hezekiah is reported to have destroyed the serpent, "for until those days the people of Israel burned incense to it" (2 Kgs 18:4).[13] Another case in point is the "calf" of Bethel. The animal (in fact, a young bull) was traditionally hailed with the liturgical formula "This is your god, O Israel, who brought you up out of the land of Egypt" (1 Kgs 12:28).[14] The interpretation of the tauromorphic image as a divine seat, Yahweh himself remaining invisible,[15] is invalidated by the presentation formula just quoted, as well as by the account of the bull image at the temple of Dan, since the latter is alleged to be identical with the 'metal-covered wooden image' (pesel ûmassēkâ)[16] of Yahweh, which Micah from Ephraim once had in his shrine (Judges 17–18).[17]

---

12. See, for example, J. Patrich, "Prohibition of a Graven Image among the Nabateans: The Testimony of the Maṣṣebot Cult," *Cathedra* 26 (1982) 47–104 [Hebrew].

13. On the cult of the bronze serpent, see K. R. Joines, "The Bronze Serpent in the Israelite Cult," *JBL* 87 (1968) 245–56.

14. The phrase is usually translated as a plural on account of the verb (he⁽elûkā) The grammar does not require this translation, as the *pluralis majestatis* or *pluralis divinitatis* of *ʾelōhîm* may well take a verb in the plural, even when there can be no doubt that a single deity is being referred to (P. Joüon and T. Muraoka, *A Grammar of Biblical Hebrew* [Rome, 1991] 553 §150f). For a careful discussion of the alternative translation, see H. Donner, "Hier sind deine Gotter, Israel!" in *Wort und Geschichte: Festschrift für Karl Elliger zum 70. Geburtstag* (ed. H. Gese and H. P. Rüger; AOAT 18; Kevelaer: Butzon & Bercker / Neukirchen-Vluyn: Neukirchener, 1973) 45–50. Donner argues that, grammatically, both translations can be defended but thinks a plural is preferable on the basis of a comparison with Neh 9:18. According to H. Motzki ("Ein Beitrag zum Problem des Stierkultes in der Religionsgeschichte Israels," *VT* 25 [1975] 470–85, esp. 470–77), Jeroboam made only a single image to be set up in Bethel; the reference to the counterpart in Dan would be a fiction designed to elicit an understanding of the *ʾelōhîm* in the presentation formula as a plural.

15. So, for example, Mettinger, "The Veto on Images," 21–22.

16. The expression is a hendiadys; see *HALAT* 895 s.v. פסל [with lit.]; Dohmen, *Das Bilderverbot*, 55–59 (pace J. Scharbert, in his review of this book in *BZ* 31 [1987] 306–7); M. Haran, *Temples and Temple-Service in Ancient Israel* (Repr.: Winona Lake, Ind.: Eisenbrauns, 1985) 35 and n. 39.

17. On the role of bull images in the Israelite cult, see J. Hahn, *Das "Goldene Kalb": Die Jahwe-Verehrung bei Stierbildern in der Geschichte Israels* (unpub. dissertation summarized in *TLZ* 106 [1980] 700–701). For an interesting proposal finding a

(4) Both the Samarian and Judahite Yahweh had a consort called Asherah. A pithos from Kuntillet ʿAjrūd, a north Israelite caravanserai 50 km south of Kadesh-barnea, contains a blessing by "Yahweh of Samaria and his Asherah."[18] Alongside "Yahweh of Samaria," then, there was "Asherah of Samaria"; she is even found under this name in the Bible (reading אשרת שמרון for אשמת שמרון in Amos 8:14). A Judahite grave inscription from Ḥirbet el-Qôm also mentions "Yahweh and his Asherah,"[19] which shows that the gods were a pair in Judah as well. An image of Asherah was present in the Temple of Jerusalem (1 Kgs 15:14; 2 Kgs 21:7, 23:6; for an image of the Samarian Asherah, see 2 Kgs 23:15; cf. Deut 33:2).[20] The goddess had a female staff to weave garments for her (2 Kgs 23:7), which suggests her image was anthropomorphic—or rather, gynaecomorphic.

(5) If "his Asherah" was represented in Jerusalem under the guise of an anthropomorphic image, there is reason to suspect that Yahweh himself was also anthropomorphically present. The Judahite polemics against the bull cult in Bethel may have been inspired, not by iconoclastic sentiments, but by an aversion to a theriomorphic representation of the deity.[21] The Yahweh of Judah is the king enthroned, whose dimensions baffle human spectators.[22] Several cultic actions, such as the glorious entry of God during the enthronement festival procession (Psalm 24),[23] could hardly have been performed

reference to the bull-cult in Psalm 22, see G. Coats, "The Golden Calf in Psalm 22," *Horizons in Biblical Theology* 9 (1987) 1–12.

18. G. I. Davies et al., *Ancient Hebrew Inscriptions* (Cambridge: Cambridge University Press, 1991) 80–81.

19. Ibid., 106 no. 25.003 and literature there.

20. H. S. Nyberg, "Deuteronomium 33,2–3," *ZDMG* 92 (1938) 320–44, esp. 335; M. Weinfeld, "Kuntillet ʿAjrud Inscriptions and Their Significance," *SEL* 1 (1984) 121–30, esp. p. 124.

21. The tension between the theriomorphic vision and the anthropomorphic vision may be present in the confrontation between Zedekiah ben Chenaanah and Micaiah ben Imlah recorded in 1 Kings 22. Zedekiah uttered his prophecy while holding horns of iron and saying: "Thus says Yahweh: with these you shall push the Syrians until they are destroyed" (1 Kgs 22:11). Since it is Yahweh himself who does battle, according to the Israelite theology of warfare, Zedekiah is impersonating Yahweh as he makes himself the latter's mouthpiece. The visualization of Yahweh as a bull is fitting from a Northern perspective. Micaiah ben Imlah, on the other hand, sees "Yahweh sitting on his throne, and all the host of heaven standing beside him on his right hand and on his left" (1 Kgs 22:19). This vision is in keeping with the visions of Yahweh as Southern texts, such as Isa 6:1–3, have recorded it.

22. Isa 6:1–3, and cf. J. C. Greenfield, "Baʿal's Throne and Isaiah 6:1," *Mélanges bibliques et orientaux en l'honneur de M. Mathias Delcor* (AOAT 215; Kevelaer: Butzon & Bercker / Neukirchen-Vluyn: Neukirchener Verlag, 1985) 193–98.

23. J. Day, *Psalms* (Old Testament Guides 15; Sheffield: Sheffield Academic Press, 1990) 67–87; K. van der Toorn, "The Babylonian New Year Festival: New

without a statue—moreover, one of respectable size. Also the references to "seeing God" or the contemplation of his 'beauty' (nō'am, Ps 27:4; compare v. 13) are most likely taken as indications that there was a divine image in the temple.[24]

Another indication may be found in the dream reports that speak about beholding God's 'face' (pānîm) and 'form' (tĕmûnâ, Ps 17:15).[25] Since the stuff of dreams is a reflection, however distorted and mangled, of waking experiences, the visio Dei at night must be modeled on the visual reality of God's image by day. The description of the goddess Isis as she appeared to the asinine Lucius in his dream (Apuleius Metamorphoses 11) is in perfect agreement with her cultic image. Only people familiar with Mary's iconography will see her, perhaps, in their dreams; prior knowledge is a prerequisite. The vision of Yahweh as an anthropomorphic deity, then, reflects the existence of his image.

Possible Contexts of Figurines
outside the Official Cult

I have dwelled at some length on the issue of Israel's supposed aniconism, because it affects the discussion of the figurines. Though the latter may in fact belong to the domain of Israel's popular religion, there is no a priori reason that they should. If the official cult was centered around images, some of them anthropomorphic, both the anthropomorphic and the theriomorphic figurines that have been found in Israel may have been related to it.

I do not mean to suggest that the figurines that have been found served as cultic images in shrines and temples. Only very few of them did; the bronze bull image from Dharat et-Tawileh, between Dothan and Tirzah, is probably

---

Insights from the Cuneiform Texts and Their Bearing on Old Testament Study," in *Congress Volume: Leuven, 1989* (VTSup 43; ed. J. A. Emerton; Leiden: Brill, 1991) 331–44.

24. Thus, defying the established opinion of the exegetical community, O. Loretz, *Leberschau, Sündenbock, Asasel in Ugarit und Israel* (UBL 3; Altenberge: CIS, 1985) 71–75. The presence of an image is implied by the observations of M. L. Barré, "An Unrecognized Precative Construction in Phoenician and Hebrew," *Bib* 64 (1983) 411–22, esp. 417 n. 30. On the notion of "seeing God's face" in surrounding civilizations, see F. Nötscher, *"Das Angesicht Gottes schauen" nach biblischer und babylonischer Auffassung* (Würzburg, 1924; repr. Darmstadt: Wissenschaftliche Buchgesellschaft, 1969); T. Abusch, "Gilgamesh's Request and Siduri's Denial: Part I," in *The Tablet and the Scroll: Near Eastern Studies in Honor of William W. Hallo* (ed. M. E. Cohen et al.; Bethesda, Md.: CDL, 1993) 1–14, esp. 6 n. 26.

25. The psalm refers to a dream vision, not to actual observation; see my "Ordeal Procedures in the Psalms and the Passover Meal," *VT* 38 (1988) 427–45, esp. 434.

a rare example.[26] The reason the majority of the figurines cannot be interpreted as cult images has little to do with their size; if comparative Mesopotamian evidence may be used as a standard, the divine images of the major
shrines could have had rather modest proportions (even if some images were
reportedly huge).[27] But if the size of the Israelite figurines does not disqualify
them to serve as cult images, their poor quality does. Even in a minor sanctuary, the cult image was presumably an object of value. The story of Micah's
silver image (Judg 17:1–6), meant to be placed in his family chapel (bêt ʾelōhîm), illustrates the importance that people attached to the quality of their
local cult images. Yet, if most of our figurines were not themselves cult images, they may have been connected with the cult in some way.

However, before we explore the possible relations between the figurines
and the official cult, I wish to discuss some of the other possibilities of interpretation. Let me begin by considering the possibility of toys and puppets of
clay. At first sight, the interpretation of the figurines (or some of them) as
playthings is quite attractive.[28] In the past, both archaeologists and biblicists
were known for their penchant to interpret as cultic almost every piece of archaeological evidence for which they saw no apparent use. Let us rejoice,
therefore, if they open their minds to the profane possibility of children's
games. Puppets as playthings are mentioned in Mesopotamian texts,[29] and

26. A. Mazar, "The 'Bull Site': An Iron Age I Open Cultic Place," *BASOR* 247
(1982) 27–42; R. Wenning and E. Zenger, "Ein bäuerliches Baal-Heiligtum im sa-
marischen Gebirge aus der Zeit der Anfänge Israels," *ZDPV* 102 (1986) 75–86; M. S.
Coogan, "Of Cults and Cultures: Reflections on the Interpretation of Archaeological
Evidence," *PEQ* 119 (1987) 1–8, esp. 1–2; A. Mazar, "On Cult Places and Early Israelites: A Response to Michael Coogan," *BARev* 14/4 (1988) 45; G. W. Ahlström,
"The Bull Figurine from Dharat et-Tawileh," *BASOR* 280 (1990) 77–82.

27. J. Renger, "Kultbild," *RlA* 6.307–14, esp. §5. Agnès Spycket thinks it impossible that "the Mesopotamians would have worshipped statuettes of 20 or 30 cm in
length in their public cult, whereas divine omnipotence in their view went together
with extraordinary size" (*Les statues de culte dans les textes mésopotamiens des origines à
la Iʳᵉ dynastie de Babylone* [CahRB 9; Paris: Gabalda, 1968] 11). Cult and mythology
are separate matters, however; it is dangerous to base one's view of the former on data
from the latter. For literary evidence on a divine statue of great size, see S. Parpola,
Letters from Assyrian Scholars: Commentary (AOAT 5/2; Kevelaer/Neukirchen-Vluyn,
1983) 5 comm. to no. 1:22–23.

28. The interpretation has been defended by H. de Genouillac, *Fouilles de Telloh
II: Epoque d'Ur IIIᵉ Dynastie et de Larsa* (Paris: Geuthner, 1936) 38; L. Woolley, *Ala-
lakh: An Account of the Excavations at Tell Atchanah in the Hatay 1937–1949* (Oxford:
Oxford University Press, 1955) 249. For further references, see Holland, "A Study of
Palestinian Iron Age Baked Clay Figurines," 134.

29. See B. Landsberger, "Einige unerkannt gebliebene oder verkannte Nomina
des Akkadischen," *WZKM* 56 (1960) 109–29, esp. 117–29: *passu* = 'Puppe' und an-
dere Bezeichnungen für 'spielen' und 'Spielzeug'.

various examples of toys have in fact been found.[30] Even if there is no word for "Barbie" in the Hebrew Bible, Israelite girls would certainly have had their dolls.[31] Unfortunately, however, these dolls can hardly be identified with the figurines that have been found. The typology of the figurines does not militate against their interpretation as puppets and toys, but their distribution over the various sites does. The very same type of figurine found in a domestic context is also discovered in graves; they must have had similar, if not identical, functions—functions that can hardly be reduced to those of toys.

The context of the finds is also an argument against their interpretation as occasional artifacts for purposes of sorcery. Mesopotamian rites of healing and measures of counter-magic prescribe the preparation of images, at times from clay and at times from tallow, to be damaged, destroyed, or buried. Similar practices are known from Egypt. Magical ways of dealing with adversaries were not unknown in Israel either.[32] It is possible that some Israelites used figurines for the purposes of sorcery: in the Septuagint rendering of Ps 58:9, there is a reference to a wax image. The figurines found so far, however, are hardly to be interpreted as sorcery props: the fact that most of them show no traces of maltreatment does not favor the assumption that they served as implements of sorcery or counter-sorcery; nor does the variety of places where quite similar images were found.

Another view, which still enjoys considerable popularity, holds that the figurines were used for purpose of imitative magic. Because the so-called "pillar figurines" tend to accentuate the issue of fertility by their protruding breasts, in combination at times with the presence of an infant, they have been characterized in general terms as "fertility figurines" or even "fertility amulets." Their purpose, it is then assumed, was to bring about conception, to facilitate parturition, and to guarantee the production of mother's milk.[33] Another group of images, the so-called "Astarte plaques," has been given a similar interpretation. Miriam Tadmor has argued that they were given to the dead to ensure that they would have the services of a concubine in the afterlife. This is why fertility seems less important a factor with them than sex appeal.[34]

30. For a survey, see N. Cholidis, "Tiere und tierförmige Gefäse auf Radern: Gedanken zum Spielzeug im Alten Orient," *MDOG* 121 (1989) 197–220.

31. For archaeological evidence of games, see H. Weippert, "Spielgerät," *BRL²*, 310–11.

32. Cf N. Nicolsky, *Spuren magischer Formeln in den Psalmen* (Giessen: Töpelmann, 1927).

33. See, for example, W. F. Albright, "Astarte Plaques and Figurines from Tell Beit Mirsim," *Mélanges Dussaud* (2 vols.; Paris, 1939) 1.107–20, esp. 119.

34. M. Tadmor, "Female Relief Figurines during the Late Bronze Age in Canaan," *ErIsr* 15 (Aharoni Volume; 1981) 79–84 [Hebrew]; idem, "Female Cult Figurines in Late Canaan and Early Israel: Archaeological Evidence," in *Studies in the Period of David and Solomon and Other Essays* (ed. Tomoo Ishida; Winona Lake, Ind.:

An analysis of the Hebrew texts, both biblical and epigraphical, does not produce arguments in favor of the interpretation of the figurines as forms of "imitative" or "sympathetic" magic. It does show that issues of fertility and childbirth were of great concern to many Israelites and that women might resort to such means as 'love apples' (dûdāʾîm, Gen 30:14–14; Cant 7:14)[35] to increase their chances of sex and pregnancy. Certainly the biblical silence about fertility figurines does not mean that they did not exist; whether our figurines are in fact fertility figurines must be decided on archaeological grounds. To a nonarchaeologist like me, it would seem that here, once more, the variety of finding places of figurines of one and the same type does not render their interpretation as fertility amulets very likely. Concerning the interpretation of the Astarte figurines as concubines: though the prospect of a concubine in the afterlife, well attested in the Egyptian material, may have been alluring to Israelite men, it was hardly what they expected. The Israelite view on afterlife is scarcely joyful; in the dim existence of the netherworld, all that the spirits really care for is some food and cool water.[36]

A type of figurine one does expect to find, on the basis of a study of the texts, is a figurine of the ancestor. Ancestor figurines, at times somewhat imprecisely referred to in the literature as household gods, are called teraphim (těrāpîm) or simply 'gods' (ʾelōhîm) in the Hebrew Bible.[37] The teraphim were relatively small, measuring 30–35 cm at most, and were roughly anthropomorphic. Their production entailed little cost, which suggests that they were made (ʿŚH, Judg 17:5) of relatively cheap material, such as clay or wood.[38] According to the biblical texts they could be found in a variety of locations: in the private quarters of the house (1 Sam 19:11–17) or near its entrance

---

Eisenbrauns, 1982) 139–73. Her views are accepted by H. Weippert, *Palästina in vorhellenistischer Zeit* (Handbuch der Archäologie, Vorderasien 2/1; Munich: Beck, 1988) 305; E. Lipiński, "The Syro-Palestinian Iconography of Woman and Goddess," *IEJ* 36 (1986) 87–96, esp. 89.

35. See *HALAT* s.v., for literature.

36. Othmar Keel and Christoph Uehlinger have presented other objections against Tadmor's interpretation They note that many of the plaques were found in a domestic, not a funerary, context; that "Astarte" is standing and not lying on a bed; and that at least in some cases the plaque imitates a shrine (*Göttinnen, Götter und Gottessymbole*, 110–22).

37. For a fuller discussion of the nature and use of the teraphim, see my "The Nature of the Biblical Teraphim in the Light of the Cuneiform Evidence," *CBQ* 52 (1990) 203–22, esp. 205–17.

38. According to 2 Kgs 23:24, Josiah "removed" the teraphim; the verb BʿR (piʿel) 'to destroy, to do away with' must be distinguished from BʿR (qal) 'to burn, to set afire'.

(Exod 21:22);[39] in temples (Hos 3:4) and local shrines (Judges 17–18; 2 Kgs 23:24); or in a temporary resting-place en route (Gen 31:19, 30–35; Ezek 21: 26). Besides divine images, the teraphim are the only kind of figurines explicitly mentioned in the Bible.[40]

The logical question, then, is: have examples of teraphim been found? I believe the answer must be affirmative, though the identification of specific Israelite figurines as ancestor images must remain provisional. Let me say right away that the association of pillar figurines and Astarte plaques with ancestor images is erroneous; if men and women died in equal proportions, why should there be far more female than male teraphim?[41] If ancestor figurines have been found, they are most likely identified with the so-called "schematic statues" such as the ones from the Stelae temple at Hazor. Pirhiya Beck has recently devoted an article to these statues, in which she make a tentative case for their interpretation as ancestor idols.[42] The images are quite small, about 20–25 cm in height; the lower portion may be carved as a base so as to suggest a seated posture. In corroboration of her view one could refer to the somewhat similar anthropoid busts found in ancient Egyptian houses; they evidently were part of the cult of the dead.[43] The Israelite images also resemble the pre-Islamic Arabian ancestor statues; they are about the same size,

39. Cf H. Niehr, "Ein unerkannter Text zur Nekromantie in Israel," *UF* 23 (1991) 301–6, esp. 304.

40. The custom of having figurines of the ancestors in the house is attested for Mesopotamia as well. The fact that Gilgamesh put the oil-containing horns of the Bull of Heaven in his bedroom to anoint his god Lugalbanda (*ana piššat ilišu* ᵈ*Lugalbanda iqīš/ušērimma itattal ina urši ḫammūtišu*; R. C. Thompson, *The Epic of Gilgamesh* [Oxford: Clarendon, 1930] pl. 25, lines 174–75) "implies that Gilgamesh kept a statue or statuette of him [i.e., his father Lugalbanda—KvdT] in his bedroom where he anointed it regularly" (S. Dalley, *Myths from Mesopotamia* [Oxford: Oxford University Press, 1989] 129 n. 68). For evidence of the worship of ancestor images at Emar and Nuzi, see my "Gods and Ancestors in Emar and Nuzi," *ZA* 84 (1994) 38–59.

41. Pace J. Gray (*I & II Kings* [OTL; Philadelphia, 1964] 745), who associates the *tĕrāpîm* with "the many figurines with the features of Asherah and Astarte found at Palestinian sites." These figurines, suggested Gray, "rank as *tĕrāpîm*" and were used "in rites of imitative magic to promote fertility." Gray here is following W. F. Albright, who once made a similar claim (Albright, *From the Stone Age to Christianity* [Garden City, N.Y., 1957] 311). See also H. G. May (*Material Remains of the Megiddo Cult* [OIP 26; Chicago, 1935] 27), who says that it is "extremely probable" that the term *tĕrāpîm* was used to designate mother-goddesses and other fertility figurines.

42. P. Beck, "A Note on the 'Schematic Statues' from the Stelae Temple at Hazor," *TA* 17 (1990) 91–95.

43. See R. J. Demarée, *The Ꜣḫ iḳr n Rˁ-Stelae: On Ancestor Worship in Ancient Egypt* (Leiden: Nederlands Instituut voor het Nabije Oosten, 1983) 289–90 with literature.

schematic in form, and usually in a seated position.[44] My only problem with Beck's identification is the fact that no "schematic statues" have been found in a domestic context.[45]

Figurines and the Official Cult

The discussion of the "schematic statues" from the Hazor Stelae temple may serve as a bridge to a survey of the possible connection between the Israelite figurines and the official cult. If their function as full-fledged cult images must be ruled out, what connections can there have been? I believe there are three possibilities, which I shall discuss in the order of increasing probability.

(1) The first possibility concerns the presence, in the temple, of lower-ranking companion gods (the so-called *theoi sunnaoi*) and apotropaeic deities alongside the image of the main god. According to the Deuteronomist, the Temple in Jerusalem contained cultic 'vessels' (*kēlîm*) for Baal, for Asherah, and for all the host of heaven (2 Kgs 23:4). Even if the term 'vessels' is not a euphemism for images—which it may very well be—the expression implies a cult for the deities mentioned. For astral gods ("the host of heaven") such a cult may have been aniconic, but for Baal this is hardly likely. During the first half of the 6th century B.C.E., the Babylonian god Tammuz also received worship in the temple (Ezek 8:14), though this may have been a disguised form of Baal worship. From Mesopotamian evidence we know that temples often harbored images of defeated divine adversaries demoted to guardian spirits: Humbaba and Anzu are examples.[46] In Jerusalem, Nehushtan and the Bronze Sea (*yam hannĕḥōšet, yam hammûṣāq*) may have been regarded as the trophies of Yahweh, the god being assimilated to Baal as the victor of Yam and Leviathan.

(2) The second possibility to relate the figurines to the cult would be to interpret them as votive gifts. Votive images are quite familiar from Mesopotamian archaeology. The temple of Gula at Isin, for instance, has yielded large groups of terra-cotta body parts, small dogs (the emblem animal of the

44. C. Rathjens, *Sabaeica:Bericht über die archäologische Ergebnisse seiner zweiten, dritten und vierten Reise nach Sudarabien, II: Die unlokalisierte Funde* (Hamburg: Appel, 1955) 61–78, "die Grabstatuetten."

45. The possibility that the approximately thirty figurines found in excavated courtyards on the Golan (see C. Epstein, "Household Idols from the Golan," *Qadmoniot* 13 [1980] 20–21) are chalcolithic precedents of such ancestor figurines deserves consideration.

46. See F. A. M. Wiggerman, *Mesopotamian Protective Spirits: The Ritual Texts* (Groningen: Styx, 1992) 146.

goddess), and images of the goddess herself. Such images are called "votive," even though many of them were offered in anticipation of answered prayers or simply to win the goodwill of the goddess (and to cut a good figure in the eyes of the neighbors). The diversity of iconographic *Motivs* needs to be stressed: usually there is a relation between the votive object and the characteristics of the deity and/or the worshiper. Thus Gula receives dog figurines because the dog is her sacred animal;[47] Baal-zaphon received miniature anchors because the worshipers were often sailors.[48] Many worshipers offered worshiper figurines[49] or representations of ailing (or healed) body parts.[50]

(3) The third and last explanation of most of the Israelite figurines would see them as reflections of official cult images or symbols, used for a variety of purposes outside the cult. In illustration of such practices I refer, once more, to Mesopotamian customs. In Mesopotamian religion, according to A. Leo Oppenheim, "the role of the image was central in the cult as well as in private worship, as the wide distribution of cheap replicas of such images shows."[51] It is true that terra-cotta figurines, often not unlike the Israelite ones, have been found in substantial numbers in a domestic context.[52] They presumably served there as "icons" of sorts.[53] They had functions comparable to those of

47. See, for example, M. A. Mustafa, "Kassite Figurines: A New Group Discovered Near Aqar Qûf," *Sumer* 3 (1947) 19–22 and 5 plates.; B. Hrouda (ed.), *Isin-Išān Bahriyat* (Munich, 1977) 1.40–41; Taf. 8–9:IB 41, 42, 47, 50, 5 a–b.

48. A. Caquot and M. Sznycer, *Ugaritic Religion* (Iconography of Religions 15/8; Leiden: Brill, 1980) 3.

49. E. Sollberger, "Old Babylonian Worshipper Figurines," *Iraq* 31 (1969) 90–93; E. Braun-Holzinger, *Frühdynastische Beterstatuetten* (Berlin: Mann, 1977); A. Spycket and K. Karstens and U. Kramm, *Ein frühdynastische Frauen-Statuette in der prähistorischen Staatssammlung München* (Munich: Profil, 1990).

50. A. Spycket, "Ex-voto mésopotamiens du IIe millénaire av. J.-C., *De la Babylonie à la Syrie, en passant par Mari: Mélanges offerts à Monsieur J.-R. Kupper à l'occasion de son 70e anniversaire* (ed. Ö. Tunca; Liège: Université de Liège, 1990) 79–86 and pls. 1–3 (feet to Gula of Isin).

51. A. L. Oppenheim, *Ancient Mesopotamia: Portrait of a Dead Civilization* (Chicago: University of Chicago Press, 1964) 184. For an interpretation of female figures as replicas of cult images, see also M.-T. Barrelet, *Figurines et reliefs en terre cuite de la Mésopotamie antique, I: Potiers, termes de métier, procédés de fabrication et de production* (Paris: Geuthner, 1968) 233.

52. See, for example, E. Douglas Van Buren, *Clay Figurines of Babylonia and Assyria* (YOSR 16; New Haven: Yale University Press, 1930) esp. 2–70; Barrelet, *Figurines et reliefs*, esp. pp. 164–69, 233–76; E. Klengel-Brandt, *Die Terrakotten aus Assur im Vorderasiatischen Museum Berlin* (Berlin: VEB, 1978) passim.

53. I. M. Diakonoff, "Women in Old Babylonia Not under Patriarchal Authority," *JESHO* 29 (1986) 225–38, esp. 232.

the clay models of sacred architecture also found in Mesopotamian (and Syrian) houses.[54] Replicas of cult images as well as miniature shrines kept the memory of the real images and the real shrines alive and kindled the devotion of those who possessed them. The prophylactic powers ascribed to these figurines (or clay models) may account for the variety of contexts (including burials) in which they have been found.

Assessing the three possibilities of cultic interpretation that I have just mentioned (the word *cultic* being used in a rather extended sense), we must probably dismiss the first one as quite improbable. The cheapness of our figurines makes it unlikely that they ever served as cult statues, even of modest *theoi sunnaoi* or guardian spirits; only some of the rare bronze figurines found so far might qualify as such.[55] The second possibility, which takes the figurines as votive gifts, is more promising. Considering the needs to which the national temples catered, one would expect them to contain impressive numbers of votive figurines—assuming that, in this respect, the Israelite cult resembled the Mesopotamian. In response to answered prayers, people might demonstrate their gratitude by celebrating a sacrificial meal, to which they invited family and friends (Ps 22:23–32). As a lasting display of their gratitude, they might leave a commemorative inscription, similar to the *miktab* (see LXX *stēlografia* in Ps 15[MT 16]:1; 55[MT 56]:1; 56[MT 57]:1; 57[MT 58]:1; 58[MT 59]:1; 59[MT 60]:1) of Hezekiah (Isa 38:9–20).

In view of the comparative evidence, the Israelite temples must have received lasting material tokens of hope and gratitude as well. Elements of the booty were customarily consecrated this way, and the sword of Goliath kept at Nob could be regarded as such a votive gift. A few archaeological examples have been found. A votive gift from the late 13th century is the Lachish ewer, whose inscription says that it is an offering (*šy*) to the goddess Elat.[56] At Arad, two votive offering dishes with a Phoenician inscription were found in the sacred area, probably from the 7th century.[57] A bronze disk from Tell Shiqmona bears the inscription "Hammer-work which Yahonbaal made, son

54. For examples, see R. Hachmann, "Rapport préliminaire," *BMB* 30 (1978) figs. 28, 29, 32, 33, 35; H. Seeden, "A Small Clay Shrine in the AUB Museum," *Berytus* 27 (1979) 7–25. It cannot be excluded that the clay models of domestic architecture are to be interpreted in a similar vein; for those who had left the family home, devotion to their ancestors may have entailed the attachment to a model of the family house.

55. For a discussion of some of the anthropomorphic bronze figurines, see Keel and Uehlinger, *Göttinnen, Götter und Gottessymbole*, 152–53.

56. F. M. Cross, The Origin and Early Evolution of the Alphabet, *ErIsr* 8 (1967) 8*–24*, esp. 16*.

57. See F. M. Cross, "Two Offering Dishes with Phoenician Inscriptions from the Sanctuary of ʿArad," *BASOR* 235 (1979) 75–78.

of Mathor. May you bless him, Baal. May it give protection."[58] The so-called El-qoneh-ʾereṣ ostracon from Jerusalem also seems to be dedicatory: it bears several names followed by the theonym El-qoneh-ʾereṣ.[59] Jars and pots inscribed "holy to Yô" (Yô being short for Yahweh) may also be interpreted as votive gifts.[60] Yet while all of this suggests that votive gifts of different kinds were by no means unknown, there is not one example of a figurine demonstrably donated as a votive gift.[61]

This brings us then to the final possibility: are the figurines to be interpreted as cheap imitations of cult images for purposes of devotion and protection? There are several arguments in support of this possibility. In our own time, people who have come to such pilgrimage centers as Lourdes in southern France do not like to leave empty-handed; healed or not, they often procure for themselves a souvenir of their passage in the form of a devotional picture or a miniature replica of the Virgin of Lourdes. There is no reason to believe that people acted differently in the past. Demetrius and his fellow silversmiths had a thriving business in the production of miniature shrines of Artemis of Ephesus; they presumably owed much of their wealth to the pilgrims (Acts 19:23–41). Pilgrimages were common enough in ancient Israel; the centralistic religious politics of both Samarian and Judahite kings favored the development. Being unable to visit the Temple daily, many people would have regarded the possession of a replica of a cult image, with the attendant cultic utensils, as a kind of substitute.

The word *replica* suggests a high degree of similarity between the clay figurine and the far more precious cult image. In some cases, this correspondence may have been present in fact. Some of the Astarte plaques depict the goddess within a frame. Though Miriam Tadmor interprets the frame as a bed, which fits her contention that the plaques represent human concubines, the frame could also—and more plausibly, in my opinion—be seen as a schematic representation of the shrine. The plaques, then, are not just replicas of the image but of the image in context.[62]

Yet while the replica theory may hold good for the Astarte plaques, it does not entirely fit the so-called pillar figurines. These, it would seem, are an

---

58. A. van de Branden, "Le disque de bronze de Shiqmona," *BeO* 22 (1980) 219–25.

59. P. D. Miller Jr., "El, the Creator of the Earth," *BASOR* 239 (1980) 42–46.

60. See R. P. Gordon, "Inscribed Pots and Zechariah XIV 20–21," *VT* 42 (1992) 120–23.

61. An interpretation of the figurines as votive gifts is defended by Leila Badre, *Les figurines anthropomorphes en terre cuite de l'âge du bronze en Syrie* (Paris: Geuthner, 1980).

62. Keel and Uehlinger, *Göttinnen, Götter und Gottessymbole*, 113–18.

iconographic type of very great antiquity and do not correspond to a specific localized cult image. The naked female whose fertility is stressed by the size of her breasts, the way in which she holds her body, or the presence of a child, represents the oldest type of figurine known from the Near East.[63] She is indeed a type rather than a personality; as such, she can be identified with a variety of specific goddesses. A subcategory of this type is described in an inventory text from Qatna: the temple treasury includes "a necklace with four lapis lazuli *šassūrātu*, each holding a child on her lap."[64] The word *šassūru* means 'womb' and, as a personification, 'mother goddess'.[65] Against this background, the customary characterization of the Israelite pillar figurine and related types as 'mother-goddesses' or *dea nutrix* is not without precedent in antiquity.

The unspecificity of the 'mother-goddess' type does not preclude its identification with one of the major goddesses of the ancient Near Eastern pantheon. In fact, quite a number of goddesses participate in her nature. In Mesopotamia, the mother-goddess may be identified with Ninḫursag, Bēlet-ilī, Mami, and several others.[66] In Canaan and Israel, the most likely identification of the mother-goddess, and thus of the pillar figurines, is Asherah. She is, according to the Ugaritic texts, mother of the gods and spouse of El, the creator of humanity. In contrast to Anath and Astarte, whose associations are far more erotic, she is connected with motherhood.[67] Since Asherah is well attested in Israelite religion, better than Anath and certainly as well as Astarte, there is no reason not to admit an identification to which so many indications point. The reluctance of Pritchard to commit himself to a specific identification[68] seems unnecessary, particularly in the light of the new epigraphic evidence of the cult of Asherah in ancient Israel.[69]

---

63. Barrelet, *Figurines et reliefs en terre cuite de la Mésopotamie antique*, 1.54–55. See also G. F. Dales, *Mesopotamian and Related Female Figurines: Their Chronology, Diffusion, and Cultural Function* (Ph.D. diss., University of Pennsylvania, 1960) 182–84.

64. J. Bottéro, "Les inventaires de Qatna," *RA* 43 (1949) 137–215, quotation from p. 160 iv 223–24: *kišādu* (GÚ) *libbi* (ŠÀ) *4 šassūrātu uqnî mārēšunu ina burkīšunu ukâl.*

65. CAD Š/2 145–46 s.v. *šassūru.*

66. The iconographic type has been identified with Šala, the spouse of the storm-god

67. Cf. also Keret's vow to Athirat of Tyre and Elath of Sidon in connection with his plan to marry Ḫurray and beget children from her (KTU 1.14 iv 195–207).

68. J. B. Pritchard, *Palestinian Figurines in Relation to Certain Goddesses Known through Literature* (Philadelphia: American Oriental Society, 1943) 86–87; so too M.-T. Barrelet, "Deux déesses syro-phéniciennes sur un bronze du Louvre," *Syria* 35 (1958) 27–44; Hübner, "Das Fragment einer Tonfigurine aus *Tell el-Milḥ*," 54.

69. In addition to the references to Asherah from Kuntillet ʿAjrūd and Ḫirbet el-Qôm, see also the dedication 'to Asherah' (*lʾšrt*) on a 7th-century B.C.E. oil jar

A question that remains to be answered concerns the predominance of female figurines over male ones. If Yahweh could be iconographically represented, why is it that he so seldom was? Let me say, first of all, that I am not sure that the horse-with-rider figurines should not be connected with Yahweh; in other words, the assumption Yahweh was hardly ever represented in clay is open to doubt.[70] Yet it must be admitted that, when it comes to the sheer quantity of terra-cotta figurines, Asherah outstrips her male consort by far. The reason must be sought in Asherah's role as mediatrix. Already in Ugaritic mythology, Asherah intercedes with El on behalf of Baal (KTU 1.4 iv–v 1–97). Her position as intermediary is also reflected by the Ḫirbet el-Qôm inscription, which says that the author has been saved (or hopes to be saved?) from all his troubles (or enemies?) by Yahweh 'through his Asherah' (לאשרתו).[71] Asherah mediates the blessing of El and, once Yahweh has taken the place of El, of Yahweh. She thus provides progeny and protection. Her power even extends to the grave, witness the funerary inscription of Ḫirbet el-Qôm and the frequency of pillar figurines in burial contexts.[72]

---

from Tel Miqne/Ekron (S. Gitin, "Ekron of the Philistines, Part II: Olive-Oil Suppliers to the World," *BARev* 16 [1990] 33–42, 59, esp. 41 and 59 n. 18). The identification of the pillar figurines with Asherah was made as early as 1967 by R. Patai, *The Hebrew Goddess* (New York: Ktav, 1967) 29–52. It is also made by M. Rose, *Der Ausschliesslichkeitsanspruch Jahwes*, 182ff.; R. Hestrin, "The Lachish Ewer and the ʾAsherah," *IEJ* 37 (1987) 212–23, esp. 221–22; R. Wenning, "Wer war der Paredros der Aschera?" *BN* 59 (1991) 89–97, esp. 92–94; Keel and Uehlinger, *Göttinnen, Götter und Gottessymbole*, 378. In a recent article on clay figurines from Jerusalem, Abdel-Jalil ʾAmr has made a case for the identification with Ishtar ("Ten Human Clay Figurines from Jerusalem," *Levant* 20 [1988] 185–96, esp. 195).

70. Cf. J. G. Taylor, "The Two Earliest Known Representations of Yahweh," in *Ascribe to the Lord: Biblical and Other Studies in Memory of Peter C. Craigie* (ed. L. Eslinger and J. G. Taylor; JSOTSup 67; Sheffield: JSOT Press, 1988) 557–66.

71. For this interpretation of the *lamed*, see H.-P. Müller, "Kolloquialsprache und Volksreligion in den Inschriften von Kuntillet ʿAǧrūd und Ḫirbet el-Qôm," *ZAH* 5 (1992) 15–51, esp. 43; Jeffrey Tigay renders ("Israelite Religion: The Onomastic and Epigraphic Evidence," in *Ancient Israelite Religion: Essays in Honor of Frank Moore Cross* [ed. P. D. Miller, P. D. Hanson, and S. D. McBride; Philadelphia: Fortress, 1987] 174–75) the *lamed* as 'for the sake of' (but turns the goddess Asherah into a cultic symbol in the sanctuary). For a photograph and drawings of the inscription, see Z. Zevit, "The Khirbet el-Qôm Inscription Mentioning a Goddess," *BASOR* 256 (1984) 39–47, with an interpretation I cannot share. It may be of interest in this connection to note reference to a blessing for Baal *lšm ʾl* 'by name of El' in one of the fragments from Kuntillet ʿAjrūd (for a convenient transcription of the text, see S. Aḥituv, *Handbook of Ancient Hebrew Inscriptions* [The Biblical Encyclopaedia Library 7; Jerusalem: Bialik, 1992] 160).

72. Wenning surmises that every dead person was given a pillar figurine or a symbol (such as the terra-cotta dove) of Asherah ("Wer war der Paredros der Aschera?"

Final Consideration

Many of the publications on Israelite (or "Palestinian," as they used to be called) figurines strike a note of caution by saying that our knowledge is limited "at the present state of archaeological research."[73] In addition to caution, there is optimism here: since the answers lie below, it is assumed that the increase of data will result in a better understanding of what has been discovered so far. Reading Pritchard's study on Palestinian figurines, which appeared in 1943, one senses that the last fifty years have indeed witnessed some progress. This progress is due not only to a less fragmentary knowledge of the history of development of the various types of figurines but quite as much to the epigraphical discoveries that have been made, as well as to an improved understanding of the Hebrew Bible as a source on early Israelite religion. These three factors favor the idea that many of the figurines had a cultic function; more specifically, they lead us to believe that the Israelites identified their pillar figurines with Asherah. What they also suggest, finally, is that the distance between the official cult and the popular religion was not as great as is commonly believed. Once it is accepted that the official cult of preexilic times was quite different from the orthodoxy of postexilic times, the devotional life reflected in the figurines, be it in a domestic or a funerary context, can be seen as derived from and dependent on the official religion. Instead of being nonconformist, popular religion conformed to the established cult.

[*Manuscript completed, December 1994*]

89–90); a similar count is given by Keel and Uehlinger, *Göttinnen, Götter und Gottessymbole*, 376.

73. Holland, "A Study of Iron Age Baked Clay Figurines," 154.

On the Use of Images in Israel and the Ancient Near East

A Response to Karel van der Toorn

Jack M. Sasson
Vanderbilt University

I begin with three obvious points:

1. It is a fact that no new texts are being added to Hebrew Scriptures, whether by excavating in Jerusalem or in library vaults. In effect, to press our favorite individual points we still mine the same scriptural passages.
2. It is also a fact that archaeologists are recovering very few types of statues and images that were unknown to recent generations of scholarship. The material from Kuntillet al-ʿAjrûd is one exception, the true usefulness of which, however, is compromised by sensationalizing articles in such publications as the *Biblical Archaeology Review* and *Bible et Archéologie*.
3. It is further a fact that the range of comparative material we can bring to bear on the issue of cult figurines, both textual and archaeological, has not changed much since the first decades of decipherment, although the testimony for each type of material has increased and our tools to analyze them have added in sophistication. If one draws on classical texts as witness, it will be seen that the evidence has been staring at us for a long time now.

Van der Toorn's approach to the problem of Israelite cultic practices is to avoid privileging one sort of documentation (for example, archaeological) over another (for example, textual). By leaning on comparative data drawn mostly from western Asia, van der Toorn has concluded that, prior to the Deuteronomistic reforms, worship in Israel was likely iconic. The arguments he gives are fivefold. I comment as I review them.

(1) While acknowledging the existence of a debate in ancient Israel about the cultic use of images, van der Toorn locates the sharpest interdictions against the cultic use of images in Deut 5:8 and 4:16 and therefore

presumes that before that time the issue was more fluid. Even if we grant his premise, must we nevertheless assume that the most effective application of a legal formulation necessarily coincided with its fullest or most decisive codification? Especially in the case of Israel, when we have no extrabiblical materials, I think it behooves us to be wary. What if we operated on the assumption that a given social condition in Mesopotamia must be coeval with its formulation by Hammurabi and no earlier? Obviously, such an assumption would not be a fruitful premise.

(2) Van der Toorn's second argument: Israel's neighbors had temples, where they had images; Israel had temples, so Israel should have had at least one cultic image. If it did not have such an image, it would have carried out its worship in the open-air sanctuaries. Thin, very thin.

In fact, in antiquity, willingly or otherwise, the gods traveled constantly, spending quite a bit of time outside of their temples and receiving adoration at designated shrines. At Emar, images of the gods were displayed in the open air, where they doubtless received worshipers. Relevant for our discussion is the disagreement among specialists whether before the second millennium Mesopotamians ever worshiped the gods themselves, anthropomorphically or otherwise, rather than just their symbols. If so, at least for Mesopotamia, the worship of the gods incarnated into images may well have to be set within a move in historical times toward greater intimacy between gods and human beings. Applied to Israel, this observation suggests the opposite of van der Toorn's scheme: Deuteronomy might be a last-ditch attempt at retaining *aniconic* worship.

(3) For his third point, van der Toorn writes about the bronze serpent, the bulls of Bethel, and the idols of Micah. Although the implication of Flaubert's famous quip "Le Bon Dieu est dans le bétail [Flaubert has 'détail']" must never be dismissed in connection with religious symbolism, I nevertheless think that we need to accentuate the difference between cult images, figurines in which the divine presence was invested, and figurines that were merely decorative or served as acolytes. I will come back to this point below.

(4) For his fourth argument, van der Toorn focuses on the testimony of Kuntillet al-ʿAjrûd regarding Yahweh and his Asherah, a testimony that in its wake has led to a profitable search for the mention of Asherot in published Northwest Semitic texts. The point he makes is about the existence of a consort for the Hebrew God. The material he brings into comparison is good and should not be dismissed out of hand. Yet I do want it remembered that, while at Elephantine and in gnostic texts (not to speak of medieval Jewish cabalistic texts), all sorts of brides were promoted for Yahweh, we must not assume that all these *shiduchs* originated in Israel's highest priestly circles or that such arrangements were deemed equally vital to the conduct of its cult.

(5) Van der Toorn's fifth point deals with the psychology of worship—specifically, with the difficulty of disassociating the anthropomorphic from our experience of the divine. This is true, and Voltaire said it most pungently when he claimed that if donkeys had gods they would conceive them in their own image. Still, I do not think we will advance too far if we take this analytic path. For in ancient Israel, as well as among its neighbors generally, the condition was at least partially caused by language, since Hebrews could not avoid creating anatomical metaphors when they reached for the abstract. I for one would not have students search for red-nosed figurines just because in Hebrew this is what is said to happen to Yahweh's nose when he lost patience. Further, we all know what it cost Ezekiel when in his early chapters he tried to avoid anthropomorphisms while speaking about God: he fractured grammar, blurred gender, ignored number, and played havoc with syntax; in short, he gave us bizarre, realistically impossible, visions. For his troubles, his text is now mercilessly emended, especially by biblical scholars with little appreciation of what he was trying to do.

In the second portion of his essay, van der Toorn does us a great service by suggesting diverse contexts for the use of figurines. Myself, I would not worry about the distribution of figurines within or beyond the "official cult," because to me the distinction is artificial. Van der Toorn categorizes as "votive" the largest number of figurines found in Israel. This is attractive, although it bears repeating that, when inscribed, Mesopotamian votive figurines tended to represent the worshipers as readily as the deities to whom they were offered. I find very quaint his suggestion that figurines dug up in Israel were clones that were destined for something like a tourist trade. I would ask van der Toorn to speculate about how much divinity remained stuck to such replicas. If not much, what was the point of shelling out shekels for their purchase? But if they retained enough of the divine aura, then I do not think there could have been much haste in wishing to purchase them, for the average worshipers of antiquity, especially those not belonging to priestly or royal circles, would not have relished transporting deities or their symbols. (Think of what 2 Samuel 6 says happened to poor Uzza when he accidentally touched a holy object!) To the contrary, fear and trembling were the prevalent reactions about coming into contact with them, as for instance when the veracity of litigants was tested through the handling of divine paraphernalia—so much so, that in many texts we are told that people would rather accept penalties than anger the gods. Having a god in your midst was also very unsettling to say the least. Think also of what happened to the poor Philistines when they commandeered the ark of Yahweh!

Among his final remarks, van der Toorn leaves open the possibility that Yahweh figurines may well have existed, especially among the figurines that portray riders and horses. Let me address this issue by connecting temples and cult figurines.[1]

When we hear about the building of temples in the ancient Near East, those taking credit for the endeavor are almost uniformly rulers and elite. This is not surprising, because most of our records on this topic, especially foundation inscriptions and the like, were sponsored by kings. Now and then, however, we learn that temples, doubtless more modest in size, were raised by private individuals. Among the more arresting of these documents is one from Emar where a Pilsu-Dagan built a temple for an avatar of Nergal. Then, at a convocation of the city's elders, Pilsu-Dagan had his own descendants declared perpetual priests.[2] Such enterprises may not have been uncommon, especially beyond the walls of administrative capitals. Thus, Judges 17, which tells how Micah supplied his temple with cult figurines and priestly personnel, may be testimony to it. Interestingly enough, central administrations may have encouraged the burgeoning of smallish temples, for they facilitated their control of outlying regions merely by inviting these local gods for extended stay in the palace temple. Thus, in the Saggaratum district of Mari, the gods of local villages—really hovels—were gathered into the central palace, to be released in time for local festivals.[3]

Mari documents tell us also about the fabrication of cultic figurines. These figurines must not be confused with protective spirits or votive representations of rulers. The manufacture of a potential host for the god was carried out under the most deliberate steps. We are told of oracular measures taken "regarding the god Lagamal, whether to give him a human face or to set a tiara of 8 horns topped by golden disk."[4] We also have queries on how to position the statues of acolytes around a statue of the god. Writes a Mari administrator, "On a raised platform, to the left, stands the statue of the god Amurru, bearing a scimitar (*gamlum*). Across from him stands my lord's statue

---

1. Some of the ideas expressed below are duplicated, with kind permission of the editors and publisher, in "The Image of Ancient Israel: Reacting to Conference Presentations," in *Text, Artifact, and Image: Revealing Ancient Israelite Religion* (ed. Gary Beckman and Ted J. Lewis; Philadelphia: University of Pennsylvania Press, forthcoming).

2. D. Arnaud, *Textes syriens de l'Âge du Bronze récent* (Aula Orientalis Supplementa 1; 1991) 143–44, text no. 87. For an accessible treatment, see H. Avalos, "Legal and Social Institutions in Canaan and Ancient Israel," in *Civilizations of the Ancient Near East* (ed. J. M. Sasson et al.; New York: Scribners, 1995) 623.

3. See text no. 8 in Maurice Birot, *Lettres de Yaqqim-Addu, gouverneur de Sagaratum* (ARMT 14; Paris: Geuthner, 1976).

4. This fragment is extracted from M.7515 and cited by D. Charpin and J. M. Durand, "Notes de lecture: *Texte aus dem Sînkāšid Palast*," MARI 7 (1993) 372.

in worship. Atop the statue (of Amurru?), there is a sun-disk and moon-crescent."[5]

Above all, no figurine could serve as object of worship if it were not first consecrated. This process required time-consuming rituals, such as rituals to open or wash the mouth of the potential god. Among the steps taken during such a ceremony was the formal disavowal that human hands were ever responsible for the creating of divine statues.[6] Once these rituals were executed, what might look like a statue to an undiscerning mind had in fact become a visible manifestation of the unknowable, a palpable transfiguration of a "cosmic implosion," in which all that ever could be was rendered accessible to the human senses.[7] This is why we should really not be completely taken in by the Hebrew prophets when they mock pagans for their worship of dead wood and inert stone. In fact, like flags, crucifixes, and torah scrolls, the consecrated idol acquired sacralization because people, realizing how pathetically limited were their natural senses, had no other recourse by which to bridge the chasm separating them from their gods. If I were asked to elaborate on this observation, I would draw attention to the fact that in India (but also now in the United States) images of the gods are constructed, made divine, and then worshiped.[8]

The above remarks bring me back to the likelihood of archaeologists' ever finding cultic figures for Yahweh. For me it is not enough to dig up figurines of bulls or of humanoids riding equids; I would insist, rather, that before

5. This fragment is quoted from A.975, as cited in ibid.

6. This point is well made by Thorkild Jacobsen, "The Graven Image," in *Ancient Israelite Religion: Essays in Honor of Frank Moore Cross* (ed. P. D. Miller Jr., P. D. Hanson, and S. D. McBride; Philadelphia: Fortress, 1987) 15–32. See now Angelika Berlejung, *Die Theologie der Bilder: Herstellung und Einweihung von Kultbildern in Mesopotamien und die alttestamentliche Bilderpolemik* (Göttingen: Vandenhoeck & Ruprecht, 1998) and her essay, "Washing the Mouth," in *The Image and the Book: Iconic Cults, Aniconism, and the Rise of Religion in Israel and the Ancient Near East* (ed. K. van der Toorn; Leuven: Peeters, 1997) 45–72. Also, Christopher Walker and Michael Dick, *The Induction of the Cult Image in Ancient Mesopotamia: The Mesopotamian Mīs Pî Ritual* (State Archives of Assyria Literary Texts 1; Helsinki: The Neo-Assyrian Text Project, 2001).

7. The phrase is taken from J. Preston, who applies it to the *mūrti* in Hindu worship: "Creation of the Sacred Image: Apotheosis and Destruction in Hinduism," in *Gods of Flesh, Gods of Stone: The Embodiment of Divinity in India* (ed. J. P. Waghorne et al.; Chambersburg, Penn.: Anima, 1985) 9–30.

8. J. P. Waghorne, "The Divine Image in Contemporary South India: The Renaissance of a Once Maligned Tradition," in *Born in Heaven, Made on Earth: The Making of the Cult Image in the Ancient Near East* (ed. M. B. Dick; Winona Lake, Ind.: Eisenbrauns, 1999) 211–43.

scholars would offer as a serious hypothesis the existence of Yahweh figurines in the Hebrew cult, they should first refer to Scriptural evidence, manifest or vestigial, for consecrative ceremonies such as those discussed above.

So I remain skeptical about the conclusions of my colleague; but not about the need to periodically debate the place of cultic figurines in Israelite worship. Van der Toorn has correctly sensed that this debate, which is already a few centuries old, has recently come back to the fore, and with a vengeance. He offers three reasons for this situation:

1. The realization that religion addresses the senses as well as the mind;
2. The sentiment that popular religion is different from official cult;
3. The awareness that we have neglected the place of women (as in figurines).

I do not wish to argue with any of these points, although I would not want it imagined that Israel's religious practice is less sensuous when it is aniconic.[9] I also do not want to debate a definition for *popular religion*, because, to be blunt about it, I don't think that we can distribute the textual and archaeological data about worship incontestably among the ranks, positions, and classes of an ancient society. When I hear talk of "popular religion," I feel carried back to the debate launched by the Social Gospel movement in America.[10]

I do, however, want to introduce another potentially cogent reason for our renewed fascination with the topic, because elucidating when we keep on rehashing old themes may also be worth our while.

It seems to me that beyond its intrinsic merits the debate about the place of cultic figurines in Israel's worship is quickened by cultural stresses of the type first described in biblical texts. The most spectacular of these debates lasted over a century and was launched most immediately when Leo III, emperor of Byzantium in the first half of the 8th century, championed the cause of iconoclasm and ordered the removal of icons and statues throughout the empire. He was challenged by powerful leaders, such as Popes Gregory II and III. What is interesting is that at the Second Nicean Council of 754 were paraded the same biblical texts that van der Toorn and others cite for proving or disproving the purity of Israel's worship. Thus, when Leo cited Hezekiah's destruction of Nehushtan, the bronze serpent, Gregory told him, "Yes, Heze-

---

9. To have witnessed Hebrew priests, in full raiment, slaughtering, butchering, burning, then dispensing of animals would certainly have quickened each of our senses—hearing, seeing, smelling, tasting, and touching—not to speak of the bother of having scads of buzzing flies, had we come upon the scene in midsummer.

10. If not also to German romanticism when the *Volk* was invested with better creative instincts, in literature as well as in moral values

kiah was certainly kin to you, displaying the same audacity as you, and in like manner tyrannized over the priests, for that serpent was brought into the temple by the holy David himself, together with the holy ark."[11] Leo learned then what we all now know: you can argue antithetical positions, just by citing from Scripture.

Now specialists still ponder the causes that impelled Leo to arm the polemic with words when for centuries it was fought mostly with swords. I have come across many suggestions; but because I know so little about the context, I can unabashedly favor one of them. Under Leo, who was a usurper (most of them were in those days), "iconoclasm was the climax of caesoropapism, the traditional reestablishment of imperial cult." His reforms came from the heart, but they also made it such that none but the central administration could define and control what was an image and where to locate it.[12] The parallels with what happened in Israel, in my opinion, are manifest.

I need not rehearse the iconomachy that took place at the Reformation; but I do want to stress that in the 19th century, when the issue was still driven by Protestants, the debate was ostensibly about the history of Israel and of its religion; but, not unlike what occurred in the creation of the documentary hypothesis, it was also about who, Catholic or Protestant, could claim the mantle as the truest inheritor of Israel's faith. During the 20th century, claims and arguments have not changed markedly. Within recent generations, the same evidence that van der Toorn has used to back up his thesis was called upon to explain the baleful influence Canaanite worship had on Israel's, and only a few voices (most prominently that of Erwin Goodenough) protested that the conjectures were dependent on biblical records that were accommodatingly sanitized.[13]

What has happened since those days to make the conclusions of van der Toorn more plausible today? Yes, we have refined our methodologies somewhat and have posed our questions differently; but I believe that the most radical change has taken place, not in our materials and methods, but in us and in our environment.

Since the early 1960s, Western Europe and America have been assimilating people from Asia, Africa, and the Caribbean who were once readily called "pagans." In many of our neighborhoods, we now have temples where the

11. Quotation adapted from p. xxii of J. Mendham, *The Seventh General Council, the Second of Niceae, in Which the Worship of Images Was Established* (London: Painter, 1849).

12. See A. Cutler and P. A. Hollingsworth, "Iconoclasm," *The Oxford Dictionary of Byzantium* (ed. A. P. Kazhdan; Oxford: Oxford University Press, 1991) 2. 975–77.

13. See now Kalman Bland, *The Artless Jew: Medieval and Modern Affirmations and Denials of the Visual* (Princeton: Princeton University Press, 2000).

worship of images is carried out: graven, theomorphic, anthropomorphic, gynecomorphic, and the like. I have noticed that a few more embellishments are now slipping into the decoration of Protestant churches than used to be found. I have also observed that Jewish ceremonial art, which once was relegated to secular buildings, is now being housed in museums attached to Jewish synagogues. We may well be adapting to a more tolerant, multicultural, and pluralistic phase of religious observance, where profundity of faith is not automatically linked to the suppression of artistic symbols. If so, then what better way to legitimize our gains than by showing, in meetings such as these, that even if Israel is proved to have worshiped through images of wood and stone, it was no less true to its instinct on the one and only God.

Part III

The Mythology of Sacred Space:
Structure and Structuralism

Preamble to a Temple Tour

ZIONY ZEVIT

University of Judaism, Los Angeles

I

The most famous temple in Western religious tradition, the best known, most studied, and perhaps the most represented in art is one that no living person has seen. What would interest the archaeologist professionally lies unexcavated somewhere on the grounds of the *Haram esh-sharif* 'the Noble Enclosure', under what is left of Herod's Temple. But it is also to be found in the biblical text partially excavated by philological-historical scholarship from beneath thousands of years' layers of misunderstanding. I refer, of course, of the *miqdash* constructed by Yedidyah ben Dawid, a.k.a. Solomon.

Israelite naology, the study of temples, is maturing beyond the early stages of typological studies. Ami Mazar and Ephraim Stern provide sophisticated typological and comparative studies of shrines found in Eretz Israel sites that address matters of plan, size, access, and orientation to points of the compass.[1] Their work is of a pure archaeological nature. In 1970, Theodor Busink provided what remains the most extensive study of the art and architecture of the Temple from a comparative perspective, one that all subsequent work must engage. Othmar Keel and others continue to gather rich comparative data for the artistic motifs in the Temple from throughout the ancient Near East, while Elizabeth Bloch-Smith, among others, has recently explored the symbolic significance of some images and appurtenances used in the Temple and its court, advancing the discussion beyond the parameters of Busnick's work into the symbolism of mythic texts.[2] Avidgor Hurowitz has

---

1. A. Mazar, *Excavations at Tell Qasile I* (Qedem 12; Jerusalem: Institute of Archaeology, the Hebrew University, 1980) 61–73; idem, "Temples of the Middle and Late Bronze Ages and the Iron Age," in *The Architecture of Ancient Israel* (ed. A. Kempinski and R. Reich; Jerusalem: Israel Exploration Society, 1992) 161–87; E. Stern, *Excavations at Tel Mevorakh: Part II* (Qedem 18; Jerusalem: Institute of Archaeology, The Hebrew University, 1984) 28–39.

2. T. A. Busink, *Der Tempel von Jerusalem I Band* (Leiden: Brill, 1970); O. Keel, *Jahwe-Visionen und Siegelkunst* (Stuttgart: Katholische Bibelwerk, 1977); E. Bloch-Smith, "Who is the King of Glory? Solomon's Temple and Its Symbolism," in *Scripture*

situated the Temple plans of 1 Kings 6–7 within their broader contemporane-
ous ancient near eastern cultural context.[3] Other research agendas contributing to Israelite naology come from anthropology, sociology, ritual studies,
art history, comparative mythology, biblical studies, ancient Near Eastern
studies in general, and religiology. Some of these are hard disciplines; others
soft. Some are philologically based; others not. Some have a hard-nosed positivistic quality to them; others a more imaginative and intuitive quality. Although religiology is classified properly with the latter group, it provided the
theme for the 1995 ASOR session.

II

A significant contribution of religiological research to our understanding
of religion has been its isolation of a spatial dimension.[4] The pertinence of
time, text, ritual, story, and belief to understanding religion has been long
recognized; not so the spatial dimension. However, it is obvious nowadays
that when we come to study the Jerusalem Temple and its implements, we
move into this dimension.

The concept *sacred space*, widely bandied about as a self-evident truism,
is actually vague and diffuse. For example, John M. Lundquist, in a book
about temples, incorporates the concept when he writes about them this way:

> The temple incorporates within itself most of the ideas that make up our
> concept of religion. These include the idea of the centre, the sacred
> mountain, sacred waters and trees of life, sacred geometry, orientation to
> the four cardinal directions, initiation ritual, sacred dance, the myster-
> ies, New Year festivals, ideas of cosmos/chaos and creation myths. It was
> within the setting of the temple that these other symbols, rituals, and
> sacred textual traditions arose, and it is within the temple that they still
> have their deepest and truest meaning. Indeed, they can only be fully

---

and Other Artifacts: Essays in Honor of Philip J. King (ed. M. D. Coogan et al.; Louisville: Westminster John Knox, 1994) 18–31.

3. V. A. Hurowitz, *I Have Built You an Exalted House: Temple Building in the Bible
in Light of Mesopotamian and Northwest Semitic Writings* (JSOTSup 115; Sheffield:
Sheffield Academic Press, 1992).

4. The notion entered religiological discussions through the insights of M. Eli-
ade and was subsequently developed by others into a wieldy conceptualizing tool. In
applying the concept to Iron Age Israel, care must be taken to demystify the term lest
layers of homogenized Buddhist and Hindu lore be imposed anachronistically and
anatopically onto Israelite civilization.

understood when they are reincorporated back into the context of the temple, and seen in that wider relationship.[5]

This enthusiastic description of a temple is, of course, a composite, drawn from many understandings of religion and many religions, primarily Eastern. It is according to Lundquist realized in only one known temple, Brobudur in Java. He writes of Brobudur: "It is a sacred site, an object of pilgrimage, a symbolic mountain, an allegory of progress through rising terraces to divine revelation, and an exposition in stone of a whole theological doctrine."[6]

The conceptual substructure for such appreciations is the notion that architecture, the art of shelter, expresses through design an implicit set of values.[7] This way of reading and criticizing architecture has its roots in 19th-century romanticism with its ideas about the truth and the spiritual in nature that were applied to architecture and made famous, at least in the English-speaking world, through the essays of John Ruskin.[8] I do not point this out in the spirit of exposé as the Achilles heel of the approach, but rather as a point of fact. The approach is applied appropriately to Israelite naology at the dawn of the 21st century, but the move from Java to Jerusalem should be made cautiously.

In the narratives about Moses at the burning bush and about Joshua before the battle of Jericho, a divine apparition instructs both: "Remove your sandals from your feet because the place on which you stand is holy ground" (Exod 3:5, Josh 5:15).[9] If the instructions represented proper behavior on holy ground, then it is odd that barefootedness was not prescribed for either the Tabernacle or Temple.[10] Furthermore, P prescribes that foodstuffs considered "holy" be consumed only by priests, presumably shodden, within the

---

5. J. M. Lundquist, *The Temple: Meeting Place of Heaven and Earth* (London: Thames & Hudson, 1993) 5.

6. Ibid., 38.

7. It is important to distinguish between buildings that are common (sense) structures, houses and barns, and uncommon ones that are expressions of art. The former too may be read semiotically, but that is not the task of this paper.

8. J. Ruskin, *The Seven Lamps of Architecture* (New York: Appelton, 1899; first printed, 1844).

9. The word for 'ground' is absent in Joshua and the words for 'sandals' and 'feet' are morphologically singular there.

10. The passages are obviously related, and it is likely that the Moses episode has been transformed for use in the Joshua tales as a way of making the latter more "Mosaic." One could argue for a reverse development also. For the purposes of this paper, what is significant is that the different circles of individuals using this story maintained similar notions of norms concerning a sacred place.

confines of the Tabernacle temenos, indicating that its status on some scale of holiness differed from that of space beyond it (Lev 6:9–10, 19–22; 7:6).

The juxtaposition of passages suggests that the places of revelation in the Moses and Joshua narratives were not "holy ground" in the same way that the courtyards of the portable Tabernacle and the permanent Temple were considered "holy ground." And if so, it cautions us that the concept *holy space* may not be applied globally and uncautiously to Israelite contexts. It has to be honed somewhat so that it may be used as an analytical tool.

As it applies to the study of the Israelite Temple, the concept has three facets.

(1) *Geographical space.* This facet is concerned with the topography of the site and its physical environment, the location of buildings, chambers, altars, lavers, and the like. It focuses on the human geographical element also. Inasmuch as real people in a real city saw and experienced the Temple on the Zion hill north of the royal palace, it asks: What impact did it have on them and what impact did they have on it? Was it accessible? Was it "user friendly"? How did visitors and priests move through its courts between the furnishings?

(2) *Thematic space.* This facet is concerned with ideas held about geographical space, some of which are reflected in psalmodic and prophetic literature: dwelling place of YHWH, dwelling place of the *kabod* 'glory' of YHWH, mountain of YHWH, his holy mountain. The themes add an evaluating valence, a psychological and emotional charge to the place. Thematic space is fraught with meaning on the liminal level. Perception of thematic space encourages questions such as: What did it mean for this altar to be there, or for this priest to enter the Temple this way? Why was it important? What do the rituals mean and what do they achieve?

(3) *Mythic-symbolic space.* This facet reflects less accessible matters, some of which may have been experienced subliminally by people visiting the site or may have been appreciated metaphorically by others: the place as *axis mundi*, sitting atop the great watery depths of the *těhôm* but under an uplifted throne; the place as the center of the world. The perception of mythic-symbolic space encourages questions such as: Why did it mean? How did it come to be a holy mountain? How do rituals mean and how do they achieve?

Although mythic space may be considered an extension of thematic space, mythic space is primal, part of a comprehensive religious world view that supplies the orientational key for interpreting thematic space.

III

Archaeology is familiar primarily with geographical space, and when considering buildings in this context, views the size, position, and distribution of buildings in space as expressions of social prestige and a social pecking order. Religiology, in contrast, tends to consider a site in terms of its thematic and mythic space, viewing sacred space as timeless and eternal. History is informed by both of these disciplines.

Archaeologists know that people actually build the spaces that they consider sacred and then build over them. For example, at Megiddo, cult places of different shapes replaced earlier ones, in the Early Bronze III strata XVII–XVI–XV, while at Lachish, one sacred space replaced another, differing greatly or slightly from what had come before in the three Late Bronze fosse temples. The third fosse temple burned during the destruction of Lachish VII was left in ruins during the final Canaanite phase, level VI, which continued the material culture of level VII. Philistine examples are found at Tell Qasile and at Ekron. An Israelite example of the same phenomenon is the Arad Temple, where sacred space was juggled, rearranged, and eventually buried, all by Israelites.[11]

The archaeological experience, coupled with awareness that metaphysical reality is socially constructed, suggests that changes in geographical space reflect changes in thematic and mythic space, in underlying conceptions and matters of interpretation. This is perhaps obvious when Muslims conquered Byzantium, converting churches into mosques, or when Christians overbuilt pagan shrines. But the archaeological examples just cited do not coincide with known changes in the ethnic composition of inhabitants or in their material culture. It is therefore puzzling that scholars do not suppose that there was any change in the attendant nonmaterial culture.[12]

IV

Some sacred places in Israel were sites that for some reason elicited belief because of an awe-generating experience there—such as is reported for Jacob at Bethel or the tradition linking the Temple site with Mt. Moriah, place of

---

11. This experience poses nonarchaeological questions: Is there an eternal, timeless element to sacred space? Wherein lies the sacredness? How is sacred space desacralized?

12. The case of the temple is somewhat more complicated than the above examples. There, a Phoenician king and devotee of Baal sent the child of a Tyrian father and northern Israelite mother to construct a temple for a Judahite Israelite king, a devotee of YHWH (1 Kgs 7:14, 2 Chr 2:11–16; cf. S. Japhet, *I and II Chronicles* [OTL; Louisville: Westminster John Knox, 1993] 540–47). Thus, at some point, there may have been discordance between the temple's external appearance in geographical space and its clarification at the mythic level. For example, the basin on the backs of twelve bulls, the *yām*, may have had nothing to do with the Canaanite deity Yam but may have symbolized the *mābūl* over which YHWH sat enthroned (cf. Ps 29:10). That is to say, it may have been a second throne for YHWH paralleling the cherub throne in the *děbîr*.

the *akedah*—while others were built on convenient real estate and "sacrilized" after the fact, for example, the building rendered the ground holy, as in the case of the Tabernacle or Micah's shrine. (These two explanations may clarify some of the Canaanite and Philistine examples mentioned above.) In both cases, liturgical texts such as the psalms recited within the precincts were linguistic expressions of the belief that the place was divinely sanctioned, just as rituals performed, such as the daily *ʿôlâ*, were physical expressions. The difference, however, is that the physical structure communicated to people, whereas the texts and rituals were directed to the deity.

*   *   *

In his book on temple-building, Hurowitz notes that Assyrian temple construction was considered a reflection of royal wisdom. Therefore, placement of the story about the Israelite Temple's construction after narratives describing how Solomon obtained wisdom as a divine boon, applied it in judgment, and employed it in establishing a royal administration is purposeful (1 Kings 3–5).[13] Explicit references and implicit allusions to his divine wisdom recur six times in these narratives (1 Kgs 3:12, 28; 5–9, 14, 21, 26). The significance of their rhetorical placement in these chapters is clarified by noting that in the ancient Near East wisdom was considered the practical reflection and adaption of metaphysical principles, a sort of pre-Platonism expressed with notions of Egyptian *maʿat*, the Sumerian *ME*s, and Hebrew *ḥokmâ*.[14]

The romantic intuition about architecture finds historical-philological justification in some wisdom texts. In Prov 8:22–23, personified Wisdom speaks:

> YHWH created me at the beginning of his path, as the first of his works of old. I was fashioned in the far past, at the first, at the origin of earth.

In Prov 24:3, an aphorism is taught:

> A house is built by *ḥokmâ* 'wisdom', and established by *tĕbûnâ* 'discernment'; its rooms are filled by *daʿat* 'knowledge' with all precious and beautiful things.

With these verses in mind, the Deuteronomistic historian's description of the Tyrian artisan sent to Solomon is noteworthy: "and he was filled with *ḥokmâ* 'wisdom', *tĕbûnâ* 'understanding', and *daʿat* 'knowledge' to execute all the

---

13. Hurowitz, *I Have Built You an Exalted House*, 134.

14. In Egyptian culture, *maʿat* means 'truth-justice' as an expression of order. It is not a parallel to Hebrew *ḥokmâ*. Cf. M. V. Fox, "World Order and Maʿat: A Crooked Parallel," *JANES* 23 (1995) 38.

craftwork in bronze" (1 Kgs 7:14). A reference to his professional knowledge *da'at* would have sufficed. Reference to the other attributes indicates that he brought additional qualities to his work and that therefore the Temple is something other than a well-constructed building.[15]

The implication of these texts is that, in Israel, architecture is linked with anthropology, and anthropology with cosmology.[16] Architecture speaks, but what does it say?

* * *

Solomon's Temple appears to have been a tripartite structure: at its rear was a square adyton, the *děbîr*, before which was a rectangular long house nave, the *hêkāl*. Here, a small altar, a showbread table, lights, and some utensils were kept. Before the *hêkāl*, on the other side of its doors, was a broad room type of vestibule, the *'ûlām*, that faced an open courtyard, where the large altar was located.[17] The dimensions of the *děbîr* were 20 × 20 cubits; of the *hêkāl* 40 × 20; of the *'ûlām* 20 × 10.

15. Bezalel, craftsman of the tabernacle, and others who shared the task with him are also described as being endowed by YHWH with *ḥokmâ* and *těbûnâ* so as to know how to execute the work (Exod 36:1–2). Although *ḥokmâ* is the general term for 'wisdom', *těbûnâ* indicates pragmatic wisdom directed at accomplishment, making proper decisions, and competence (M. V. Fox, "Words for Wisdom: *tbwnh* and *bynh* : *'rmh* and *mzmh* : *'ṣh* and *twšyh*," ZAH 6 [1993] 152–58, 165). Similarities between the descriptions of Bezalel and Hiram are to be explained along lines used to clarify the Moses-Joshua similarities alluded to in n. 10 above.

16. R. Pannikar, "There is No Outer without Inner Space," in *Concepts of Space, Ancient and Modern* (ed. K. Vatsyaya; New Delhi: Abhinav, 1991) 7–38, at p. 17.

17. Oulette suggests on the basis of the plan of the *'ûlām* and on the basis of his argument that the two pillars called "Jachin" and "Boaz" were located within the portico supporting its roof and a decorated architrave (cf. 1 Kgs 7:19–21) that the Temple is modeled after a porticoed structure, the *bît ḥilāni* ("Le vestibule du Temple de Salomon était-il un *bit hilani?*" RB 76 [1969] 376–78). If correct, these two pillars, though highly decorated, were structural and of no particular consequence. However, if 2 Chr 3:17 is accepted, and "he erected the columns *'l pny*, in front of, the *hêkāl*" is preferred over 1 Kgs 7:21, "he erected the pillars *l'wlm hhykl*, for the vestibule of the *hêkāl*," an argument could be made that they were not integrated into the structure and were free standing. If so, the huge, bronze columns, decorated with capitals and rings of pomegranates, endowed with names, may have been of some cultic consequence. What this was, however, is not yet known. I suspect that Egyptian naology may help clarify their significance. Both types of plans have architectural antecedents in the ancient Near Eastern archaeological record, but resolution of the issue is hindered by complex lower-critical problems. See C. F. Burney, *Notes on the Hebrew Text of Kings* (Oxford: Oxford University Press, 1903) 85–90.

Among the excavated temples catalogued and analyzed by Mazar and Stern, Solomon's Temple remains an architectural isolate, finding its closest parallel in a small Phoenician temple from the 8th century B.C.E., at Tell Tainat in Syria. [18] However, if the vestibule, the *'ûlām*, is considered an architectural flourish belonging with the three-storied structure built against its external walls, then the basic Temple was bipartite. Such a basic temple is attested in the Tent shrine of meeting described in Exodus where a square adyton, 10 × 10 cubits, was fronted by a rectangular nave, 20 × 10 cubits, and at Arad, where a squarish 1.3 × 1.5 m deep adyton is fronted by a 2.3 × 9.6 m broad room nave.

Unlike these two, however, at Jerusalem the basic Temple, paneled and decorated with symbolic images, was encased in a protective building. This is similar to the adyton of Greek temples from the classical period that were surrounded by rows of pillars; and to the Holy Sepulcher, a cave enclosed in a small building that is enclosed in a larger one.

According to the Deuteronomistic historian (Dtr), the basic Temple in Jerusalem remained untouched throughout most of its history, even as the *temenos* around it changed. Dtr noted in particular (1) the reign of Ahaz, when a new altar was introduced and the old bronze one set aside for royal divination, Solomonic lavers removed from their stands, the huge hemispheric basin called the *yām* removed from the backs of twelve bronze oxen, and various architectural changes made (2 Kgs 16:10–18); (2) the reign of Manasseh, who sponsored a host of cultic activities accommodating both Baal and Asherah worship and introduced altars and symbols of non-Yahwistic cults to the Temple courts as well as on the roofs of some structures (2 Kgs 21:4, 23:11–12); and (3) the reign of Josiah, who attempted to restore the Temple to what it had been prior to Manasseh's entrepreneurial undertakings (2 Kgs 23:4–7, 11–14). Some of the changes affected the YHWH rituals conducted before the main Temple. For example, Ahaz's introduction of the Damascene altar into the courtyard led to changes in the Temple ritual of the *ḥaṭṭā't* offering. [19]

18. What is particular interesting about the exemplars in Mazar and Stern is that, although some structures are parallel, no two are congruent in the same way that gate structures at Hazor, Megiddo, and Gezer were. It is as if Temple architects in Palestine worked with a general notion of what components constituted a temple, but were free with regard to their size, shape, and articulation. This situation is parallel to medieval practice, in which specific sections of structures were left to the skill and imagination of the workman doing the actual construction and not to a micromanaging master architect.

19. Z. Zevit, "Philology, Archaeology, and a Terminus a Quo for P's *ḥaṭṭā't* Legislation," in *Pomegranates and Golden Bells: Studies in Biblical, Jewish, and Near Eastern Ritual, Law, and Literature in Honor of Jacob Milgrom* (ed. D. P. Wright, D. N. Freedman, and A. Hurvitz; Winona Lake, Ind.: Eisenbauns, 1995) 29–38.

These geographic changes and innovations in thematic space influenced the choreography of ritual. For the changed choreography on the new cultic stage, mythopoets most likely created explanations clarifying and even justifying the presence or absence, the addition or removal of the constellation of divinities and cultic accoutrements and appurtenances in the corners of YHWH's courtyard.[20] Israelite mythopoets knew the meaning of the incense offering and how it drew YHWH's attention to the small altar, they knew how the blood of the ʿôlâ on the large altar atoned and how ḥaṭṭāʾt blood on the altar's horns purged, they knew how a pinch of frankinsence and semolina flour cast into the altar's flame was used by YHWH. They knew the narratives that linked mythic with geographical space. They knew; we do not. And we may not assume that we know what they knew on the basis of models derived from Far Eastern religions.

*   *   *

Each of the following essays in this section is a sondage, a sounding into some aspect of the ancient shrine. Each comes to the Temple seeking to understand, but each enters with a different agenda. The questions of one differ from those of the others because the methodology underlying each is different. And so, inevitably, the answers will all be different. They attempt to enhance our common knowledge through symbology, typology, and phenomenology.

In aggregate, these essays demonstrate that a multidisciplinary effort by biblicists familiar with the archaeology and by archaeologists familiar with biblical scholarship is necessary for a multidimensional understanding of Israelite religion in its complexity. The paper of Elizabeth Bloch-Smith examines artistic motifs on structures that define geographical space as an expression of thematic space, while Sy Gitin's classifies a defining artifact, the small altar, as a prop that bridges between thematic and mythic space. The third paper, by Baruch Levine, clarifies sets of choreographed temple rituals that connected offerers in geographic space with the indwelling deity in mythic space. It illustrates the physical dynamics of such connections at charged moments in sacred space.

20. G. A. Klingbeil interprets the itinerary of the ritual in Leviticus 8 in the geographic-thematicized space of the Tabernacle as reflecting the separation of Aaronides from Israel and their transition to sacerdotal status ("Ritual Space in the Ordination Ritual of Leviticus 8," *JNSL* 21 [1995] 59–82). Although highly intuitive, this study, which is based in Hebrew philology and historical commentary as well as in religiology, is suggestive for future lines of research.

Solomon's Temple:
The Politics of Ritual Space

ELIZABETH BLOCH-SMITH

Bala Cynwyd, Pennsylvania

Solomon adopted and adapted common Near Eastern cultic elements for the new Yahwistic royal Temple. As the ambitious and successful king of a young nation, he had political and religious reasons to build a temple, as well as the necessary resources and political connections. This essay explores the religious and political symbolism of the structure, offers a new interpretation of the 'lampstands' (měnōrōt) and concludes with the distinctive Israelite aspects of the Temple. Nothing remains of the Solomonic Temple allegedly built approximately 950 B.C.E.; all discussion is based on the descriptions in 1 Kings, Chronicles, and Ezekiel.

The Courtyard Objects

According to the account in 1 Kings 6 and 7, the Temple was a small structure adjacent to the much larger palace in the royal compound. The rectangular building measuring 100 × 50 cubits (165 × 84.5') was divided into three rooms. In the outer courtyard of the Temple stood an immense tank called 'the molten sea' (hayyām mûṣāq), ten gigantic 'lavers' or stands (měkônôt), and two towering pillars (ʿamûdîm), all of which Hiram of Tyre had cast in bronze (1 Kgs 7:13–40). The lavers were positioned five to the right of the entrance and five to the left, and the tank was placed on the right, at the southeast corner (1 Kgs 7:39). The bronze altar constructed during the reign of David or Solomon (1 Kgs 8:64, 9:25; 2 Kgs 16:14–15; 2 Chr 6:13) is not mentioned in descriptions of the Temple outer court.

Each of the courtyard items was of unusually great size and, in the case of the tank and stands, significantly larger than ancient Near Eastern parallels. The immense tank measured 10 cubits (over 16') in diameter and held nearly 10,000 gallons of water. Its size and capacity render unlikely the Chronicler's explanation of the "Sea" as a sink for priestly ablutions (2 Chr 4:6). Each stand/"laver" measured 4 cubits (approximately 6.5') square and 7 cubits (over 11') high, well out of human reach. The basin supported by each of the

10 stands had a capacity of 40 baths (approximately 240 gallons). The same type of basin, *kîyyôr*, is mentioned in the context of boiling sacrificial meat at Shiloh (1 Sam 2:12–16). These giant stands may have functioned as "hot carts" for tribal sacrifices or for rinsing parts of the burnt offering, as recorded in 2 Chr 4:6.

The immense cherub throne in the Temple holy of holies (*děbîr*), 10 cubits high and 10 cubits wide (over 16' high and 16' wide), attests to the Israelites' vision of their god as superhuman in size. Baal's throne of superhuman size and the meter-long footsteps at the 'Ain Dara Temple (Abu Assaf 1990: 15–16) are further attestations to the late-second- to early-first-millennium conception of gods of superhuman size.

Accordingly, the exaggerated size of the structures in the Solomonic Temple courtyard would suggest that they were not intended for human use but belonged to the realm of the divine. Lacking archaelogical remains of the bronze Molten Sea and stands or corroborating evidence of their size, one can only determine by faith whether or not they were cast to the biblical specifications. Superhuman-sized objects likely stood in the courtyard, conveying to ancient Israelites that they served a divine function.

Symbols are effective only when their meaning is known. Israelite cultic texts may have served to articulate the symbolic meaning of the courtyard objects. The cultic repertoire, exemplified by early verses from Psalms 18 (Ps 18:8–16 = 2 Sam 22:8–16), 29, 89, and 93 (Cross 1973: 135, 152, 158–62; but see Kraus 1988: 258; 1989: 201–2, 232–33 for difficulty in dating these psalms), recount Yahweh's victories over the earth and its creatures, including the sea, and conclude with a description of the warrior god enthroned in his Temple for eternity.

The political function of the conflict story between the storm-god and the cosmic sea has been recognized by the dashing young professor Smith (1990: 56). Smith cites an 18th-century B.C.E. letter from the prophet Nur-Sin of Aleppo to Zimri-Lim of Mari in which the god defeats Sea and then bestows the weapons upon the earthly king. The storm god Adad proclaims, "I s[et] you on the th[rone of your father]; the weapons with which I had battled against Sea I gave to you" (Bordreuil and Pardee 1993). Just as Adad provided Zimri-Lim with the weapons to defeat Sea, so Yahweh empowered David to subdue Sea and River, "I will set his [the king's] hand upon the sea, his right hand upon the rivers" (Ps 89:26[25] NRSV). The Molten Sea may have symbolized Yahweh's cosmic victories and extension of divine powers to the king.

The Temple courtyard objects were designed to convey Yahweh's triumphant enthronement with its implicit endorsement of the monarchy (Bloch-Smith 1994). After defeating the chaotic forces of nature, symbolized by the Molten Sea, Yahweh extended his powers to the monarch (Ps 89:26) and des-

ignated Zion, the holy mountain won in battle, to be the seat of eternal divine (and human) sovereignty (Ps 18:8–16 = 2 Sam 22:8–16; Psalms 29, 89,
93). Sated with offerings from the stands or *mĕkônôt*, Yahweh entered his
Temple, bestowing blessings on the king and the people, as recorded on the
pillars *Yachin* and *Boaz* that flanked the Temple entrance. Thus the courtyard
objects conveyed Yahweh's enthronement in the royal chapel with the attendant empowerment of the king and divine blessings for all Israel.

The Interior Decoration

What was the choice of repeating interior motifs meant to convey? As
with the outdoor objects, religious and political considerations likely dictated
the interior decoration. Gilded wood reliefs of cherubs (*kĕrûbîm*), palm trees
(*timōrôt*), and calyxes (*pĕtûrê ṣiṣṣîm*) were carved on the doors and wall pan-
eling. The configuration of cherubs, palms, and calyxes is not specified. Ezekiel describes wainscoted walls decorated with a pattern of "cherubim and
palm trees, with a palm between every two cherubim" (Ezek 41:18). The calyxes may have formed a floral border for the repeating cherubs and trees.

The cherub was the prominent motif in the Temple interior. As represented by its bodily parts, this mythical creature combined the strength, fe-
rocity, and regalness of a lion with the flying capability of a bird and the
higher reasoning of a human. The resulting composite creature possessed
superior intelligence and physical abilities. A human face for the biblical
cherub is inferred both from Ezekiel's description of the creature with a human and a lion face (Ezek 41:19) and from the standardized depiction on Syrian glyptic and ivory and metal objects. Cherubs were enlisted to guard the
Tree of Life in the Garden of Eden (Gen 3:24). In addition, cherubs served as
chariots to transport the deity (Ps 18:11 = 2 Sam 22:11; Ps 80:2, 99:1) and as
the divine throne over the ark in the Tent of Meeting, at Shiloh, and in the
Solomonic Temple (Exod 25:18ff.; 1 Sam 4:4, 1 Kgs 6:23–27). The cherub's
role at Shiloh may be inferred from the description of the Ark of the Covenant of Yahweh of Hosts Enthroned on the Cherubim (1 Sam 4:4).

The Egyptian sphinx and Mesopotamian *kuribu* could be winged or non-
winged, male or female (CAD K 559). By contrast, the biblical cherub was
winged but of unspecified gender. It is difficult to distinguish the *kuribu* from
the sphinx in Syrian art; therefore, all extrabiblical examples will be referred
to as "sphinxes" in comparison to the biblical "cherub."

Dessenne proposes an Egyptian origin for the sphinx, while noting that
sphinxes existed in both Egypt and Mesopotamia by the end of the third
millennium B.C.E. (Dessenne 1957: 175). Most of the examples of winged
sphinxes are on cylinder seals from the region of modern-day Syria. Not surprisingly, northern Levantine sphinxes are closer in style to Anatolian (with

Canby 1975) and Mesopotamian examples than to Egyptian depictions. Northern sphinxes had clearly delineated wings in contrast to Egyptian sphinxes, which were often wingless or had such stylized wings that they were unrecognizable.

The motifs of facing winged sphinxes guarding and eating from a stylized sacred tree developed in Late Bronze Age Mitanni and from there spread through northern Syria and the southern Levant (Vollenweider 1967: 114). While animals besides sphinxes feed from the branches or repose to either side of the stylized sacred tree, they do not raise a paw or foreleg in a protective stance. A seal from Alalakh level I–II, dated 1225–1175 B.C.E., depicts facing sphinxes protecting a stylized plant with raised paws meeting over the plant's apex (Collon 1982: fig. 105; 1987: fig. 307). Sphinxes flank a stylized plant on a Cypriot rod tripod from the 12th or early 11th century B.C.E. The tripod, measuring 0.34 meters in diameter, is adorned with nine cast plaques: five with winged male sphinxes standing at attention to either side of a stylized plant, likely sacred, because it is clearly not realistic, and four with goats mounting a variant highly stylized plant (Catling 1964: pl. 29 c, e).

Did the stylized tree represent a goddess, either Asherah or Hathor? None of Asherah's proponents have argued for her presence on the Jerusalem Temple walls and doors. Had she been present, then Manasseh need not have introduced a sculpted image (1 Kgs 21:7). A stylized tree or decorated pole supporting a solar symbol was a common motif on Middle and Late Bronze Age Syrian cylinder seals. Two Middle Bronze Age examples depict the tree/pole as Hathor, the celestial mother of the sun calf who, according to the ancient myth, raised the youthful sun up to heaven with her horns (Lurker 1980: 59). On a seal found in the Karnak Temple but attributed to Alalakh VII, the stylized pole supporting the winged sun-disc is depicted as an upside-down winged Hathor, her head resting on the ground with wings, torso, and arms extended upward (Schroer 1989: fig. 176). A second seal depicts a wingless but armed figure topped by a sun-disc flanked by cow horns (Schroer 1989: fig. 177). From depictions on Middle and Late Bronze Age seal impressions, Schroer illustrates Hathor's metamorphosis into a stylized tree or plant. The body became the stem or trunk, and the head, headdress, and horns the stylized, ornamental parts of the plant (Schroer 1989: 144, figs. 118, 120). Late Bronze Age sheet metal pendants fashioned as a female with Hathor hairstyle and a tree on the belly (Negbi 1976: 98, figs. 114–16) may be related to these cylinder seal depictions. Hathor as a tree/pole raising her son up into the sky may be represented on the golden (and silver) pendants, which evoke the sun by their luminescence when reflecting light. There is no iconographic indication either in specific details or in general context to suggest that the trees carved on the Temple walls and doors symbolized either Asherah or Hathor, both represented as a pole or tree. To paraphrase Freud, sometimes a sacred tree is just a sacred tree.

What did the tree in the Temple represent? In Hebrew, the trees are called *timōrôt*, from the root *tmr*, meaning 'erect' or 'stiff'. Words derived from this root include *tāmār* ('palm tree'), *tōmer* ('post, palm tree') and *tîmārâ* ('column'; BDB 1071). *Timōrôt* may be reconstructed as stylized palms similar to the sacred trees depicted in Late Bronze and Iron Age art. On cylinder seals, the stylized tree providing sustenance for the animal kingdom was similar in depiction to the tree protected by sphinxes. The stylized tree represented either divine bounty, when flanked by animals nibbling from the branches or reposing in the shade, or a sacred tree such as the biblical Trees of Life and Knowledge, when guarded by sphinxes. The sacred tree was represented in the Solomonic Temple to recreate the Garden of Eden.

The image of the bull rather than the cherub might have been chosen to adorn the Temple walls and serve as Yahweh's throne or pedestal. Symbolizing strength, virility, and aggression, the bull was associated with the storm- and warrior-gods, Mesopotamian Adad, Hittite and Hurrian Teshub, West Semitic Baal/Haddu, and Israelite Yahweh. Biblical passages, all from the North, attest to the association of Yahweh and the bull-calf image. Aaron and the people recite nearly the same Yahwistic confession over the golden calf as Jeroboam I recited over the calves he installed in the temples to Yahweh at Dan and Bethel (Exod 32:4 = 1 Kgs 12:28). F. M. Cross persuasively aruges that Jeroboam's goal was to create a Northern Yahweh cult independent of the Jerusalem Temple. In order to do so, Jeroboam chose established Yahwistic elements—such as the bull-calf (Cross 1973: 73–74, 199).

The bull as the symbol or attribute animal of the storm god enjoys a long iconographic history. Already on a 19th-/18th-century B.C.E. provincial Old Babylonian cylinder seal, the storm- or weather-god stands on his attribute animal, the bull (Schroer 1989: fig. 2). By the 18th–17th century in the Middle Bronze II Levant, the storm-god representation was standardized. The god stood in a smiting pose brandishing a mace, axe, or throw stick in his raised hand with the bull's leash and often a second weapon in his other hand. Typically dressed in a short kilt with a dagger secured in his belt, the god donned a horned crown or cap and styled his hair with a long curl down the back (Collon 1987: 170). A shapely young woman wearing only jewelry, a cape that hung down her back, or a skirt raised in the front to reveal all, often accompanied the storm god (Collon 1987: fig. 777; Schroer 1989: fig. 30; Keel and Uehlinger 1992: 43–45, fig. 30).

Bronze Age cylinder seals were replaced by Iron Age stamp seals. In a study of Iron I seals from the region of modern-day Israel, Shuval found that in the north and along the coast (and through the lowlands?), the Bronze Age god with attribute animal was replaced by a god standing on a quadruped. As an example, a Jericho Tomb 11 seal depicts a bearded figure with a horned headpiece standing on a bull (Shuval 1990: 95–96, fig. 25). No bull is recorded from the southern highlands.

Three-dimensional bulls of clay and of bronze abound in Syro-Palestinian archaeological contexts. Given the expense and expertise required to produce metal figurines, as well as the cultic context of some, all are assumed to have cultic significance. They may have represented the god, the pedestal on which the god stood, or attributes of the god. The Middle Bronze II silver-plated bull-calf from Ashkelon found in a model shrine in the city-gate "temple" is an early example from a likely cultic context (Stager 1991: 3). Both the Ashkelon calf and a bronze bull from the 13th-century Stratum IA Megiddo Temple H have pegged feet, probably for mounting the figures on poles to parade in cultic processions. Mazar published a bronze bull from a 12th-century site in the Northern Samarian hills (Mazar 1990: 350–52). The bovine or young bull without horns in the top register of the Taʿanach cult stand demonstrates the continuing role of the bull from the Middle Bronze Age down into the 10th century B.C.E. These bull and bull-calf figurines, like the stamp seals with gods standing on quadrupeds, were found at Northern and coastal sites.

Given the long-standing association of the bull with storm- and warrior-gods, including Yahweh, why was the cherub selected for the Solomonic Temple? For both religious and political purposes, the sphinx had a leg up on the bull. First, while the bull as attribute animal for the storm-god was a northern motif, the cherub as a symbol for royal as well as divine rule had both northern and Egyptian credentials. Second, the bull was generally associated with the storm- or weather-god (with the possible exception of the basalt torso and bull fragments found at the entrance to the Hazor Late Bronze I Stratum IB Temple H; Yadin 1975: 84–85). The cherub was not identified with any one god and may therefore have better served a new national god who subsumed various divine functions. Third, Solomon built the Temple to be Yahweh's terrestrial residence. To create the divine abode, the walls and doors were covered with cherubs and sacred trees from the mythological Garden of Eden.

The Ten Lampstands

Within the virtual Garden of Eden, manifest in the interior decoration, the Temple objects functioned in the interaction between Israel and Yahweh. Ten *mĕnōrôt*, or 'lampstands', stood five to either side of the entrance into the holy of holies. The Kings account does not describe the lampstands; it merely provides the number and their placement. A single menorah is described in the detailed instructions and description of the Tent of Meeting (Exod 25:31–36, 37:17–22). Meyers understands *yĕrēkāh wĕqānāh* to be a hendiadys meaning 'central shaft', and *kaptōr wāperaḥ*, also a hendiadys, to mean 'floral capital'. The resulting form is a cylindrical shaft, flaring at the base and perhaps also the top (Meyers 1979; 1992a). In the Tent of Meeting description, seven lamps are described as discrete objects to be fashioned separately and placed on top of the lampstand (Exod 25:37, 37:23; 1 Kgs 7:49; cf. also Zech 4:2). Referred to collectively as the *nēr tāmîd* or 'eternal light', the lamps were lit from evening to morning (Exod 27:20, Lev 24:2–3).

The lights of the *mĕnōrôt* may have represented the stars of the heavenly host, the physical referent of the prophet Micaiah's testimonial, "I saw the Lord seated on His throne, with all the host of heaven standing in attendance to the right and to the left" (1 Kgs 22:19). These stars, considered lesser divinities, Job's *bĕnê ʾĕlōhîm* (Job 38:7), battled on Israel's behalf (Zatelli 1991). "The stars fought from heaven, from their courses they fought against Sisera" (Judg 5:20), sang the prophetess Deborah.

More specifically, the seven lights of each lamp may represent the Pleiades, a constellation associated with divination. Biblical *kîmâ*, literally 'herd, group' or 'family' (BDB 465), is identified as the constellation Pleiades on the basis of a Sumerian equivalent meaning 'stars' in a lexical list from Ebla (Zalcman 1995). The Pleiades is a galactic cluster of over 400 stars with 5 to 7 stars visible to the naked eye. The symbol of seven dots is known from as early as the Old Babylonian period and referred to as *sibittu*, literally, 'group of seven' (CAD S 230–31). Van Buren suggested that the symbol evolved from the seven pellets or pebbles used in casting lots for divining the fate of individuals to the rosette-star of Ishtar and finally, with the growing Babylonian interest in astronomy, to the constellation of the Pleiades. A 2d-century c.e. north Syrian example of seven inscribed stones used for casting lots demonstrated the enduring association of the number seven with divining practices (Van Buren 1945: 74–82).

Excavations have yielded seven-spouted lamps in the form of a rosette dating from the Middle Bronze Age (Nahariyah) through the 7th/6th century b.c.e. (Tell es-Safi, Tell en-Nasbeh, Megiddo) (Keel 1977: 278–80, figs. 202–4). These rosette-shaped lamps resemble the Middle Bronze to Iron I iconographic representations of the Pleiades on cylinder seals.

Each biblical lampstand with seven lights was lit only at nighttime. Like the stars of the heavenly host, the lights shone from dusk to dawn. The ten Temple lamps with seven lights each may also have served the ten tribes (all Israel) to divine Yahweh's will.

Halpern (1987) and Taylor (1993), among others, have argued that the sun, moon, and stars were kosher ingredients of the Yahwistic cult into the 7th century b.c.e. If the interpretation of the *mĕnōrôt* is correct, then stars shone in the Temple. The threat of the 7th-century Assyrian star cult was not that it introduced astral worship into Israel but that the stars already in place became a greater threat to the exclusive worship of Yahweh. While the evidence is tenuous and the resulting hypothesis highly speculative, heavenly manifestations of the Yahwistic cult in the Jerusalem Temple should be contemplated.

Distinctive Aspects of the Solomonic Temple

The Solomonic Temple was decorated and furnished with cultic motifs and symbols from the 1000-year Bronze Age to Early Iron Age repertoire rather than with new Iron I elements, as detailed by Shuval (1990). While the constituent elements, sphinxes/cherubs and sacred trees, are attested in Egypt, their combination and the repetition that is characteristic of cylinder seal impressions are both northern features.

The ʿAin Dara Level II temple (1000–900 B.C.E.), located in modern-day northern Syria, provides several parallels to the contemporary Solomonic Temple. Both were built on the same tripartite plan, with columns flanking the entrance. At ʿAin Dara, immense lions and cherubs depicted with stylized palms guarded the entrances onto the temple platform and into the temple proper and cella. The deity inhabiting the temple was also of superhuman size. Divine footprints, each nearly one meter long, were carved into the portico entrance and the interior thresholds, first left foot and then right foot, marking the deity's procession into the cella (Abu Assaf 1990).

What distinguished the new Israelite royal Temple from other cultic expressions? The ʿAin Dara Temple and Taʿanach cult stand are the best contemporary cultic manifestations in relation to which we can identify Solomon's innovations. Certain common Bronze Age cultic elements were not adopted in the Solomonic Temple. The first element is an anthropomorphic representation of the deity, in this case a god. In contrast to the Solomonic Temple, at ʿAin Dara anthropomorphic footsteps were carved into threshold stones and divinities among others were depicted on basalt orthostats lining the interior and exterior walls. In seal impressions, northern Bronze Age anthropomorphic gods in sitting and smiting poses were replaced by Iron Age gods mounted on quadrupeds (Shuval 1990: 117). Neither the Bronze nor the new Iron Age anthropomorphic representation of the deity was adopted, though the quadruped was!

A second element from the Bronze Age cultic repertoire missing from the Solomonic Temple is the naked goddess, or consort. For nearly 1000 years, from the last quarter of the third millennium through the Middle Bronze Age, the storm-god was accompanied by a nude female. A naked goddess posed on the bottom register of the Taʿanach cult stand, but no explicitly female image graced the Solomonic Temple (the sculpted image of a/Asherah was subsequently added; see 1 Kgs 21:7).

Third, the ubiquitous winged sun-disc inexplicably was not depicted in the Solomonic Temple. This manifestation of the solar cult, a familiar symbol in Egypt and in the north, appeared at the top of the Taʿanach cult stand but not in the Jerusalem Temple. Horses and chariots dedicated to the sun standing at the Temple entrance (2 Kgs 23:11) and the possibile positioning of the

Temple toward the sun in conjunction with the evidence of solar worship in Israel gathered by Taylor (1993) render the omission all the more noteworthy.

How can these omissions be explained? The evidence supports Mettinger's (1979, 1995b) argument for the aniconic tendency. Anthropomorphic god and goddess representations were wholly unacceptable. While images of known creatures from the heavens, earth, and waters were prohibited (Exod 20:4, Deut 5:8), the composite cherub was permissible. The mythical cherub, the stylized sacred tree, and the lights symbolizing stars recreated Yahweh's Garden of Eden and attendant heavenly host.

Without explicit royal imagery, but by means of the placement of the Temple and the choice of courtyard objects and interior motifs, the Temple conveyed divine endorsement of the Davidic kings. Solomon adopted a prevalent Near Eastern architectural plan and built a Palace-Temple compound, or "edifice complex," with the national shrine in the shadow of the much larger, adjacent palace (Ottosson 1980: 51). Courtyard objects symbolically conveyed Yahweh's victories and patronage of the Davidic king. The interior decoration recreated the mythological Garden of Eden, expressing Yahweh's presence in the Temple with implied endorsement of the monarchy. Solomon's temple design was successful; the Davidic dynasty with its patron deity endured.

Bibliography

Abu Assaf, A.
> 1990   *Der Tempel von ʿAin Dara.* Damaszener Forschungen 3. Mainz: von Zabern.

Barnett, R. D.
> 1982   *Ancient Ivories in the Middle East.* Qedem 14. Jerusalem: The Institute of Archaeology of the Hebrew University of Jerusalem.

Bloch-Smith, E.
> 1994   "Who Is the King of Glory?" Solomon's Temple and Its Symbolism. Pp. 18–31 in *Scripture and Other Artifacts: Essays on the Bible and Archaeology in Honor of Philip J. King,* ed. M. Coogan, C. Exum, and L. Stager. Louisville: Westminster/John Knox.

Bordreuil, P., and Pardee, D.
> 1993   Le combat de Baʿlu avec Yammu d'après les textes ougaritiques. *MARI* 7: 63–70.

Busink, T. A.
> 1970   *Der Tempel von Jerusalem von Salomo bis Herodes, Band I: Der Tempel Salomos.* Leiden: Brill.

Canby, J. V.
> 1975   The Walters Gallery Cappadocian Tablet and the Sphinx in Anatolia in the Second Millennium B.C. *JNES* 34/4: 225–48.

Catling, H. W.
    1964   *Cypriot Bronzework in the Mycenean World.* Oxford: Clarendon.
Collon, D.
    1982   *The Alalakh Cylinder Seals: A New Catalogue of the Actual Seals Excavated by Sir Leonard Woolley at Tell Atchana, and from Neighboring Sites on the Syrian-Turkish Border.* British Archaeological Reports International Series 132. Oxford: British Archaeological Reports.
    1987   *First Impressions: Cylinder Seals in the Ancient Near East.* Chicago: University of Chicago Press.
Cross, F. M.
    1973   *Canaanite Myth and Hebrew Epic: Essays in the History of the Religion of Israel.* Cambridge: Harvard University Press.
Dessenne, A.
    1957   *Le Sphinx—Étude iconographique, I: Des origines à la fin du second millénaire.* Bibliothèque des écoles françaises d'Athènes et de Rome 186. Paris: Boccard.
Halpern, B.
    1987   "Brisker Pipes Than Poetry": The Development of Israelite Monotheism. Pp. 77–115 in *Judaic Perspectives on Ancient Israel,* ed. J. Neusner, B. Levine, and E. Frerichs. Philadelphia: Fortress.
Kantor, H.
    1956   Syro-Palestinian Ivories. *JNES* 15: 153–74.
Keel, O.
    1977   *Jahwe-Visionen und Siegelkunst: Eine neue Deutung der Majestätsschilderungen in Jes 6, Ez 1 und Sach 4.* Stuttgarter Bibelstudien 84–85. Stuttgart: Katholisches Bibelwerk.
Keel, O., and Uehlinger, C.
    1992   *Göttinnen, Götter und Gottessymbole: Neue Erkenntnisse zur Religionsgeschichte Kanaans und Israels aufgrund bislang unerschlossener ikonographischer Quellen.* Freiburg: Herder.
Kepinski, C.
    1982   *L'Arbre stylisé en Asie occidentale au 2ᵉ Millénaire Avant J.-C.* Bibliothèque de la Délégation Archéologique Française en Iraq 1. Travaux du Centre de Recherche d'Archéologie Orientale—Université de Paris 1/1. Paris: A.D.P.F.
Kraus, H.-J.
    1988   *Psalms 1–59: A Commentary.* Trans. H. C. Oswald. Minneapolis: Augsburg. [Originally published in German, 1978]
    1989   *Psalms 60–150: A Commentary.* Trans. H. C. Oswald. Minneapolis: Augsburg. [Originally published in German, 1978]
Loud, G.
    1939   *The Megiddo Ivories.* OIP 52. Chicago: Oriental Institute of the University of Chicago Press.
Lurker, M.
    1980   *The Gods and Symbols of Ancient Egypt.* London: Thames & Hudson.

Mazar, A.
1990   *Archaeology of the Land of the Bible, 10,000–586* B.C.E. New York: Doubleday.

Mettinger, T. N. D.
1979   The Veto on Images and the Aniconic God in Ancient Israel. Pp. 15–29
in *Religious Symbols and Their Functions*, ed. H. Biezais. Scripta Instituti
Donnerians Aboensis 10. Stockholm: Almqvist & Wiksell.
1995a   Cherubim. Cols. 362–67 in *Dictionary of Deities and Demons in the Bible*,
ed. K. van der Toorn, B. Becking, and P. van der Horst. Leiden: Brill.
1995b   *"No Graven Image?" Israelite Aniconism in Its Ancient Near Eastern Context*. ConBOT 42. Stockholm: Almqvist & Wiksell.

Meyers, C. L.
1979   Was There a Seven-Branched Lampstand in Solomon's Temple? *BARev*
5/5: 46–57.
1992a   Lampstand. Pp. 141–43 in vol. 4 of *ABD*, ed. D. N. Freedman. 6 vols.
New York: Doubleday.
1992b   Temple, Jerusalem. Pp. 350–69 in vol. 6 of *ABD*, ed. D. N. Freedman. 6
vols. New York: Doubleday.

Negbi, O.
1976   *Canaanite Gods in Metal: An Archaeological Study of Ancient Syro-Palestinian Figurines*. Publications of the Institute of Archaeology 5. Tel Aviv:
Tel Aviv University Institute of Archaeology.

Ottosson, M.
1980   *Temples and Cult Places in Palestine*. Boreas: Uppsala Studies in Ancient
Mediterranean and Near Eastern Civilizations 12. Uppsala: Uppsala University Press.

Schroer, S.
1989   Die Götten auf den Stempelsiegeln aus Palästina/Israel. Pp. 89–212 in
Studien zu den Stempelsiegeln aus Palästina/Israel Band II, ed. O. Keel,
H. Keel-Lev, and S. Schroer. OBO 88. Freiburg: Universitätsverlag /
Göttingen: Vandenhoeck & Ruprecht.

Shuval, M.
1990   A Catalogue of Early Iron Stamp Seals from Israel. Pp. 67–161 in *Studien
zu den Stempelsiegeln aus Palästina/Israel, Band III: Die Frühe Eisenzeit, Ein
Workshop*, ed. O. Keel, M. Shuval, and C. Uehlinger. OBO 100. Freiburg:
Universitätsverlag / Göttingen: Vandenhoeck & Ruprecht.

Smith, M. S.
1990   *The Early History of God: Yahweh and the Other Deities in Ancient Israel*.
New York: Harper & Row.

Stager, L.
1991   When Canaanites and Philistines Ruled Ashkelon." Pp. 2–19 in *Ashkelon
Discovered: From Canaanites and Philistines to Romans and Moslems*. Washington, D.C.: Biblical Archaeology Society.

Taylor, J. G.
1993   *Yahweh and the Sun: Biblical and Archaeological Evidence for Sun Worship in
Ancient Israel*. JSOTSup 111. Sheffield: JSOT Press.

Tessier, B.
  1984   *Ancient Near Eastern Cylinder Seals from the Marcopoli Collection.* Berke-
          ley: University of California Press / Beverly Hills: Summa.
Van Buren, E. D.
  1945   *Symbols of the Gods in Mesopotamian Art.* AnOr 23. Rome: Pontifical Bib-
          lical Institute.
Vollenweider, M.-L.
  1967   *Catalogue raisonné des sceaux cylindres et intailles,* vol. 1. Geneva: Musée
          d'Art d'Histoire de Genève.
Yadin, Y.
  1975   *Hazor: The Rediscovery of a Great Citadel of the Bible.* New York: Random.
Zalcman, L.
  1995   Pleiades. Cols. 1240–42 in *Dictionary of Deities and Demons in the Bible,* ed.
          K. van der Toorn, B. Becking, and P. van der Horst. Leiden: Brill.
Zatelli, I.
  1991   Astrology and the Worship of the Stars in the Bible. ZAW 103/1: 86–99.

The Four-Horned Altar and Sacred Space: An Archaeological Perspective

SEYMOUR GITIN

W. F. Albright Institute of Archaeological Research

Traditionally, textual analysis has been used to determine what constituted sacred space in the ancient Near East (Levine 1987; 1997: 245–49). Archaeological data, such as structures defined as temples and shrines, a natural focus of the investigation of sacred space, have mainly served as referents in the discussion of religious architecture (Aharoni 1969: 71–73; Burdajewicz 1990: 60–103; Dever 1987: 222–25; Holladay 1987: 252–65; Mazar 1992: 187; Ottosson 1980: 115–18; Renfrew 1985: 293– 444; Shiloh 1979; Wright 1985: 215–69). Artifacts considered "cultic" objects, such as figurines, statuary, masseboth, chalices, altars, and astragali, have been primarily the focus of the study of religious worship and practice (Coogan 1987: 2–3; Gitin 1989b: 52*–60*; 1992: 45*–47*; Keel and Uehlinger 1998: 393–95, 400–405; Kletter 1996: 73–81; May 1935: 12–42; Mettinger 1995: 135–97; Uehlinger 1997: 111, 139, 152–55).[1] The strong emphasis and reliance on written evidence has resulted from the ready availability of detailed texts and the lack of well-defined archaeological data.

The recent excavations at Tel Miqne-Ekron, however, provide an exceptional opportunity to reexamine the question of sacred space on the basis of secure archaeological data (Gitin 1989a: 25–40; Dothan and Gitin 1993: 1056–59). The core evidence is the corpus of well-documented Iron Age II four-horned altars from Ekron (Gitin 1989b: 61*–64*; 1992: 43*–44*), examined within the context of antecedent Syrian forms (Margueron 1976: 196–207; Muller-Pierre 1992: 39 n. 22) and Mesopotamian, Anatolian, Canaanite, Aegean (Diamant and Rutter 1969: 175–77) and Cypriote (Loulloupis 1973: 242–44) iconographic parallels for the altar's primary form

---

1. For a treatment in which artifacts are employed as criteria for identifying sacred sites, see Fowler 1985.

feature—its horns.[2] These data are critical to the discussion of sacred space in antiquity, especially when considered in light of the textual evidence presented below, which describes the form of the four-horned altar and its cultic function. This combination of text and realia not only demonstrates the sacred character of the four-horned altar in its role as an incense burner but, most significantly, the relationship between its form and function. The evidence of a continuous long-term tradition in the ancient Near East constitutes the basis for maintaining that the four-horned altar had an intrinsic quality of sanctity, an attribute symbolically transmitted to the physical space it occupied, even when that space was not already defined as a sacred area by conventional standards.[3] The implication of this conclusion that the four-horned altar serves as a criterion for defining sacred space is the focus of this paper.

The earliest examples in the archaeological record of objects with a four-horned-altar form are the Late Bronze Age terracotta-tower models from Emar, Mumbaqat, and Tell Faqʾous in the Syrian Middle Euphrates region (Muller 1997: 258, fig. 2a, e, f, i). These are generally dated to the 14th–12th centuries B.C.E. (Muller-Pierre 1992: 40–41). The examples with the most secure context, Tower J from Emar and Tower G–V from Faqʾous, can be dated to the 13th–12th centuries B.C.E. (Muller-Pierre 1992: 41; Muller 1997: 258, fig. 2e, f). The tower models, which may have mirrored Syrian architecture, were used as altars or stands for burnt offerings, and Towers A (fig. 1) and J from Emar provide the best examples (Muller-Pierre 1992: 40–41). The body of each tower narrows toward the top, where there are two overhangs, creating the effect of a rim or ledge. The crowning, with edges or horns at each corner stretching outward and upward, as if pointing heavenward, forms merlons, which represent the battlement at the top of the tower (Holloway 1996:

2. The Tel Miqne-Ekron excavations and publications are a joint project of the W. F. Albright Institute of Archaeological Research and Hebrew University, directed by T. Dothan and S. Gitin. The research for this paper was completed during my 1996–97 sabbatical semester as a Fellow of the Center for Judaic Studies at the University of Pennsylvania. The Ekron altar corpus was drawn by E. Cohen, T. Solskina, S. Halbreich, and M. Zeltser; the altars from other sites were drawn by G. Hasel and M. Zeltser; and the altar plates and map were prepared by J. Rosenberg. Support for this work came from the Dorot Foundation. The manuscript was read by V. Hurowitz, E. Sachar, and H. Flusfeder, who made much-appreciated suggestions.

3. Support for such a long-term form-function tradition, extending into modern times, can be seen in the incense burners from Yemen. "Used in uninterrupted tradition . . . some of their shapes changed very little over millennia . . . an uncovered altar shape with four protruding corners, so called horns . . . reminiscent of ancient archaeological types . . . The lime incense-burner from 10th-century B.C. Megiddo is specially similar" (Muchawsky-Schnapper 1998: vi–viii).

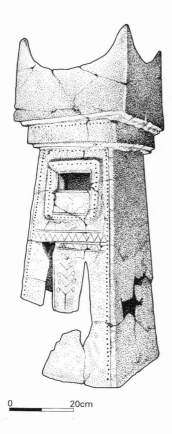

Fig. 1. Ceramic model of Tower A from Emar,
based on drawing in Muller-Pierre 1992:40, fig. 8.

0 _____ 20cm

27). Body features include triangular and oblong-shaped windows and an assortment of incised and relief decorations (Margueron 1976: 193–213, 197,
fig. 1, 203, fig. 5, pls. 1–2). Similar features are indicated on fragmentary examples from Emar and other sites (Muller 1997: 258, fig. 2), as well as on an
unprovenienced example in the Louvre (Muller-Pierre 1992: 37).[4]

In the 10th century b.c.e., the form and function of this Syrian altar tradition continued in two forms, both more stylized than the earlier tower-
shaped models, as attested by the straight-sided ceramic cult stand and altar

_____

4. These data demonstrate that the antecedent of the Iron Age Israelite four-
horned stone altar is to be found in the Late Bronze Age, contrary to what Dever has
suggested: "The only innovation in Iron I remains that cannot be derived from LB is
the small four-cornered or 'horned' altar, which may perhaps be considered as evidence
for the introduction of incense offerings by the Israelite cult" (Dever 1987: 233).

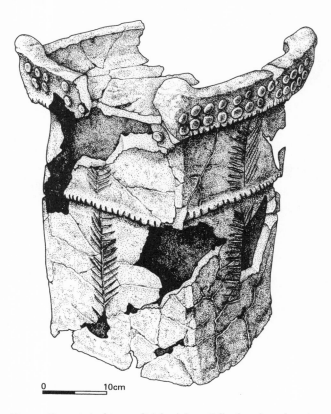

*Fig. 2. Ceramic 'cultic stand' (altar) from Pella, based on photo in
Smith and Potts 1992: pl. 70.*

from Pella (Smith and Potts 1992: 97). The cult stand has an elaborate decoration and a perforated top or grate that was thoroughly blackened and covered with soot. The altar, although lacking the triangular-shaped windows of
the Late Bronze Age examples, is closed on top and has horn-like swellings at
each of its top corners, a pronounced rim, and a rope-like molded band
around its body (fig. 2), (Potts 1985: 204, pls. 41–42).[5] While the ceramic
cult stand continues to appear elsewhere in the form of a typologically-

5. A similar ceramic altar with horns and a molded figure was found in the recent excavations (July, 2000) at Tel Rehov (personal communication, A. Mazar).
Other examples are also known from Jordan, a corpus of which is currently being prepared by H. Katz.

related ceramic shrine (May 1935: 13–17, pls. 13–15), the ceramic altar, continuing the form tradition of the antecedental tower models, develops into a stone model, as seen in the Iron Age II Israelite four-horned altars (Smith and Potts 1992: 97, 100).

The long-term use of the form of the tower-shaped altar to symbolize the roof tops on which offerings were made, reflects the well-established ancient Near Eastern tradition of the roof ritual, which was an integral element of East and West Semitic cult practices. For example, the Assyrian Gilgamesh Epic describes Ninsun, the great queen, going up to the roof to offer incense to the god Shamash (Gilgamesh III ii 1–10 [Pritchard 1969: 81]). In a Ugaritic text, King Keret is described as ascending to the roof for sacrifice and prayer and thereafter descending from the *mgdl*, that is, from the tower (Krt 73–80 [Gray 1964: 12, 37, 38]; Gordon 1965: 295). Roof rituals are also mentioned on an Aramaic incantation bowl (Gordon 1941: 342). In the Bible, Josiah is described as "the King [who] tore down the altars made by the kings of Judah on the roof by the upper chamber of Ahaz" (2 Kgs 23:12). Making offerings on roofs, using the verb *qtr*, usually understood as 'to burn incense', also appears in Jeremiah, which mentions offerings made to "the whole host of heaven" (19:13), and "to Ba'al" (32:29).

The symbolism of one of the most prominent features of the tower models—the horns—is also a well-known cultic phenomenon in the ancient Near East. Horns frequently appear in Mesopotamian cultic iconography—for example, the often multi-horned cap of a god placed on an altar, especially on *kudurru* stones (Black and Green 1992: 102). In Anatolia, most examples have a domestic rather than a ritualistic association, although some horned objects are found in a temple context (Diamant and Rutter 1969: 165–70, 176). In Canaanite cult, the storm god Ba'al is portrayed with horns, as in the well-known example from Ugarit (Schaeffer 1949: pl. 24). By the middle of the second millennium B.C.E., horns of consecration were a common phenomenon in Minoan and Mycenaean cultic contexts. Among the best examples are the stone, clay, and alabaster horns on the altars and on the roofs of shrines at Knossos, Phaistos, and Haghia Triada (Davaras 1976: 289–92; Gesell 1985: 188–89; Schoep 1994: 193, 203–6). This feature is also well attested in Cyprus (Loulloupis 1973: 225–42). In addition, horns are a well-established symbol in the biblical text, representing strength and political power—an image based on bulls pushing with their horns (Deut 33:17). In prophetic symbolism, horns signify royal or military power (Dan 7:8; 8:21). The hallowed status of the horns is demonstrated by the fact that fugitives could claim asylum from temporal authority by grasping the horns of the altar (1 Kgs 1:50; 2:28).

The horned altar first appeared in Israelite religious practice as part of the paraphernalia of the Tabernacle, the movable sanctuary or tent of meeting, constructed in the wilderness. There it is defined as a *mzbḥ mqṭr qṭrt* 'an altar for burning incense'. Made of acacia wood, its dimensions were one cubit long, one cubit wide, and two cubits high. It was gold-plated and had horns, a *zr* 'a gold molding' or body band around it, and two gold rings to hold poles so that it could be carried (Exod 30:1–4). It is also described as a *qṭrt smm*, for burning "aromatic incense" (Exod 30:7), and as *mzbḥ qṭrt hsmm* 'the altar of aromatic incense' (Lev 4:7). The smoke produced from the burning may have symbolized the ascendancy of an offering to God on high (Nielsen 1986: 87). The sweet smell of aromatic smoke may have been considered a special fragrance reserved for the deity and could have served as an expression of his personality (Houtman 1992: 462). Although portable, the prescribed place for the altar in the Tabernacle was in front of the curtain covering the shrine of the Lord that housed the Ark of the Covenant (Exod 30:6). Solomon's Temple contained a similar incense altar, described as a *mzbḥ ʿrz* 'a cedar altar', overlaid with gold, located near the shrine of the Ark of the Covenant (1 Kgs 6:22). It is also referred to as a *mzbḥ hzhb* 'an altar of gold', clearly distinguishing it from the table of gold for the bread of display (1 Kgs 7:48). A later source describes King Uzziah (8th century) entering the Temple *lhqṭr ʾl mzbḥ hqṭrt* 'to offer incense on the incense altar' (2 Chr 26:16).

Although the biblical altar was made of wood (unlike the ceramic-tower models), it continued the traditional relationship between the form and function of the tower models in the following ways: In terms of form, the biblical altar emulated the overall rectangular shape and most characteristic feature of the early Syrian tower models—its horns. In addition, the biblical altar had a rope-like molded band around the center of the body, which is also a prominent feature of the 10th-century Pella altar. The altar's function, its role in the cultic tradition of making burnt offerings—that is, burning incense in roof rituals—is known from the Bible and other ancient Near Eastern texts, as cited above. This practice is supported by the archaeological evidence from Ashkelon, where a non-horned altar was found on top of the remains of a destroyed roof (Stager 1996: 66*, 68*). The roof ritual should also be considered symbolically inherent in the four-horned image, based on the form-function relationship, which continues the Syrian tower-model tradition, with burning taking place on the top surface of the altar, that is, its roof.

The biblical evidence is significant for two reasons. First, it defines the horned altar as an incense burner integral to official religious praxis, with a prescribed sanctified or sacred space. Second, because the form of the four-horned altars found in archaeological contexts, some of which are cultic, accords with the form described in the text, it is possible to conclude that these excavated altars also functioned as incense burners. It is this relationship between form and function, based on the cultic tradition of roof rituals, and the inherent symbolic sacred character of the four-horned altar that provides the basis for extending the definition of sacred space to contexts in which excavated altars were found that were not already considered sacred as defined by conventional criteria. [6]

The relationship between the altar's textual image and its representation as an artifact has been discussed intensively since the 1920s, when, as a focus of the debate on the early or late dating of the Priestly (P) code, it became a major issue for biblical scholarship (Wiener 1927: 1–22). At the time, a number of biblical scholars held the position that rituals such as the burning of incense, which were part of the P code and associated with early Israelite religion in the Bible, were actually introduced during the postexilic period (Haran 1957: 778; 1985: 9–12). This conclusion was based on the then widely-accepted Kuenen-Wellhausen evaluation of Israelite cult (Albright 1929: 50, 53; Wellhausen 1957: 64–66). In defense of the early dating of P, Wiener maintained that incense was used in Israelite religious practice during the preexilic period (Wiener 1927: 23–31). His assumption was based on the similarity of the 3 four-horned stone objects (altars) found at Israelite Iron Age sites—one at Gezer and 2 at Shechem (Wiener 1927: 30–32)—to the altar of incense described in the Bible (Exod 30:1–4). Over the years, the majority of scholars (Albright 1929: 52–53; May 1935: 12; McCown 1950: 210; Haran 1957: 778–79; de Vaux 1965: 286–87; and Milgrom 1971: 767; among others) supported this position and, in so doing, strengthened the equation of the excavated altars with the biblical altar. As archaeological excavations produced more altars, an expanded data base was created with 8 additional four-horned examples: 7 from Megiddo (fig. 3), one from Nineveh, and one non-horned altar from Megiddo (Gitin 1989b: 65*).[7] Further support for the equation came from the 11 altars subsequently found at Arad (2 non-horned), at Dan (6; 5 of them non-horned), and at Kedesh, Lachish, and Megiddo (one each), bringing the total number of excavated altars to 23 (Gitin 1989b: 58*–59*, 64*–65*). Although 8 of these are non-horned,

6. These criteria include cultic contexts, such as a temple or a room with a cluster of established cultic objects, as cited above on the first page of this article. One of the best examples of the former is from Ekron, where a dedicatory inscription indicated that the building in which it was found was a sanctuary (Gitin, Dothan, and Naveh 1997: 5, 9). A more common phenomenon is a corner of a room with an assemblage of established cultic objects, such as those found in Megiddo, Stratum VA/IVB, in the southwest corner of Room 2081. Clustered there were 2 four-horned altars, astragali in a ceramic bowl, 2 chalices, 1 offering stands, and a number of votive items (Loud 1948: 44, 161–62).

7. Nineveh actually produced three other similar altars that were not found in situ. Unfortunately, neither illustrations nor photographs were published, so they are not included in the current altar corpus (Holloway 1996: 27 n. 1).

Fig. 3. Stone altar from Megiddo, based on photo in May
1935: pl. XII, 2982.

other features, such as the block/rectangular shape of the biblical altar and
the Syrian tower-model tradition, as well as the body band of the biblical altar
and the Pella example, provide the basis for considering them incense altars.
Some examples also have rims, as do a number of horned altars. This feature
is characteristic of the Syrian tower-model tradition and can be equated with
the *karkov* 'ledge' of the bronze or burnt offering horned altar of the Tabernacle (Exod 27:5).

Other scholars dealing with Israelite religious practice, including Shiloh
(1979: 150), Dever (1983: 573), and Holladay (1987: 265, 272), also accepted the equation of the excavated altars with the biblical altar as the basis
for defining the function of the excavated altars as an incense burner. These
scholars, however, implicitly or explicitly expressed the qualification that

substances other than incense could also have been burned on these altars (for example, see Shiloh 1979: 150). In one of the most detailed investigations of incense and its cultic uses in ancient Israel, Nielsen (1986: 46–47) designated the four-horned altar as one of seven types of incense utensils. He acknowledges, however, that these altars may not have been used exclusively as incense burners (Nielsen 1986: 38). Thus, although some scholars suggest that more than one substance could have been burned on these altars, the long-held consensus has been that the excavated four-horned altars, like the altars described in the Bible, were used to burn incense. This consensus formed the basis for my conclusion that the Tel Miqne-Ekron altars should be identified as incense altars, including 17 published examples: one non-horned and 15 four-horned altars from the 7th century B.C.E., and one possibly from an earlier context (fig. 4, nos. 1–3, 6–7, 9–12; fig. 5) (Gitin 1989b: 53*; 1992: 44*; MacKay 1995: 4, pl. 9); and 2 previously unpublished four-horned examples (fig. 4, nos. 4, 8) (object nos. 4188 and 4530). This same consensus is also the basis for the conclusion that the 3 more recently excavated examples at Ashkelon were also incense altars. These include a 7th-century non-horned altar (Stager 1996: 66*, 68*) and one horned and one non-horned altar (material cultural nos. 43844 and 41072) that predate the 6th century. These bring the total altar corpus to 45 (fig. 6).

Menahem Haran, however, formerly a supporter of the consensus (Haran 1957: 778–79), subsequently sharply attacked the identification of the four-horned altars from archaeological contexts as incense burners following the publication of the first assemblage of 12 altars from Tel Miqne-Ekron (Gitin 1989b: 53*). Initially, he argued that such altars were not used to burn incense (Haran 1993: 239–41). Later, however, he took the more extreme position of attempting to prove that four-horned altars found in Iron Age contexts could not have been used for the burning of incense (Haran 1995: 33–35, 37). The following discussion of Haran's criticism, based on my earlier response (Gitin 1992: 45*–47*), will show that the evidence, contrary to supporting Haran's position, is totally consistent with the relationship between the textual tradition and the excavated altars as defined by the consensus position.

In Haran's approach to the textual evidence, his point of departure stems from two a priori judgments, both based on the biblical text. The first is that burning incense was the sole prerogative of the Temple priests, who performed this ritual only in the Temple in Jerusalem (Haran 1985: 237–38). Consequently, according to Haran, Iron Age II four-horned altars found outside the Temple in Jerusalem could not have been incense altars (Haran 1993: 239–41). The second is that temples did not exist outside of Jerusalem, except for those built before Solomon's Temple (Haran 1977: 13). Thus, according to Haran, the altars from the Arad temple could not have been

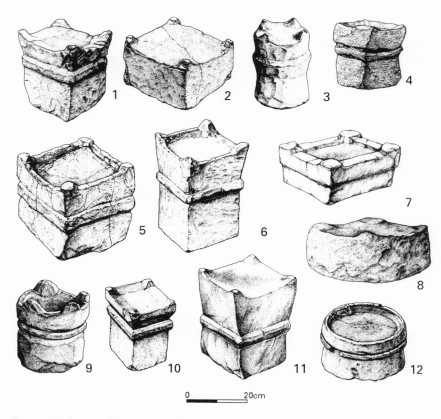

Fig. 4. Twelve portable stone altars from Ekron.

incense altars, since "what was found at Arad cannot possibly be interpreted as a temple" (Haran 1977: 14).[8]

In holding to these views, "Haran ignores the fact that scripture itself sanctions—though on emergency grounds—for incense to be burned on pans outside the sanctuary (Num 17:11). The fact that incense was offered privately after the destruction of the Second Temple (*m. Zebaḥ.* 13:5–6), indi-

8. The consensus does not support Haran's interpretation of the Arad "temple." For example, B. Levine contends "that it had served as a proper, Yahwistic sanctuary ever since its initial construction in the tenth century" (Levine 1997: 251–52). For further support of the existence of sanctuaries outside of Jerusalem, see the discussion of *mqm* in n. 16 (p. 114).

cates that it was not an innovation, but a continuous practice" (written communication, J. Milgrom, 1995). In addition, Haran also does not consider the possible *tendenz* of the biblical writer, who may have had reason to deny the existence of a long-established popular religious practice. It has been suggested that these altars were an expression of local *Volksreligion*. Therefore, P, in his exposition of Israelite religion, would have wished to convey the image that incense burning from the outset was restricted to a selected, centrally-located priesthood and thus that local Israelite incense burning was unlawful (Nielsen 1986: 51).

Haran's lack of appreciation of the relevance of the study of folk religion is indicated by his failure to relate to its broad treatment in the literature, which shows the important role played by altars, the burning of incense, and the offering of libations on roofs. For example, Weinfeld in his study of the extensive biblical evidence for the worship of the host heaven after the penetration of Assyria into the region, points out the significance of offering incense on rooftops. One of his main conclusions is that what distinguishes this cultic practice is its private character, performed by nonpriests outside the official setting of the Jerusalem Temple (Weinfeld 1972: 151–53). In another study, Halpern emphasizes the official character of this folk religion: "For the Judahites of the late 7th and early 6th century, worship of these 'other gods,' including the Queen of Heaven, was indeed traditional practice, part of the folk and state religion of Judah" (Halpern 1993: 117). Support for this can be found in Jer 44:17: "We will do everything which we have vowed—to make offerings to the Queen of Heaven and to pour libations to her, as we used to do, we and our fathers, our kings and our officials, in the towns of Judah and the streets of Jerusalem."

In regard to the specific arguments that Haran has published recently against the view that excavated altars are incense burners, one of his main points is based on an interpretation of the biblical texts that use the verb *qṭr*. In the past, in most English versions of the Bible, this verb in the piel was understood to refer to the "burning of incense" and in the hiphil to the more general category of "making offerings," which could also include instances of "burning incense." Haran, however, points out, "In more recent translations this verb is rendered as burning sacrifices or making offerings," citing the new translation by the Jewish Publication Society (NJPSV) as one of his proof texts (Haran 1995: 36). A careful examination of the NJPSV, however, indicates that this is not quite the case. While in the majority of examples the NJPSV does change the traditional "burning incense" to "making offerings," in a number of instances this was because the translators were not certain what kind of offering was intended and did not wish to commit themselves to a specific meaning of the term (private conversation, Weinfeld 1995). Thus, "making offerings" does not necessarily preclude "burning incense" but, rather,

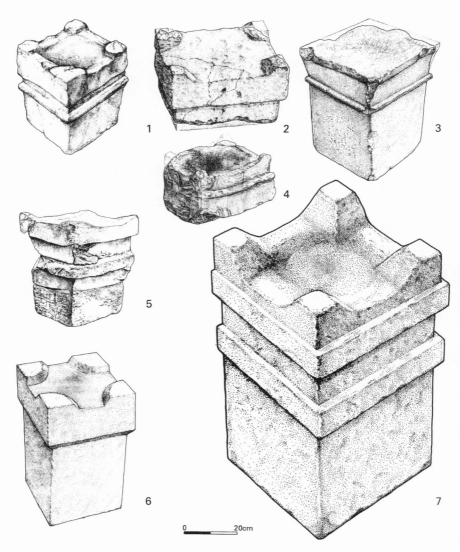

Fig. 5. Seven stone altars with fixed locations from Ekron.

includes it as a possibility. Moreover, in a number of passages, the NJPSV translates the piel of the verb *qṭr* 'burning incense'—for example, in Isa 65:3 and Jer 44:23 and 25, the latter involving burning an incense offering to the Queen of Heaven. In addition, elsewhere Haran acknowledges that some

spices were added to grain offerings and, therefore, incense was burned in
some cases in combination with other substances (Haran 1985: 230). He also
acknowledges that, on occasion, when both spices and grain offerings are
mentioned, it is difficult to determine whether a separate spice offering is
meant or whether the reference is to a combination of substances (Haran
1985: 231).

Concerning the archaeological data, Haran presents four arguments on
the basis of which he rejects the obvious implications of the size, context, and
the geographic and chronological distribution of the altar corpus. First, he
maintains that burning incense on the large number of four-horned altars
found in archaeological excavations would have been precluded by the high
cost of incense. Second, burning incense was a royal or upper-class activity
and would not have occurred in industrial and domestic zones, such as those
at Ekron, which produced four-horned altars. Third, incense was only burned
indoors and could not have been used in the outdoor areas in which four-
horned altars were found. Fourth, evidence of burning is rarely found on the
excavated four-horned altars (Haran 1993: 239–41; 1995: 32–35).

Haran's argument that the cost of incense was prohibitive is based on the
assumption that large numbers of four-horned altars were being used simultaneously. On the contrary, only 45 altars have been found in the course of 100
years of excavation (fig. 6) and, given the number of sites excavated and the
size of the population in Iron Age II, the corpus is relatively small. [9] More importantly, 7 of these altars can be assigned to the 10th, 6 to the 8th, 3 to the
8th/7th, and 19 to the 7th century. Ten, in uncertain contexts and primarily
on typological grounds, are assigned a pre–6th century date (Gitin 1989b:
54*–57*; 1992: 44*; MacKay 1995: 4; Stager 1996: 66*; unpublished examples from Ekron, object nos. 4188, 4530; and unpublished examples from
Ashkelon, material culture nos. 43844 and 41072). Thus, a large amount of
incense would not have been required to be burned in any one century (Gitin
1989b: 54*–57*). The cost would have been negligible—especially if, as Haran posits, only royalty used incense, for whom the price would not have been
prohibitive (Haran 1993: 241).

In discussing the cost of incense, the economic situation prevalent in the
last phase of the Iron Age should also be taken into consideration. The price
of incense in the 7th century, like that of other internationally traded com-
modities, was probably affected by Neo-Assyrian economic interests that
stimulated the expansion of commerce during the *pax Assyriaca* (Postgate
1979: 198–99; Knauf 1992: 50–51; Gitin 1997: 78–79 nn. 4–7). New trade
routes were established and political and economic relations formed with the

9. For estimates of the size of the population of ancient Israel in Iron Age II, see
Broshi and Finkelstein 1992: 54.

Arab tribes renowned for their involvement in the incense trade (Elat 1990: 77–78; 1994: 23). These developments should have normalized the supply and lowered the cost of incense. Haran apparently came to the same conclusion, despite his statement regarding the prohibitive cost of incense. Based on Jer 17:26 and 41:5, he notes that "towards the end of the First Temple period, ordinary folk could manage to bring a piece of frankincense and offer it in Jerusalem" (Haran 1993: 240). If the use of incense became more widespread, therefore, it stands to reason that there would have been a corresponding increase in the number of altars or similar objects on which incense was burned. The evidence of the 19 altars from the 7th century b.c.e.—18 from Ekron (Gitin 1989b: 56*–57*; 1992: 44*; MacKay 1995: 4; unpublished examples object nos. 4188, 4530) and one from Ashkelon (Stager 1996: 66*)—and the appearance of a significant number of cult stands—for example, from Ekron (Gitin 1992: 49* n. 42), Jerusalem (Shiloh 1984: 19), and Lahav (oral communication, J. Hardin), among others—is consistent with an increased supply of incense, on the one hand and, on the other, with its lower price.

As for Haran's assumption that burning incense was restricted to elite groups, his own statement cited above regarding ordinary people being able to afford to offer incense in Jerusalem contradicts this view. Furthermore, the biblical text discussed above demonstrates that incense was burned outside of Jerusalem in private contexts, not necessarily in a temple or shrine or even by priests (Jer 44:21, 25). Thus, in the waning days of the First Temple Period, that is, the 7th/6th century b.c.e., burning incense was gradually becoming a widespread practice. This development is supported in the archaeological record, in a Late Iron Age II context at Beer-sheba and at other sites, by the appearance of the tiny cuboid incense altar, probably the successor of the four-horned altar, which was to become the dominant form in the Persian period (Stern 1973: 52). That these altars were used to burn incense is indicated by the word *lbnt* 'frankincense', inscribed on one of the postexilic examples from Lachish (Nielsen 1986: 48). By the Persian period, these cuboid altars are found in large numbers throughout the ancient Near East—for example, more than 200 at Lachish (Stern 1982: 182–95). Surely this phenomenon indicates the extensive use of incense, probably as a result of the increased incense trade with the Arabian Peninsula, under the expanding influence of the Neo-Babylonian and Persian Empires (Eph'al 1982: 210). It also strongly suggests that groups other than the upper classes were burning incense in the 6th–4th centuries b.c.e. This data base provides a model for explaining the relationship between supply and usage, which is consistent with the presence of the large assemblage of altars at Ekron at the end of the 7th century, when the incense trade began to flourish.

Haran also argues that the outdoor archaeological contexts of the four-horned altars precluded their use for burning incense because the effect would

45 limestone altars: 33 horned ☖ & 12 non-horned ☐
Iron Age II 10th-7th c BCE

Fig. 6. Distribution and period map of corpus of 45 altars.

have been dissipated in the open space. The text traditions cited above, however, refer to burning incense and making offerings on the roof—that is, in an
open area. Confirmation of this practice can be seen, as mentioned above, in
the location of one of the three altars from Ashkelon, which was found on top
of the collapsed roof of a building burned in the 604 B.C.E. Babylonian destruction (Stager 1996: 66*, 68*). Of all the archaeological evidence that Haran brings to bear on the issue, most strongly emphasized is the argument that
the outdoor contexts of the altars negate their use as incense burners (Haran
1993: 241; 1995: 35). This argument, however, is totally without any basis in
fact. Not only is there evidence of roof ritual incense burning, but many of the
altars were used indoors. The find-spots of the seven in situ altars excavated
in Israel and Judah indicate that they were in enclosed (that is, roofed) buildings; for example: the 2 altars in the Arad temple, the 2 in the Dan altar room,
the one in the Lachish cult room, and the 2 in the Megiddo cult room (Gitin
1989b: 64*–65*). In addition, the 14 in situ altars from Ekron were solidly
sealed beneath the burned roofs of buildings destroyed in the 604 B.C.E. Babylonian campaign (Gitin 1989b: 59*; 1992: 43*; MacKay 1995: 3–4; and unpublished example object no. 4530). The remains of steps leading up to a
second floor were found in some of these buildings, further evidence that the
rooms in which the altars were located had ceilings or were roofed (Gitin
1997: 89, fig. 7).

Finally, Haran states that the four-horned altars, with only two excep-
tions, do not show evidence of burning on their top surfaces. Four altars,
however, have produced evidence of burned residue (Gitin 1989b: 64*–65*).
The absence of this evidence on the other altars may be explained by Albright's suggestion that incense was burned in a bowl placed on the altar.
Albright's conclusion was based on the example of the altar from Nineveh
(fig. 7), which included a bowl carved out of the same piece of limestone from
which the rest of the altar was made. The bowl gave the appearance of being
held in place by the altar's four horns (Albright 1929: 52). Burning incense
in a bowl is logical, since this would be the most efficient way of handling the
incense before, while, and after it was burned.

If, as Haran claims, the altars were not used for burning incense, what
then was their purpose? He suggests that they were used for Minhah, a grain
offering. He links this with the worship of the Queen of Heaven, which was
first mentioned during the 7th-century reign of Manasseh, when Judah was
under Assyrian hegemony (Haran 1993: 241–43; 1995: 35–36). Therefore,
Haran concludes, the altars erected by Manasseh were similar in shape to the
four-horned altars found in archaeological assemblages (Haran 1993: 244;
1995: 37). There are three problems with this conclusion. First, the Minhah
offering is also a burnt offering and, consequently, would have produced
burned residue, the absence of which Haran points to as proof that incense

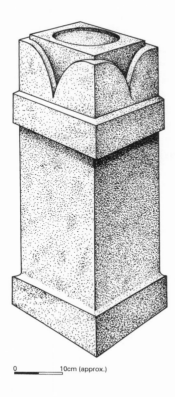

0 _____10cm (approx.)

Fig. 7. Stone altar from Nineveh, based on
drawing from Thompson and Hutchinson 1929:
pl. 56:335.

could not have been burned on the altars.[10] Second, the biblical text, according to Weinfeld, indicates that in the worship of the Queen of Heaven,
incense was burned on altars on rooftops (Weinfeld 1972: 149–52). Third, no
four-horned altars have been found in the archaeological context of the kingdom of Manasseh, and the few Late Iron Age examples from the Northern
Kingdom of Israel cannot be dated with certainty to the time of Manasseh
(Gitin 1989b: 54*–57*). Thus, Haran's attempt to link the altars erected by
Manasseh with the excavated four-horned altars is not supported by the
evidence.

     In addition, in using the archaeological record, Haran does not take into
consideration the ramifications of this evidence for his own position, which is
based on the biblical text. For example, he assumes that the restrictions of the

     10. If a bowl was used to hold the Minhah offering, as suggested above in the
case of burning incense, then one should not expect to find evidence of burning on
the altar itself.

biblical tradition, which reflect the status of Judahite religious practice (ideal or otherwise), applied to all of ancient Israel and Philistia. In so doing, he does not fully appreciate the implications of the geographical distribution of the altars. The largest assemblage of altars—numbering 18—as already demonstrated above, is from 7th-century Ekron, which as part of Philistia was first a Neo-Assyrian vassal city-state and subsequently under the hegemony of Egypt (Gitin 1989a: 41–48). Three other altars from Philistia came from Ashkelon, as cited above, and are either dated to the 7th century or associated with it. Thus, both Ekron and Ashkelon were not subject to the authority of Judah and therefore were not affected by its rules of cult practice, including incense burning.

The second largest group of altars—numbering 9—is from Megiddo. Of these, only 2 were in situ (Loud 1948: 44–46) and could be dated to the Solomonic part of the 10th century, when they would have been subject to the cultic rules of the Temple in Jerusalem. The remaining 7 Megiddo altars are from uncertain stratigraphic context (Stern 1990: 104–6) or from a post-10th-century Stratum (Gitin 1989a: 55–56, 65 nn. 13–18)—that is, the post–United Monarchy period, when Megiddo was already part of the Northern Israelite kingdom and, apparently, no longer subject to the cultic rules of the Temple in Jerusalem. The other 10 altars from the North are also either from the period of the Israelite kingdom or from uncertain chronological contexts (Gitin 1989b: 58*–59*). Of the 3 altars from Judah that could be considered incense burners, one is from 10th-century Lachish (Aharoni 1975: 26, 31) and 2 are from 8th-century Arad (Herzog 1997: 175). Haran's argument, therefore, would apply only to 5 altars from Megiddo, Lachish, and Arad, since only their use would have been affected by the cultic practices at the centrally located Temple in Jerusalem.[11] Thus, even if Haran's argument based on the biblical text is accepted, his conclusion would still not preclude the majority of the altars in the corpus from being used to burn incense.

In refuting Haran's attempt to prove that the four-horned altars from archaeological contexts could not have been used to burn incense, it has been demonstrated that the textual and archaeological data are entirely consistent with the relationship between the altar's form and function as defined by the consensus position. The study of this relationship has also provided a chain of literary and artifactual evidence from the Bronze through Iron Ages, which is the basis for my conclusion that four-horned altars can be used to define sacred space. This attribute would apply to 13 of the 45 altars in the Iron Age II

---

11. The 2 altars in the 45-altar corpus not included in the consideration of altars affected by the cultic rules of the Temple in Jerusalem are from Ekron, one of which was found in a post-10th and pre-7th-century fill; and from Nineveh, which was in Assyria (Gitin 1989b: 57*).

corpus (fig. 6). While these altars can be assigned to datable architectural units, they do not appear in space considered sacred as defined by conventional criteria.[12] The 13 examples are from Ekron Stratum IB, dated to the 7th century, and include 9 horned altars found in situ and sealed by a massive layer of destruction debris (Gitin 1989b: 56*–57*, nos. 22, 24, 26, 27, 30–32; MacKay 1995: 4, Loci 150007, 150009), and 4 altars (3 horned and one non-horned) that, although presumed to be in situ, were not found in a sealed context (Gitin 1989b: 56*, nos. 23, 25, 28, 29). In attributing an inherent sacred quality to these altars, which transmitted sanctity to the space they occupied, the traditional definition of sacred space is expanded effectively to include work and domestic areas.[13] Thus, the find-spots of these 13 Ekron altars in the olive oil industrial and domestic zones of occupation would be considered sacred space because of the presence of a sacred object used for a cultic purpose—that is, the burning of incense.

This broadening of cultic contexts, based on the implications of the four-horned altar's form-function relationship, represents a new dimension in defining sacred space. It also forms the basis for identifying five examples of coexistence and duality in cultic practice at Ekron during the 7th century: (1) private worship in religious and secular areas, (2) public worship in religious and secular areas, (3) the portability and fixed character of acts of religious worship, (4) centralized and decentralized systems of worship, and (5) local and foreign traditions of religious practices.

(1) The coexistence of private worship in religious and secular settings is demonstrated by the 6 altars in the Temple Auxiliary Buildings, 2 each in Buildings 651 (fig. 4, nos. 9, 10; Gitin 1989b: 56*–57*, nos. 24, 30), 653 (fig. 4, no. 7, fig. 5, no. 1; Gitin 1992: 44*, A, B), and 654 (fig. 4, nos. 4, 11; Gitin 1992: 44*, C; previously unpublished example, object no. 4530); and by the presence of 2 altars in the domestic zone (fig. 4, 12; fig. 5, no. 2; Gitin 1989b: 56*, nos. 23, 25).

(2) Public worship in a religious setting is attested by the sanctuary in Temple Complex 650 that contained the Ekron royal dedicatory inscription (Gitin, Dothan, and Naveh 1997: 3–10); and public worship in a secular area is demonstrated by the 9 altars in the olive oil industrial zone (fig. 4, nos. 1–3, 5, 6; fig. 5, nos. 4–7; Gitin 1989b: 56*–57*, nos. 22, 26–29, 31, 32; and MacKay 1995: 4, Loci 150007 and 150009).

(3) Portability of worship activities is based on the conclusion that a number of altars could be moved easily because of their small size and because

12. See n. 6 (p. 101).

13. The association of cult and industry and cultic practice in the home are documented in the archaeological record (Dothan 1981: 92–93; Karageorghis 1981: 82–83; Rutkowski 1986: 135–41, 213–21; Ottosson 1980: 97–98).

they are not engaged. An engaged altar would have one or more unfinished sides, indicating that it had a fixed placement. Fourteen of the Ekron altars are 32 cm high or less and, of these, the 12 that are freestanding would be considered portable (fig. 4; Gitin 1989b: 56*–57*, nos. 22, 24–27, 30, 32; Gitin 1992: 44*, A, C; MacKay 1995: 4, pl. 9, Locus 150009; and 2 unpublished examples, object nos. 4188, 4530).[14] The 4 engaged altars include 2 that are small, 31 cm and 18 cm high (Gitin 1989b: 56*–57*, nos. 23, 31), and 2 that are large, 48 cm and 116 cm high (Gitin 1989b: 56*, nos. 28, 29). In addition, there are 2 large freestanding altars, 37.5 and 46 cm high, that most likely were not portable (fig. 5; Gitin 1992: 44*, B; MacKay 1995: pl. 9, Locus 150007).[15]

(4) The coexistence of centralized and decentralized worship is in sharp contrast to the contemporary Deuteronomist's singular focus on the centralization of religious practice in Israelite religion in what was its formative period of development in the biblical period (Weinfeld 1992: 175, 177). Centralized worship at Ekron is well attested by the sanctuary in Temple Complex 650, which contained the Ekron royal dedicatory inscription (Gitin, Dothan, and Naveh 1997: 3–10). Also, a store jar inscription found in Temple Auxiliary Building 654 points to a central place of worship. It reads "for the shrine, 30 units of x," which could mean that 30 units of produce were set aside for the shrine as a tithe (Gitin 1990b: 251).[16] Tithing would suggest the existence of a priesthood that served the central shrine. As for decentralized worship, of the 18 altars from 7th-century Ekron, 9 are from the industrial complex (fig. 4, nos. 1–3, 5, 6; fig. 5, nos. 4–7; Gitin 1989b: 56*–57*, nos. 22, 26–29, 31, 32; MacKay 1995: 4, pl. 9), 7 are from the elite zone—that is, from the Temple Auxiliary Buildings (fig. 4, nos. 4, 7–11; fig. 5, no. 1; Gitin 1989b: 57*, nos. 24, 30; Gitin 1992: 44*, A–C; previously unpublished examples, object nos. 4188, 4530), and 2 are from the domestic area (fig. 4, no. 12; fig. 5, no. 2; Gitin 1989b: 56*, nos. 23, 25). It is significant

---

14. One portable altar was found in front of a stone niche from which it must have fallen during the 604 B.C.E. destruction, indicating that it also had a fixed position (fig. 4, no. 5; Gitin 1989b: 60*). This is similar to the situation of the altar in the Tabernacle (Exod 30:6).

15. The 19th altar in the Ekron corpus was 39.5 cm high and made of nonvesicular basalt. Its size and weight put it in the nonportable category (fig. 5, no. 3). This altar, however, is not included in the discussion, because stratigraphically it came from a post-Stratum IV and pre-Stratum IC phase and does not belong to Stratum IB.

16. In the inscription, *mqm* is the word understood as a 'shrine'. This is the meaning ascribed to it in Jeremiah (7:12), "where *byt* 'temple' and *mqm* 'cult-place' are equated" (Levine 1997: 248). For an extensive treatment of *mqm*, meaning shrine, temple, or sacred space in Biblical Hebrew, Phoenician, and Neo-Punic texts, see Vanderhooft 1999: 628–30.

that altars were found in every excavated area of the tel except in the sanctuary and in other parts of Temple Complex Building 650. Thus, in contrast to what occurred in the central shrine, worship involving altars could be practiced at different locations throughout the city—whether at a person's work, at home, or in the private quarters of the elite zone.

(5) Local religious practices are assumed, based on the evidence of long-standing cultic traditions at Ekron. Foreign cultic praxis, on the other hand, is identified by specific objects that are known from neighboring cultures, which only appear at Ekron during one cultural horizon. At Ekron, two local traditions are implied by the long-term use of the prominent architectural feature of cultic buildings, the round pillar base, and by the name of the goddess of the Ekron sanctuary—both of which imply a continuum of religious practices. In the central hall plan of the 7th-century sanctuary of Temple Complex 650, a number of round pillar bases appeared in two parallel rows (Gitin 1997: 99, fig.17). This type of pillar base is known from the earlier Iron Age cultic buildings in the lower city, that is, from Strata VI–V (Dothan 1998: 156, fig.7). The presence of round pillar bases, indicating the use of round pillars, is unique to Ekron and is not attested during the Iron Age in ancient Israel.[17] It can be assumed that at least some long-term acts of religious worship are associated with such a conservative approach to sanctuary design and construction. As for the goddess of Ekron's 7th-century sanctuary, *ptgyh*, she is recorded as such in the Ekron dedicatory inscription found in the cella of the sanctuary (Gitin, Dothan, and Naveh 1997: 9, 11, 12). The name *ptgyh* appears to reflect the Early Iron Age I Aegean origins of the Philistines, since it has been associated with the sanctuary at Delphi known as Pytho, which was the shrine of Gaia, the Mycenean mother-goddess (Schäfer-Lichtenberger 2000: 89–91).[18] Another example of a name from a 7th-century context that has an earlier Aegean origin and that supports the continuity of long-term traditions at Ekron is the name Ikausu. In the Ekron dedicatory inscription, Ikausu appears as the ruler of Ekron who built the sanctuary for his lady, *ptgyh* (Gitin, Dothan, and Naveh 1997: 11). The name Ikausu (Achish), that is, 'Akhayus' or 'Achaean', meaning 'the Greek', supports the Aegean association of the Philistines, who settled Ekron in the 12th century B.C.E. This would indicate ethnic continuity for most of the Iron Age, or at the very least, the reflex of a memory of Ekron's ethnic origins.[19]

17. The closest parallel of a central hall sanctuary with two parallel rows of pillars is the central courtyard with two rows of rectangular-shaped pillars in the 8th–7th-century Astarte temple at Kition (Karageorghis 1974: 24–25).

18. For a recent discussion of the inscription and specifically of the goddess *ptgyh*, see Younger 2000.

19. For an analysis of the continuity of Iron Age material culture at Ekron, see Gitin 1998: 162–67.

Foreign cultic practices, which were adopted in the 7th century by the inhabitants of Ekron, include the use of the ubiquitous Israelite-type four-horned altar and the dominant Phoenician-type figurine, one of which (object no. 7133) came from the inner cella of the Temple Complex 650 sanctuary. Similar figurines exist throughout the Mediterranean basin, for example, at Carthage, Motya, and Tharros (Acquaro 1988: 623, nos. 234, 235; Ciasca 1988: 358, 363), and on Cyprus (Gjerstad 1937: pl. 203:3). Additional evidence of foreign cultic elements is represented in the Ekron pantheon, which includes names from inscriptions found on pottery vessels at Ekron: the West Semitic/Canaanite god Baʿal (Gitin and Cogan 1999: 197) and the goddesses Asherat and Anat (Gitin 1990b: 250, 251, fig. 2a; Gitin, Dothan, and Naveh 1997: 13–14). The silver medallion with an Assyrian Ishtar cultic motif (Gitin 1997: 102, fig. 21) and an Egyptian Hathor Naos-shaped sistrum (Gitin 1990a: 41) also indicate the presence of other foreign cult practices.

These examples of coexistence and duality in the cultic practice of Ekron represent the structure of a complex and well-developed worship system, partially defined by its relationship to the role of the four-horned altar, and the perception that this altar can be employed to define sacred space. This worship system may have developed, at least in part, as the result of the impact of Assyrian influences on the Levant that occurred in the last phase of the Iron Age (Oded 1974: 38–39; Elat 1977: 21, 28–34). During this period, when the Neo-Assyrian Empire had destroyed the Northern Kingdom of Israel and turned Judah and the four remaining Philistine capital cities into vassal states (Ephʿal 1979a: 186–88; 1979b: 286–88), the four-horned altar no longer appears in the archaeological record at Israelite sites. It does, however, appear at Ekron, perhaps brought to Philistia at the beginning of the 7th century by displaced Israelite craftsmen from the North (Gitin 1989b: 61*). It was at this time that the four-horned altar became the dominant cultic object at Ekron, which, under the impact of Assyrian imperial commercial policy (Gitin 1997: 77–85), became the largest olive oil production center in the ancient Near East (Gitin 1995: 63).

To summarize, the practice of burning incense on an object that represents the image of a four-horned tower or altar, symbolizing a roof ritual offering to the gods, is an established cultic tradition in the ancient Near East. This phenomenon indicates a relationship between form and function that maintains its distinctive sacred quality when transmitted from one cultural horizon to another—that is, from a Late Bronze Age Syrian Middle Euphrates horizon to Iron Age Israelite society. The 13th/12th century B.C.E. terracotta-tower models and their 10th-century counterparts are the antecedents of the biblical four-horned altar used for the burning of incense in sacred space and of the Iron Age II four-horned stone altars found in cultic contexts at sites in Israel, Judah, Philistia, and Assyria. This relationship between form and function is the basis for attributing the incense-burning tradition to the four-horned altars found at Iron Age II sites in contexts not usually considered cultic, an attribution consistent with the archaeological and textual evidence. Consequently, it can be argued that the four-horned altar attested in archaeological contexts, which had over time maintained the attribute of sanctity, should be considered a criterion for defining sacred space. This has broadened the context of cultic activity beyond the traditionally defined areas, adding a new dimension to understanding what constitutes sacred space. In the process, it has also served as the means by which to identify five aspects of duality and coexistence in the cult practiced at Ekron, which form the basis of a multifaceted Philistine worship system.

Bibliography

Acquaro, E.
   1988   Catalogue. Pp. 581–754 in *The Phoenicians*, ed. S. Moscati. Milan: Bompiani.
Aharoni, Y.
   1969   Israelite Temples in the Period of the Monarchy. Pp. 69–74 in *The Proceedings of the Fifth World Congress of Jewish Studies, Jerusalem 3–11 August 1969*, ed. P. Peli. Jerusalem: World Union of Jewish Studies.
   1975   The Sanctuary and High Place. Pp. 26–32, pls. 5:1, 43:7 in *Investigations at Lachish: The Sanctuary and the Residency—Lachish V*. Tel Aviv: Institute of Archaeology, Tel Aviv University.
Albright, W. F.
   1929   Unsigned review *The Altars of the O.T.*, by of H. M. Wiener. *Journal of the Palestine Oriental Society* 9:50–54.
Black, J., and Green, A.
   1992   *Gods, Demons and Symbols of Ancient Mesopotamia*. London: British Museum Press.
Broshi, M., and Finkelstein, I.
   1992   The Population of Palestine in Iron Age II. *Bulletin of the American Schools of Oriental Research* 287:47–60.
Burdajewicz, M.
   1990   *The Aegean Sea Peoples and Religious Architecture in the Eastern Mediterranean at the Close of the Late Bronze Age*. BAR International Series 558. Oxford: British Archaeological Reports.
Ciasca, A.
   1988   Masks and Protomes. Pp. 354–69 in *The Phoenicians*, ed. S. Moscato. Milan: Bompiana.
Coogan, M. B.
   1987   Of Cults and Cultures: Reflections on the Interpretation of Archaeological Evidence. *Palestine Exploration Journal* (January–June) 1–8.
Davaras, C.
   1976   *Guide to Cretan Antiquities*. Park Ridge, N.J.: Noyes.

Dever, W. G.

1983 Material Remains and the Cult in Ancient Israel: An Essay in Archaeological Systematics. Pp. 571–87 in *The Word of the Lord Shall Go Forth: Essays in Honor of David Noel Freedman in Celebration of His Sixtieth Birthday,* ed. C. Meyers and M. O'Connor. Winona Lake, Ind.: Eisenbrauns/American Schools of Oriental Research.

1987 The Contribution of Archaeology to the Study of Canaanite and Early Israelite Religion. Pp. 209–47 in *Ancient Israelite Religion: Essays in Honor of Frank Moore Cross,* ed. P. D. Miller, P. D. Hanson, and S. D. McBride. Philadelphia: Fortress.

Diamant, S., and Rutter, J.

1969 Horned Objects in Anatolia and the Near East and Possible Connexions with the Minoan "Horns of Consecration." *Anatolian Studies* 19:147–77.

Dothan, T.

1981 The High Place of Athienou in Cyprus. Pp. 91–95 in *Temples and High Places in Biblical Times: Proceedings of the Colloquium in Honor of the Centennial of the Hebrew Union College—Jewish Institute of Religion, Jerusalem, 1977,* ed. A. Biran. Jerusalem: Nelson Glueck School of Biblical Archaeology.

1998 Initial Philistine Settlement: From Migration to Coexistence. Pp. 148–61 in *Mediterranean Peoples in Transition: Thirteenth to Early Tenth Centuries B.C.E. —In Honor of Professor Trude Dothan,* ed. S. Gitin, A. Mazar, and E. Stern. Jerusalem: Israel Exploration Society.

Dothan, T., and Gitin, S.

1993 Ekron. Pp. 1051–59 in vol. 3 of *The New Encyclopedia of Archaeological Excavations in the Holy Land,* ed. E. Stern. Jerusalem: Israel Exploration Society.

Elat, M.

1977 The Economic Relations of the Neo-Assyrian Empire with Egypt. *Journal of the American Oriental Society* 98: 21, 28–34.

1990 International Trade in the Land of Israel under Assyrian Rule. Pp. 67–88 in *Commerce in Palestine throughout the Ages,* ed. B. Z. Kedar, T. Dothan, and S. Safrai. Jerusalem: Israel Exploration Society. [Hebrew]

1994 Phoenician Overland Trade within the Mesopotamian Empires. Pp. 21–35 in *Ah, Assyria . . . Studies in Assyrian History and Ancient Near Eastern Historiography Presented to Hayim Tadmor,* ed. M. Cogan and I. Eph'al, Jerusalem: Magnes.

Eph'al, I.

1979a Israel: Fall and Exile, Pp. 180–92 in vol. 4/1 of *The World History of the Jewish People,* ed. A. Malamat. Jerusalem: Massada.

1979b Assyrian Dominion in Palestine. Pp. 276–89 in vol. 4/1 of *The World History of the Jewish People,* ed. A. Malamat. Jerusalem: Massada.

1982 *The Ancient Arabs: Nomads of the Borders of the Fertile Crescent, 9th–5th Centuries B.C.* Leiden: Brill.

Fowler, M. D.
1985   Excavated Incense Burners: A Case for Identifying a Site as Sacred? *Palestine Exploration Quarterly* (January–June) 25–29.

Gesell, G. C.
1985   *Town, Palace, and House Cult in Minoan Crete*. Studies in Mediterranean Archaeology 67. Gothenburg: Åstroms.

Gjerstad, E.
1937   *The Swedish Cyprus Expedition 1927–1931, III: Plates*. Stockholm: Petterson.

Gitin, S.
1989a   Tel Miqne-Ekron: A Type-Site for the Inner Coastal Plain in the Iron Age II Period. Pp. 15–22, 23–58 in *Recent Excavations in Israel: Studies in Iron Age Archaeology*, ed. S. Gitin and W. G. Dever. Annual of the American Schools of Oriental Research 49. Winona Lake, Ind.: Eisenbrauns.
1989b   Incense Altars from Ekron, Israel and Judah: Context and Typology. *Eretz-Israel* 20 (Yadin Memorial Volume): 52*–67*.
1990a   Ekron of the Philistines, Part II: Olive Oil Suppliers to the World. *Biblical Archaeology Review* 16: 32–42, 59.
1990b   Seventh Century BCE Cultic Elements at Ekron. Pp. 248–58 in *Biblical Archaeology Today, 1990: Proceedings of the Second International Congress on Biblical Archaeology, Jerusalem*, ed. A. Biran and J. Aviram. Jerusalem: Israel Exploration Society and Israel Academy of Sciences.
1992   New Incense Altars from Ekron: Context, Typology and Function. *Eretz-Israel* 23 (Biran Volume): 43*–49*.
1995   Tel Miqne-Ekron in the 7th Century B.C.E.: The Impact of Economic Influences on a Neo-Assyrian Vassal City State. Pp. 61–79 in *Recent Excavations in Israel: A View to the West*, ed. S. Gitin. Archaeological Institute of America Colloquia and Conference Papers 1. Dubuque, Iowa.
1997   The Neo-Assyrian Empire and Its Western Periphery: The Levant, with a Focus on Philistine Ekron. Pp. 77–103 in *Assyria 1995: Proceedings of the 10th Anniversary Symposium of the Neo-Assyrian Text Corpus Project, Helsinki, 1995*, ed. S. Parpola and R. M. Whiting. Helsinki: University of Helsinki.
1998   Philistia in Transition: The Tenth Century BCE and Beyond. Pp. 162–83 in *Mediterranean Peoples in Transition: Thirteenth to Early Tenth Centuries B.C.E.—In Honor of Professor Trude Dothan*, ed. S. Gitin, A. Mazar, and E. Stern, Jerusalem: Israel Exploration Society.

Gitin, S., and Cogan, M.
1999   A New Type of Dedicatory Inscription from Ekron. *Israel Exploration Journal* 49: 193–202.

Gitin, S.; Dothan, T.; and Naveh, J.
1997   A Royal Dedicatory Inscription from Ekron. *Israel Exploration Journal* 47: 1–16.

Gordon, C. H.
1941   Aramaic Incantation Bowls. *Orientalia* 10: 339–60.
1965   *Ugaritic Textbook*. Rome: Pontifical Biblical Institute.

Gray, J.
  1964   *The KRT Text in the Literature of Ras Shamra: A Social Myth of Ancient Canaan*. Leiden: Brill.
Halpern, B.
  1993   The Baal (and the Asherah) in Seventh-Century Judah: YHWH's Retainers Retired. *Orbis Biblicus et Orientalis* 126 (Konsequente Traditiongeschichte; Baltzer Festschrift): 115–54.
Haran, M.
  1957   Altar. Pp. 778–79 in vol. 4 of *Encyclopaedia Biblica*, ed. U. M. D. Cassuto, Jerusalem: Bialik Institute. [Hebrew]
  1977   A Temple at Dor? *Israel Exploration Journal* 27:12–15.
  1985   *Temples and Temple-Service in Ancient Israel*. Reprinted, Winona Lake, Ind.: Eisenbrauns.
  1993   "Incense Altars"—Are They? Pp. 237–47 in *Biblical Archaeology Today, 1990: Proceedings of the Second International Congress on Biblical Archaeology, Jerusalem*, ed. A. Biran and J. Aviram. Jerusalem: Israel Exploration Society and Israel Academy of Sciences.
  1995   Altar-ed States: Incense Theory Goes up in Smoke. *Bible Review* (February): 30–37, 48.
Herzog, Z.
  1997   Arad: Iron Age Period. Pp. 174–76 in *The Oxford Encyclopedia of Archaeology in the Near East*, ed. E. Meyers. New York: Oxford University Press.
Holladay, J. S., Jr.
  1987   Religion in Israel and Judah under the Monarchy: An Explicitly Archaeological Approach. Pp. 249–99 in *Ancient Israelite Religion: Essays in Honor of Frank Moore Cross*, ed. P.D . Miller Jr., P. D. Hanson, and S. D. McBride. Philadelphia: Fortress.
Holloway, S. W.
  1996   Porch Lights in Neo-Assyrian Temples. *Revue d'Assyriologie* 90: 27–32.
Houtman, C.
  1992   On the Function of the Holy Incense (Exodus 30:34–8) and the Sacred Anointing Oil (Exodus 30:22–33). *Vetus Testamentum* 42: 458–65.
Karageorghis, V.
  1974   Kition: Mycenaean and Phoenician. Pp. 1–27 in *The Proceedings of the British Academy*, vol. 59. London: Oxford University Press.
  1981   The Sacred Area of Kition. Pp. 82–88 in *Temples and High Places in Biblical Times: Proceedings of the Colloquium in Honor of the Centennial of the Hebrew Union College—Jewish Institute of Religion, Jerusalem, 1977*, ed. A. Biran, Jerusalem: Nelson Glueck School of Biblical Archaeology.
Keel, O., and Uehlinger, C.
  1998   *Gods, Goddesses, and Images of God*. Minneapolis: Fortress.
Kletter, R.
  1996   *The Judean Pillar-Figurines and the Archaeology of Asherah*. BAR International Series 636. Oxford: British Archaeological Reports.

Knauf, E. A.
  1992   The Cultural Impact of Secondary State Formation: The Cases of the
            Edomites and Moabites. Pp. 47–54 in *Edom and Moab: The Beginning of
            the Iron Age in Southern Jordan*, ed. P. Bienkowski. Sheffield Archaeologi-
            cal Monographs 7. Sheffield: Sheffield Academic Press.

Levine, B.
  1987   The Language of Holiness: Perceptions of the Sacred in the Hebrew
            Bible. Pp. 241–55 in *Backgrounds for the Bible*, ed. M. P. O'Connor and
            D. N. Freedman. Winona Lake, Ind.: Eisenbrauns.
  1997   The Next Phase in Jewish Religion: The Land of Israel and Sacred Space.
            Pp. 245–57 in *Tehillah le-Moshe: Biblical and Judaic Studies in Honor of
            Moshe Greenberg*, ed. M Cogan, B. L. Eichler and J. H. Tigay, Winona
            Lake, Ind.: Eisenbrauns.

Loud, G.
  1948   *Megiddo II: Seasons of 1935–39* (Text). Oriental Institute Publications 62.
            Chicago: University of Chicago Press.

Loulloupis, M.
  1973   Mycenaean 'Horns of Consecration' in Cyprus. Pp. 225–44 in *The
            Mycenaeans in The Eastern Mediterranean: Acts of the International Ar-
            chaeological Symposium, Nicosia, 1972*. Nicosia: Department of Antiqui-
            ties, Cyprus.

MacKay, D. B.
  1995   *Tel Miqne-Ekron: Report of the 1994 Spring Excavations Field IISW*, ed.
            S. Gitin. Miqne Limited Edition Series 5. Jerusalem: Albright Institute /
            Hebrew University.

Margueron, J.
  1976   "Maquettes" architecturales de Meskene-Emar. *Syria* 53: 193–232.
May, H. G.
  1935   *Material Remains of the Megiddo Cult*. Oriental Institute Publications 26.
            Chicago: University of Chicago Press.

Mazar, A.
  1992   Sanctuaries in the Middle and Late Bronze Age and Iron Age. Pp. 161–
            87. Chapter 19 in *The Architecture of Ancient Israel*. Jerusalem: Israel Ex-
            ploration Society.

McCown, C. C.
  1950   Hebrew High Places and Cult Remains. *Journal of Biblical Literature* 69:
            205–19.
Mettinger, T. N. D.
  1995   *No Graven Image? Israelite Aniconism in Its Ancient Near Eastern Context*.
            Stockholm: Almqvist & Wiksell.

Milgrom, J.
  1971   Altar. Pp. 760–68 in vol. 2 of *Encyclopedia Judaica*. Jerusalem: Keter.
Muchawsky-Schnapper, E.
  1999   The Use of Incense by Yemenite Jews. *Tema* 6 (Association for Society
            and Culture): iii–xxx.

Muller, B.
1997   Remarques sur les "Maquettes Architecturales" de Syrie. Pp. 256–67 in *Les maisons dans la Syrie antique du IIIe millenaire aux debuts de l'Islam*, ed. C. Castel, M. al-Maqdissi, et F. Villeneuve. Beirut: Institut Francais d'Archéologie du Proche-Orient.

Muller-Pierre, B.
1992   Un modele de tout en terre cuite du Moyen-Euphrate. *La Revue du Louvre et des Musées de France* 1: 35–41.

Nielsen, K.
1986   *Incense in Ancient Israel*. Vetus Testamentum Supplements 38. Leiden, Brill.

Oded, B.
1974   The Phoenician Cities and the Assyrian Empire in the Time of Tiglath-pileser III. *Zeitschrift des deutschen Palästina-Vereins* 90: 38–49.

Ottosson, M.
1980   *Temples and Cult Places in Palestine*. Uppsala Studies in Ancient Mediterranean and Near Eastern Civilizations 12. Uppsala: Boreas.

Postgate, J. N.
1979   The Economic Structure of the Assyrian Empire. Pp. 193–221 in *Power and Propaganda*, ed. M. T. Larsen. Mesopotamia Copenhagen Studies in Assyriology 7. Copenhagen: Akademisk.

Potts, T. F.
1985   Preliminary Report on the Sixth Season of Excavation by the University of Sydney at Pella in Jordan, 1983/84: The Late Bronze–Early Iron Ages. *Annual of the Department of Antiquities of Jordan* 29: 202–4, 339–40.

Pritchard, J. B.
1969   *Ancient Near Eastern Texts Relating to the Old Testament*. 3d edition. Princeton: Princeton University Press.

Renfrew, C.
1985   *The Archaeology of Cult*. London: British School of Archaeology at Athens.

Rutkowski, B.
1986   *The Cult Places of the Aegean*. New Haven: Yale University Press.

Schaeffer, C. F.-A.
1949   *Ugaritica II*. Mission de Ras Shamra 5. Paris: Geuthner.

Schäfer-Lichtenberger, C.
2000   The Goddess of Ekron and the Religious-Cultural Background of the Philistines. *Israel Exploration Journal* 50: 82–91.

Schoep, I.
1994   "Home Sweet Home": Some Comments on the So-Called House Models from The Prehellenic Aegean. *Opuscula Atheniensia* 20/13: 189–210.

Shiloh, Y.
1979   Iron Age Sanctuaries and Cult Elements in Palestine. Pp. 147–57 in *Symposia Celebrating the 75th Anniversary of the Founding of ASOR (1900–1975)*, ed. F. M. Cross. Cambridge: American Schools of Oriental Research.

1984   *Excavations at the City of David* I. Qedem 19. Jerusalem: Institute of Archaeology, Hebrew University.

Smith, R. H., and Potts, T.
1992   The Iron Age. Pp. 83–101 in *Pella in Jordan 2: The Second Interim Report of the Joint University of Sydney and College of Wooster Excvavations at Pella, 1982–1985.* Sydney: Meditarch, University of Sydney.

Stager, L. E.
1996   Ashkelon and the Archaeology of Destruction: Kislev 604 BCE. *Eretz-Israel* 25 (Aviram Volume): 61*–74*.

Stern, E.
1973   Limestone Incense Altars. Pp. 52–53, chap. 12, and pls. 29–30 in *Beer-sheba I: Excavations at Tel Beer-sheba, 1969–1971 Seasons,* ed. Y. Aharoni. Tel Aviv: Institute of Archaeology.
1982   *Material Culture of the Land of the Bible in the Persian Period, 538–332 BC.* Warminster: Aris & Phillips.
1990   Schumacher's Shrine in Building 338 at Megiddo: A Rejoinder. *Israel Exploration Journal* 40: 102–7.

Thompson, R. C., and Hutchinson, R. W.
1929   The Excavations on the Temple of Nabu at Nineveh. *Archaeologia* 79: 104–8, pl. 56.

Uehlinger, C.
1997   Anthropomorphic Cult Statuary in Iron Age Palestine and the Search for Yahweh's Cult Images. Pp. 97–155 in *The Image and the Book,* ed. K. van der Toorn. Leuven: Peeters.

Vanderhooft, D.
1999   Dwelling beneath the Sacred Place: A Proposal for Reading 2 Samuel 7:10. *Journal of Biblical Literature* 118: 628–30.

Vaux, R. de
1965   *Ancient Israel, II: Religious Institutions.* New York: McGraw Hill.

Weinfeld, M.
1972   The Worship of Molech and of the Queen of Heaven. *Ugarit Forschungen* 4: 133–54.
1992   Deuteronomy, Book of. Pp. 168–83 in vol. 2 *The Anchor Bible Dictionary,* ed. D. N. Freedman, New York: Doubleday.

Wellhausen, J.
1957   *Prolegomena to the History of Ancient Israel.* Reprinted, New York: Meridian.

Wiener, H. M.
1927   *The Altars of the Old Testament.* Leipzig: Hinrichs.

Wright, G. R. H.
1985   *Ancient Building in South Syria and Palestine,* vol. 1: *Text.* Leiden: Brill.

Younger, K. L.
2000   The Ekron Inscription of Akhayus (2.42). P. 164 in *The Context of Scripture,* vol. 2: *Monumental Inscriptions from the Biblical World,* ed. W. W. Hallo and K. L. Younger, Jr. Leiden: Brill.

Ritual as Symbol:
Modes of Sacrifice in Israelite Religion

Baruch A. Levine
Emeritus, New York University

In the Land of Israel of biblical times, as elsewhere in the ancient Near East and the Mediterranean world, temples and other cult installations were built with established cultic rites in mind or with the purpose of instituting new or revised rites. The result was that the architectural plans of ancient temples and the placement of installed artifacts within their sacred space expressed or reflected intended functions. Conversely, the choreography of cultic celebrations was itself conditioned by certain notions of space and location deriving from customary building methods and designs and from the relationship of human construction to the natural environment—to mountains and rivers. It would be of great value, therefore, were we able to choreograph the celebration of the biblical sacrificial rites so as to link function to form, in the same way that plans of excavated ancient temples are redrawn so that we can now visualize how they might have looked.

Ultimately, both art and architecture, as well as the choreography of performance, hark back to phenomenology, to the perceived meaning of ritual in its various forms. We need to understand how differing modes of sacrifice signified the different meanings attributed to various ritual celebrations.

A basic question poses itself at the outset: Where was the deity presumed to be, in spatial terms, when the sacrifice was initiated? Essentially, temples and other cult installations were conceived as divine residences or as visitation sites of the gods. Basic to the phenomenology of worship is the perception that the deity must be invited, often attracted to the cult-site; that we cannot presume, as a generalization, that the deity is always present or in residence at the site before the worship sequence begins. In other words, we should seek to determine from analyzing the mode of a particular sacrificial rite where the deity is perceived as being when the rite was about to commence. If the mode indicates that the deity is, indeed, perceived to be present at that point, it remains to explain how he got there. I have discussed this subject in an essay entitled "Phenomenology of the Open-Air-Altar in Biblical Israel"[1] and in scholarly lectures.

Corollary to the question of divine whereabouts is the zoning of sacred space within cult edifices and their courtyards, including the process of enclosure and the raising of terrain. The demarcation of zones on the basis of gradated sanctity, as Menahem Haran has shown, not only served to restrict and control human access but to lend a particular character to certain, more sacred areas, those in which the deity (or deities) resided, or sat, when they were present. This process was clearly expressed in architectural design and the planned use of space, and it correlates with the purificatory rites associated with temples. The requirements of purity also affected the stationing of cultic personnel and the storing of *Opfermaterie*, in addition to limiting the access of worshipers. Purity requirements thus determined to a large degree what took place in various sectors of the temple and its environs and how the temple plan was executed.

To clarify the methodology I will employ in the present inquiry I will first state how I read Priestly sources, such as those preserved in Exodus, Leviticus, and Numbers, that speak of a portable Sanctuary (variously termed *miškān*, *ʾōhel mōʿēd*). I take them to be projections of the *ritus* of the Jerusalem Temple at various periods of biblical history. What is more, it is my view that the Holiness School and the authors of the *Priesterschrift* were operating with the Deuteronomic requirement of a single, central temple. Consequently, such Priestly sources, notwithstanding their wilderness scenery and nomadic terminology, should be interpreted against the reality of a stationary temple edifice, with gates and courtyards.

With considerations of form and space in mind, an attempt will be made here to discuss the modes of biblical sacrifice, factoring in several variables as we proceed. These variables include:

1. The manner of disposing of an offering—whether or not an altar was used and whether the offering, in whole or in part, was burned on an altar and turned into smoke.
2. The primary location where the offering was presented within sacred space, whether inside a a covered edifice or under the open sky, as in a courtyard.
3. The basic state of the offering, whether prepared and/or processed or whether offered in unprocessed form—as it was harvested, for example.

1. B. A. Levine, "Phenomenology of the Open-Air-Altar in Biblical Israel," in *Biblical Archaeology Today: Proceedings of the Second International Congress on Biblical Archaeology, Jerusalem, June 1990* (Jerusalem: Israel Exploration Society, 1993) 196–205.

4. The materials or substances used in comprising or concocting the offering: the recipe.

At the risk of oversimplification, I would state at the outset that Israelite
sacrifice was realized in three primary modes: (a) The mode of presentation
and display before the deity. The deity was perceived as viewing the offering—favorably, it was hoped. Once accepted or received in this way by the
deity, the offering would be consumed by priests and in some cases by donors.
The substance of the offering may or may not have been prepared for con-
sumption before presentation. In ancient Near Eastern perspective, the
modes of presentation and display were the most pervasive. (b) The mode of
offering prepared food, intended for a sacred meal in the company of the
deity, with the deity variously perceived as host or as guest. This mode is exemplified by the *zebaḥ*, a term that I take to be cognate with Akkadian *zibū*
('meal') and that does not, in the first instance, mean 'slain offering' or the
like, although it was often realized in that way. Ugaritic temple rituals often
describe the *zebaḥ* mode (*dbḥ*, in Ugaritic), and in fact this term was generalized to connote any major celebration, including a sacred feast. (c) The mode
of the burnt altar offering. The rising, aromatic smoke of the offering is
thought to be inhaled by the deity and in this way ingested, or consumed, by
him. The ultimate logic of this mode is realized in the holocaust, which feeds
the deity food in its most extremely reduced form. At times, incense was uti-
lized in this mode, although it also had other functions.

In actual practice, most biblical sacrifices were realized in mixed modes
and methods of disposition, representing adaptations and combinations of the
primary modes. Thus, parts of them might be cooked and other parts burned
on the altar, as was the case with most prescribed forms of the *zebaḥ* and *ḥaṭṭā't*
('sin offering'). Or most of the offering might be presented, with only a small
part of it burned on the altar. Methodologically, it would be useful to trace
certain sacrifices back to their original form, to the extent that this is possible,
so as to be able to consider the development of Israelite sacrifice.

In the course of writing the Leviticus commentary, I became aware of a
pattern of development in the disposition of the grain offering, or *minḥâ*, that
clearly illustrates a process of modal adaptation and that may serve as a
model. I hope to go a bit further here in analyzing the presentational mode by
focusing on forms of the *minḥâ* in particular, making reference to other modes
by contrast.

Both etymologically and in terms of its known character, the *minḥâ* of
biblical worship is best viewed as a presentation offering, most often but not
exclusively in baked or other prepared form. The verb *nāḥâ* means 'to conduct, to lead', so that nominal *minḥâ* bears the sense of something brought.
The term *minḥâ*, like many others designating cultic gifts, comes from the

administrative vocabulary. It means 'tribute, gift' and is so used in the Hebrew Bible itself, without reference to ritual. The *locus classicus* is 2 Kgs 3:4: "Mesha, king of Moab, was a herder, and he remitted (*hēšîb*) to the king of Israel as tribute (*minḥâ*) 100,000 fattened lambs and the wool of 100,000 rams."

In the cultic vocabulary, the term *minḥâ* came to designate a grain offering, whereas it may have been a generic term for any kind of sacrificial offering. In Gen 4:3–4, both the animals of Abel and the produce of Cain are referred to as *minḥâ*, but it remains an open question whether animals and fowl were ever actually offered in ancient Israel in the purely presentational mode. It seems more likely that in relatively early times they may have been disposed of in the *zebaḥ* mode but without recourse to an altar of burnt offerings, much in the way of the paschal *zebaḥ* of Exodus 12–13, originally a domestic sacrifice. We must also bear in mind that an altar was conceived as a table and that not every altar was an altar of burnt offerings. Altars were also used for presentation, just as they served as a locus for gods to join in meals with their devotees. Archaeologists have found very early altars in Canaan of pre-Israelite times, their sides spattered with blood, but with no evidence of burning on them. The enigmatic account of 1 Sam 14:32–35 may reflect the same practice in ancient Israel of desacralizing the *zebaḥ* by offering its blood on the altar before roasting a sacrifice or cooking it in pots. So, we should not conclude that the utilization of an altar, on the one hand, and presentation, on the other, are mutually exclusive modes of sacrifice, although the preponderance of the biblical evidence might suggest this conclusion. What we do not know about the early development of Israelite ritual far exceeds what we do know.

Let us begin with a careful analysis of Leviticus 23, the festival calendar representative of the Holiness School, for information on the presentational mode in biblical worship at a rather late stage in its overall development. Leviticus 23 shows evidence of the adaptation of the *minḥâ* from a presentation offering to an expanded rite that included burnt offerings. The section beginning in Lev 23:16–17 is most relevant to our discussion. Israelites are to bring from their settlements *minḥâ ḥădāšâ lYhwh* ('an offering of new grain to Yhwh'). It is to consist of two loaves classified as *tĕnûpâ* ('raised, elevated offering') made of a specified quantity of semolina flour. These loaves are then designated *bikkûrîm lYhwh* ('offerings of firstfruits to Yhwh'). This is to occur annually, seven sabbatical weeks after the first sheaf (*ʿōmer*) of new barley grain, had been brought to the priest by the Israelites, likewise 'raised' by him (the verb *hēnîp*) in the presence of Yhwh (Lev 23:10–11). With the passage of seven weeks, wheat from the new harvest had become available, hence the prescribed semolina. The *minḥâ* of *bikkûrîm* was to be baked in a *tannûr* of unleavened dough, *ḥāmēṣ*.

There can be little doubt that what has just been described constituted a complete, or sufficient, rite in and of itself—one expressive of presentation

and display. This description contrasts with what we read immediately following, in Lev 23:18–20. There we are told what was to accompany the
bikkûrîm offering. The relevant formula is: wĕhiqrabtem ʿal hallehem 'You shall
offer in addition to the bread' or 'together with the bread', thereby implying
what the essential bikkûrîm offering had consisted of. An entire regimen of
animal sacrifices is now prescribed as accompaniment, even including additional grain offerings and libations. I take Lev 23:18–20 to be redactional, introduced by a subsequent Priestly legislator who knew of the adapted grain
offerings of Leviticus 2, for instance where we also encounter a minḥâ of firstfruits (Lev 2:14–16). The same redactional pattern is evident earlier on in vv.
12–13, where the ʿōmer was to be accompanied by a similar, though less elaborate, regimen of sacrifices.

However, the primary presentational mode of the minḥâ of firstfruits of
Leviticus 23 had not initially involved any use of the altar of burnt offerings
whatsoever. The standard Priestly adaptations, such as those prescribed in
Leviticus 2, differ in this regard; they effect an internal change in the disposition of the minḥâ itself with the result that some part of it went into the altar
fire, thereby satisfying the superimposed requirement of burnt offerings. In
Leviticus 23, the presentation offering was expanded by combination with
other rites that themselves make use of the altar while remaining unchanged.

On the face of it, I would conclude that the redactors of the Priestly
School, when working with an ancient and honorable offering, may have felt
constrained not to alter its internal character. But, when prescribing their
own regimen of rituals, as in Leviticus 2, they felt free to structure them so as
to incorporate the requirement of a burnt altar offering. We shall see below
how they did this.

Against Israel Knohl (and others who hold similar views), who has recently analyzed Leviticus 23 with an eye to demonstrating that the Priestly
Torah (PT) antedates the writings of the Holiness School (H), of which the
core of Leviticus 23 is a salient part, the above analysis may be offered as partial rebuttal. Knohl does not give sufficient weight to the redaction of Lev
23:9–23, or he may not acknowledge this redaction. Surely in structural
terms, or in terms of mode, it is arguable that the primary bikkûrîm offering of
Leviticus 23, representing the Holiness School, was entirely presentational
and for display and that its adaptation in the direction of the burnt offering is
secondary and hence subsequent. A reverse process would appear to be less
arguable.[2]

---

2. See I. Knohl, "The Priestly Torah Versus the Holiness School: Sabbath and
the Festivals," HUCA 58 (1987) 65–117; and now I. Knohl, The Sanctuary of Silence
(Minneapolis: Fortress, 1995).

That offerings of firstfruits were characteristically presentational may be inferred from Deuteronomy 26, which informs us how one kind of offering of firstfruits, presumably in the harvested state rather than having been prepared as food, was presented. An Israelite was to take of the 'first' or 'prime' fruits (Hebrew *rē'šît*) of the earth, place it in a covered basket of some sort, and proceed to the central Temple. He was to hand the basket of firstfruits over to the priest, who would then set it down (the verb *hēnîaḥ*) in front of the altar. The offerant declared that he had settled n the land in fulfillment of God's promise, and in gratitude, was now desacralizing the firstfruits of the land. Presumably, *mizbaḥ Yhwh 'ĕlōhêkā* ('the altar of Yʜwʜ, your God') of Deut 26:4 refers to the altar of burnt offerings that stood in the Temple courtyard, and yet no subsequent use of that altar is indicated in the performance of the rite. Now, this rite is not designated *minḥâ*, truth be told, although it qualifies as such. It is cited here to exemplify the presentational mode applicable to offerings of the firstfruits of the earth. I would conclude that Deuteronomy 26 is speaking of an earlier from of the *minḥâ* of firstfruits ultimately legislated in Leviticus 23.

We should now trace other adaptations of the presentational *minḥâ* in the direction of the burnt offering. One step is represented by the 'bread of display' (*leḥem happānîm*) as ordained in Lev 24:5–8. The sense of *pānîm* in this terminology relates to being in the divine presence or purvue. Twelve loaves are baked from semolina flour and placed on two purified tables constructed for that purpose. Other biblical sources, while giving evidence of the relative antiquity of the Bread of Display, also indicate that the one or two tables, as the case may be, stood inside the Sanctuary building; actually, near the altar of incense (see 1 Samuel 27; 1 Kings 7; Exod 35:13, 39:36; Num 4:7). Although the text of Lev 24:5–8 is not explicit in calling the bread of display *ḥāmēṣ*, it was, like the *minḥâ* of firstfruits, not baked as *maṣṣôt*, a point whose significance will become apparent below.

The adaptation of *leḥem happānîm* was realized by placing containers of pure frankincense on the set tables. The frankincense was lit, with the aroma ascending as a burnt offering. It served as an *'azkārâ* ('token') of the presentational *minḥâ*, thereby satisfying the requirement of a burnt, altar offering in the process.

The method of utilizing a substance pinched off from the offering in place of the whole offering, as a token representing the offering, called *'azkārâ*, is first encountered in the types of *minḥâ* ordained in Leviticus 2. The suggested sense of Hebrew *'azkārâ* as 'token' comes from the Akkadian cognate *zikru* 'effigy', an explanation first proposed by G. R. Driver. This, then, is a significant adaptation: a fistful of the dough of the *minḥâ*, now unleavened in accordance with Priestly law, is burned on the altar, and the rest of the dough is baked, fried, and so forth. The ultimate adaptation of the *minḥâ* was realized in the *minḥâ* holocaust (*kālîl*), also ordained in Leviticus 2.

Leviticus 24 shows what pains were taken to preserve the presentational character of a relatively ancient offering, the Bread of Display. We observe how a device routinely employed by legislators of the Priestly school, the *'az-kārâ* is, itself, adapted to the needs of *leḥem happānîm*. No part of the loaves ever reached any altar, inside or outside the Sanctuary building—frankincense was just placed near the loaves and lit to give its aroma.

To understand modes of presentation and their adaptation requires, of course, reviewing the substances used in the offerings themselves and the way these substances were prepared. The most significant fact pertaining to the primary *minḥâ* of firstfruits of Leviticus 23 is that it was baked of leavened dough, of *ḥāmēṣ*, not in the form of *maṣṣôt* ('unleavened cakes'). There were several offerings made of leavened dough, additional to the ones already reviewed, and in all of them recourse to the altar was either limited or absent entirely.

The *tôdâ* ('thanksgiving offering') was made of *ḥāmēṣ*, as we learn from Lev 7:12–15. The code of Lev 7:11–27 details the various types of *zebaḥ šĕlāmîm* ('sacred offerings of greeting'). It stipulates, *'im tôdâ yaqrîbennû* ('If one offers it [namely, a *šĕlāmîm*] to serve as, or for, a thanksgiving offering'), the following specifications apply. The main offering under discussion, the *šĕlāmîm*, is partially an altar offering, consisting of both animals and a grain offering, variously prepared. Then we read: *ʿal ḥallōt leḥem ḥāmēṣ yaqrîb qorbānô* ('with loaves of leavened bread added shall he make his offering'), namely, his *šĕlāmîm* offering of thanksgiving (Lev 7:13). Reference to the loaves of the thanksgiving offering is introduced almost as an aside, as an accompaniment to the *šĕlāmîm*. This is the reverse of what we saw in Leviticus 23, where it was the *zebaḥ* component that was introduced as an accompaniment.

There is, however, good reason to believe that the grain offering of *tôdâ*, made of *ḥāmēṣ* ('unleavened dough'), originated as a separate and sufficient sacrifice, one whose independent origin is submerged in Leviticus 7. This is intimated by the provision of Lev 22:29–30, where the composite *tôdâ*, as known to us from Lev 7:11–15, is prescribed separately from the other types of *zebaḥ* stipulated immediately preceding: those serving as payment of vows and as free-will offerings. The *tôdâ* is not one of a bound group of three, as was true in Leviticus 7.

More specifically, it is from Amos 4:4–5 that the distinctiveness of the *tôdâ* becomes apparent. The prophet castigates the worshipers of Bethel:

Come to Bethel and transgress;
To Gilgal and transgress even more:
Present your sacred meals (*zibḥêkem*) the next morning
And your tithes on the third day;
Burn a thanksgiving offering (*tôdâ*) from leavened dough,
And proclaim free will offerings loudly,
For you love that sort of thing, O Israelites.

The prophetic criticism voiced in the above passage hardly pertains to modes of sacrifice but, rather, to Israel's tendency to mistake the purpose of worship generally. There is, however, the problem of burning the *tôdâ*, which is what the piel form, *qiṭṭēr*, must necessarily mean. After all, in Priestly ritual law, *ḥāmēṣ* could not be burned on the altar, and what is more, it is doubtful whether the *tôdâ* was ever intended as a holocaust. Either the *'azkārâ* method was in practice in Amos's day or, as is much more likely, incense was offered in conjunction with the *tôdâ*, which was itself baked and eaten by priests, thereby making the disposition of the *tôdâ* similar to that of the Bread of Display. Generally, usage of *qiṭṭēr* refers to the burning of incense. So the problematic Amos passage does not contradict the definition of the *tôdâ* offering as presentational.

To summarize up to this point, I would say that there is ample biblical evidence for projecting a development in the mode of the *minḥâ* and other offerings of the fruits of the earth, however classified, from a presentation offering to a burnt, altar offering. This development reflects the rising importance of the burnt offering, whose phenomenology will be discussed as we proceed.

It would now be well to identify the venue of the several primarily presentational offerings that have been discussed thus far. The Bread of Display (*leḥem happānîm*) was presented inside the Sanctuary, with the pure frankincense set down next to the loaves serving as a burnt offering. We note that the altar of incense was located inside the Sanctuary. As has just been suggested, the *tôdâ* referred to by Amos may have also been accompanied by an incense offering and would have also been brought inside the Sanctuary. It is likely, however, that the *tôdâ* of Leviticus 7 was part of a larger rite performed near the altar of burnt offerings in the Sanctuary courtyard, and the same was true of the *minḥâ* of firstfruits, as prescribed in Leviticus 23. This may be inferred from Deuteronomy 26, where the offering of firstfruits was set down in front of the altar of burnt offerings in the courtyard. The conclusion is that the presentational mode was characteristic of offerings brought both inside the Sanctuary and in the courtyard. We should not dismiss the likelihood, however, that an offering may have been presented initially inside the Sanctuary, shown to the deity, and then taken out to the courtyard for disposition. This pattern is evident in Ugaritic descriptive rituals and, effectively, all over the ancient Near East. After all, few ancient ritual texts fully choreograph the sacrificial rites that they describe.

We note in passing that, practically speaking, the only type of burnt offering that could be performed inside the covered Sanctuary was an incense offering; offerings of which any part was burned in the altar fire were performed in the open-air courtyard on the altar of burnt offerings. In extreme cases, burning could take place outside the encampment when total destruction was the objective.

Passing mention was made above of the offering designated těnûpâ ('raised, elevated offering') and of the verb hēnîp ('to raise, elevate'). The priest raised the ʿōmer in this manner (Lev 23:11), and seven weeks later, the essential minḥâ of firstfruits is called leḥem těnûpâ ('the bread of the raised offering'). In addition, the accompanying offerings, consisting of animals, were raised over the bread of the firstfruits.

The character of těnûpâ has been most concisely discussed by Jacob Milgrom, who presents graphic depictions of this mode taken from Egyptian wall paintings.[3] It is the display offering par excellence, and in its essential form, no part of it ascends the altar. M. Menaḥot 5:6 provides a postbiblical description of how such offerings were displayed, one that may, for all we know, be a continuation of more ancient practice. The offering was carried to and fro and shown to the deity. Most often, this mode served in biblical rites as a prelude to other forms of disposition; first the offering was shown to the deity and then was disposed of on the altar or in some other way. It is of interest that, whereas the minḥâ is set down before the deity, the těnûpâ is raised to show to him, but essentially the mode is the same.

A remarkable application of the těnûpâ pertains to the dedication of the Levites, prescribed in Numbers 8. The těnûpâ is there projected as a multi-phased rite, performed in the courtyard of the Sanctuary, there referred to as ʾôhel môʿēd ('the Tent of Assembly'). More precisely, it took place in the area of the courtyard outward of the altar. The display character of the dedication was realized by having the Levites stand near the altar as the Israelites, most likely their representatives, laid their hands on the heads of the Levites. This was a rite of assignment used in any number of sacrificial offerings, and discussed most clearly by David Wright.[4] At this point, Aaron raised the Levites as a těnûpâ in the presence of YHWH. The Levites were an offering given by the Israelite people. They then brought their own offering of atonement, after which the text repeats that Aaron and this sons displayed the Levites as těnûpâ. What we learn from this application of the těnûpâ is that its acceptance by the deity was conceived as visual.

It remains to discuss the posture, or venue, of the deity while all of this sacrificing has been going on inside and outside the Temple building. Logically, presentation and display, aimed at having the deity view the offering and hopefully view it with favor, presume that the deity is already present inside the Sanctuary, his residence; or, at less elaborate cult-sites, he is outside

3. J. Milgrom, "The Alleged Wave-Offering in Israel and the Ancient Near East," *IEJ* 22 (1972) 33–38; repr. in *Studies in Cultic Theology and Terminology* (Leiden: Brill, 1983) 133–38.

4. D. P. Wright, "The Gesture of Hand Placement in the Hebrew Bible and in Hittite Literature," *JAOS* 106 (1986) 433–46.

on a platform (*bāmâ*) or the like, situated near the altar. In a fully built cult installation, where the altar of burnt offerings is oriented toward the entrance of a building, we may presume that the deity was thought to be able to view what was set down near the courtyard altar, or displayed there, from within the depths of the building.

Elsewhere, I speak of this as the horizontal phenomenology—the contact established once the deity has arrived at the cult site. The realization of the *zebaḥ*, in its various forms, would also seem to presume the near presence of the deity, although the matter is more complex because in its primary form the *zebaḥ* may not have been associated with the altar, or with sanctuaries, as such.

In utter contrast, it would seem that the burnt offering, the offering of fire (*'iššeh*), expresses the vertical phenomenology. In my 1974 work, *In the Presence of the Lord*, I first put forth the hypothesis that the *ʿôlâ*, routinely the opening sacrifice in a fixed series, was offered for the purpose of invoking the deity, of attracting him to the cult site.[5] This emerged from an analysis of the Elijah encounter, from the etiological narrative of Judges 6, and from the utilization of *ʿôlôt* by Balaam in his peregrinations (Numbers 22–24). Now I have added to this body of textual evidence an analysis of the open-air cult installation at Edomite Qitmit, whose plan and features I discussed in *Biblical Archaeology Today*.[6] Problems remain of course, but it would seem, as has been suggested thus far, that the growing importance of the burnt altar offering accounts for most of the adaptations of horizontally oriented presentation and display offerings in biblical Israel.

The subject of burnt, altar offerings requires much more study. It is not the typical Near Eastern mode, which is presentation or display, and outside of temples probably the *zebaḥ*. Nor is there solid evidence for its early use in Canaan of pre-Israelite times. We are now able to trace its path from Eblaite *śarapātu* to Ugaritic *šrp* to biblical *miśrāpâ*, attested only in the plural construct, *miśrĕpôt* (Jer 34:5). The verb *śārap* is, however, frequent in biblical cultic texts.

It is my sense that the introduction of burnt, altar offerings into Canaan comes from Syria and that it may have been introduced by the Israelites, suggesting that they too came from Syria. In other words, the history of burnt offerings in biblical Israel may argue for the Syrian origin of the Israelites themselves. Putting this aside for the moment, suffice it to say that the mode of burnt, altar offerings projects the process of reaching the deity in heaven or far away atop high mountains, by perceiving the deity as inhaling the ascending column of aromatic smoke. Its message is "Come down!" Of course, once the burnt, altar offering more or less took over in the disposition

---

5. B. A. Levine, *In the Presence of the Lord: A Study of the Cult and Some Cultic Terms in Ancient Israel* (Studies in Judaism of Late Antiquity 5; Leiden: Brill, 1974).

6. Idem, "Phenomenology of the Open-Air-Altar."

of Israelite sacrifices, it was expressed in those offerings brought before the present deity in horizontal perspective as well. Whereas relatively early biblical accounts speak of the altar fire coming down from heaven, it is likely that Lev 9:24 had fire emitting from within the Sanctuary at the initiation of the altar of burnt offerings and igniting the first sacrifices offered on it.

Having suggested where the deity was during the performance of certain rites, we must similarly locate the worshipers and priests. We have probably tended to underestimate how much was going on in the courtyards of ancient temples. As Thorkild Jacobsen has shown, the courtyard was the venue for many presentations before the deity. In Mesopotamian temples, the *šulmānu* ('sacred gift of greeting') was presented in the courtyard, and in biblical temples of a certain period the same was true of its cognate, the *šĕlāmîm*. Generally, notions of strict purity prevented the entry of ordinary worshipers into the temple building itself; this was even true of priests. These restrictions inevitably shifted a good deal of ritual activity to the courtyard. As temples grew in size, more courtyards were added.[7] It would be interesting to summarize all of the activities consigned to the *ḥāṣēr* of the Temple and to review biblical references to *ḥaṣrôt bêt Yhwh* ('the courtyards of Yhwh's Temple').

The phenomenology of the presentational mode directs our attention to both human and divine processionals. The deity, or deities, having alighted on earth in response to invocation or having arrived as inspectors and masters of their domain or to celebrate scheduled rites such as festivals, entered the temple edifice, circumambulated it, and so forth. It was obviously a matter of great significance to know that God was in his holy temple, present and ready to accept the offerings of his people, to hear their petitions, and to bless them. Would that biblical literature afforded more information on the processionals of the God of Israel. There are a few allusions, but the clearest reference is in Psalm 24, as is well known. This psalm is of three parts, which bear analysis. The psalm opens with a statement of God's status as creator of the world, thereby reflecting the perception of the physical Temple compound as *axis mundi*. It continues with a rite of entry, rhetorically asking who may ascend the mount of the Lord and replying with an ethical modulation of the requirement of purity, defined as clean hands and a pure heart (compare Isaiah 1). The last part of the psalm achieves the meeting of man and God. The worthy worshipers have entered, and now God enters:

> O gates, lift up your heads!
> Up high, you everlasting doors,
> So the King of Glory may enter!

Now, the presentation offerings may proceed.

7. T. Jacobsen, "The Mesopotamian Temple Plan and the Kititum Temple," *ErIsr* 20 (Yadin Volume; 1989) 79–91.

Part IV

Death in the Life of Israel

Death in the Life of Israel

ELIZABETH BLOCH-SMITH
Bala Cynwyd, Pennsylvania

Introduction

According to the 1996 American presidential election results, it is not the popular position, but I would like to build a bridge not forward into the 21st century but backward to the 10th–6th centuries B.C.E.—not to look forward to life but backward to death. Just as there is no consensus on how to proceed into the future, there is no agreement on reconstructing the past.

Reconstructing the history of biblical Israel is extremely difficult. We do not have access to many events of the time, the documents have been mediated through multiple authors, editors, and historical traditions, and the material culture is only partially preserved. All of these stumbling blocks lie before historians, and if that is not formidable enough, our vision is dimmed by current societal attitudes and world events.

Haunted by the spectre of diverging opinions regarding the dead in Israelite society, the 1996 Archaeology and the Religion of Israel Section of ASOR was devoted to resurrecting the dead through examining relevant archaeological and literary evidence and interpretive methodologies. Members of the panel advocated a minimalist-moderate and a maximilist-moderate position on the role of the dead in Israelite society. Wayne Pitard and Ted Lewis's essays conjure up varying reconstructions, portentous of lively debate.

In this introduction, I will review the 20th-century C.E. debate over the presence or absence of a cult of the dead in preexilic Israel. The changing views during the 20th century demonstrate how modern context affects the interpretation of ancient evidence. This century has witnessed a cycle of interpretation regarding the dead. Initially the dead were attributed an active role, only later to be consigned to Sheol. They were again resurrected and at present are being stripped of their powers.

Let me begin with the problem of definition, followed by a summary of 20th-century views regarding the cult of the dead.

Defining a Cult of the Dead: Proponents and Opponents

The contemporary debate uses early-20th-century anthropological and sociological definitions of the cult of the dead. In his 1915 book _The Elementary Forms of the Religious Life_, Émile Durkheim defined the cult of the dead as comprising "repeated standardized practices oriented toward the dead at ritual locations associated with the dead" (Durkheim 1915: 63). The words "repeated standardized practices" are critical, because methodologically the interpretation of unique archaeological remains is highly subjective. Also, literary references must not be isolated but considered in their broad historical and theological context.

Those who argue against a cult of the dead in preexilic Israel define cultic activity in terms of the intentions and behaviors of the practitioners and anticipated results. Unfortunately, intentions and anticipations leave little archaeological evidence. Yehezkel Kaufmann argued that biblical rites for the dead did not constitute cultic activity because they were not imbued with religious significance; they constituted "ethical behavior" not "religious acts" (Kaufmann 1972: 315). Another individual with a minimalist view of the role of the dead, Brian Schmidt, requires veneration and worship of the deceased as prerequisites for the existence of a death cult (Schmidt 1994: 5). Schmidt does not detail veneration for ancient Israel. He defines worship as acts of propitiating the dead "through the offer of _goods_, services, words, and other gestures in order to secure their favor" (1994: 10). "Goods" are retrievable through archaeology. However, Schmidt obfuscates the issue by elsewhere interpreting "care for and feeding of the dead" as a sign of the weakness of the dead who accordingly have "no power to affect the living in a beneficial way" (1994: 10). You cannot have it both ways—goods cannot be both a gift to secure favors from the powerful dead and a sign of weakness and inability to affect the living! Death cult opponents and minimalists rely heavily on literary evidence and largely ignore archaeological remains.

Proponents of a death cult in preexilic Israel agree that the dead played an active role in Israelite society, through supernatural powers that could benefit the living and/or by laying claim to the patrimony. Scholarly reconstructions of the cult vary in regard to rites practiced, how prevalent they were, their location, the occasions, the centuries during which they took place, indigenous or foreign origin, and whether or not they were kosher. For example, some scholars mandate periodic or repeated activities while others appear content with circumstantial initiatives. Proposed loci for death cult activities include the Jerusalem Temple, tombs, trees, bamot, doorposts, and local shrines. A spirited debate also rages over whether death cult activities were limited to so-called "popular religion" or were a fact of the equally ambiguous "normative/State religion."

Ugaritic texts unearthed beginning in the 1930s and the growing number of excavated hill-country burials are more often than not cited in support of an Israelite cult of the dead. Israel is considered to have followed the practices of her neighbors and predecessors; the cult is understood against the backdrop of the Mesopotamian *kispu* and the Ugaritic royal (and possibly domestic) funerary cults.

Twentieth-Century Debate over the Preexilic Israelite Cult of the Dead

The 20th century has seen both advocates and opponents of an Israelite death cult. While not an exhaustive treatment of those who have written on the subject, the following is a representative sample that reflects historical shifts in opinion.

In Fustel de Coulanges's mid-19th-century work *The Ancient City* (1864) and Sir James Frazer's early-20th-century *Folk-Lore in the Old Testament* (1919), ancient Israel was treated as a case study, in the same way that anthropologists were studying contemporary cultures. According to these early works, the divine dead were provisioned and consulted within the realm of "popular" or "domestic religion." While not a normative feature of the Yahwistic cult, death cult rites were considered regular features of Israelite religious practice.

European biblical scholars of the 1920s and 1930s, including G. Quell, J. Pedersen, and A. Lods, typically interpreted funerary and mourning rites as features of an Israelite cult of the dead (Quell 1925: 24; Pedersen 1926: 3–4. 484; Lods 1932: 224). The Deuteronomic prohibition against feeding the dead tithed food (Deut 26:14), David's familial "yearly sacrifice" (1 Sam 20: 6), and the story of the Witch of Endor (1 Samuel 28), were commonly cited as evidence of a death cult. In the 1942 publication of Samaria Tomb 103, the archaeologists Crowfoot, Kenyon, and Sukenik identified pits cut into the tomb floor as "receptacles of offerings connected with the cult of the dead as regularly practiced in ancient Israel in spite of the attacks of the prophets" (Crowfoot, Kenyon, and Sukenik 1942: 21–22).

A shift occurred beginning with the work of Yehezkiel Kaufmann in the late 1930s (1937–), followed by William Foxwell Albright (ca. 1947), G. Ernest Wright (1953), and Roland de Vaux (1957), religious men working during and in the years following World War II. The Second World War revived theological interest in the Bible, as reflected in the career of G. Ernest Wright and the Biblical Theology movement. This American movement, strongly Protestant in orientation, sought to restore the unity and theological dimension of Scripture and Israel's uniqueness in the ancient Near Eastern world. The movement lost its impetus with the publication of newly discovered ancient texts and technical studies that cast doubt on Israel's singularity. Brevard Childs identified three factors in the demise of the Biblical Theology Movement. First, philological studies refuted terminology considered to demonstrate Israel's uniqueness. Second, study of the Ugaritic and Nag Hammadi texts and the Dead Sea Scrolls demonstrated similarities rather than differences between the Bible and other ancient Near Eastern cultures. The third factor was the cultural revolution of the 1960s (Childs 1970: 74–82).

The next generation, writing between the late 1950s and the mid-1990s, resurrected the dead in ancient Israelite society. Against a backdrop of the Ugaritic texts and the increasing number of hill-country burials excavated, scholars stressed the *similarities* between ancient Israel, her neighbors, and her predecessors. The weight of new data convinced W. F. Albright to shift his opinion and write in 1957,

> biblical references to veneration of heroic shrines (e.g., Rachel and Deborah), cult of departed spirits or divination with their aid, and high places in general add up to a much greater significance for popular Israelite belief in life after death and the cult of the dead than has hitherto appeared prudent to admit. (Albright 1957: 257)

Some of the more significant contributions of this period were made by Albright in the 1950s, Mitchell Dahood and Avraham Malamat in the 1960s, John Ribar, B. Halevi, Chanan Brichto, and Marvin Pope in the 1970s, and Klaus Spronk and Ted Lewis in the 1980s.

The winds are shifting. Several of the most recent treatments of the subject, including those of Rainer Albertz, Philip Johnston, Brian Schmidt, and Wayne Pitard seek to minimize the role of the dead compared to historical reconstructions of the last approximately 30 years. There are several possible factors contributing to this nascent shift in scholarly opinion. Current scholars are rightfully reacting to the excesses in interpretation of the data of the previous generation. They are also reevaluating the role of comparative studies. Whereas the previous generation emphasized similarities between Israel and other ancient Near Eastern cultures, current scholarship stresses differences, seeking to (re)establish unique features of early Israel. Given the Biblical Theology movement's influence in the 1950s and 1960s, one may wonder if theological forces are at work in the current backlash against the cult of the dead.

This brief survey perhaps illustrates a regular cycle in scholarship. As Robert Bly wrote, "Both science and literature advance by means of ritual battles between generations" (Bly 1996: 164). Make no bones about it, we need to evaluate both archaeological and literary data and methodology in death cult studies, lest we reach a dead end.

Bibliography

Albright, W. F.
  1957   The High Place in Ancient Palestine. Pp. 242–58 in *Volume du Congrès: Strasbourg, 1956*. VTSup 4. Leiden: Brill.

Bly, R.
  1990   *Iron John: A Book about Men*. Reading, Mass.: Addison-Wesley.

Childs, B.
  1970   *Biblical Theology in Crisis*. Philadelphia: Westminster.

Coulanges, F. de
  1877   *The Ancient City: A Study of the Religion, Laws and Institutions of Greece and Rome*. Boston: Lee & Shepard / New York: Dillingham.

Crowfoot, J.; Kenyon, K.; and Sukenik, E.
  1942   *The Buildings at Samaria*. London: Palestine Exploration Fund.

Durkheim, É.
  1915   *The Elementary Forms of Religious Life: A Study in Religious Sociology*. Trans. J. Swain. London: Allen & Unwin.

Frazer, J.
  1919   *Folk-Lore in the Old Testament: Studies in Comparative Religion, Legend and Law*. London: Macmillan.

Kaufmann, Y.
  1972   *The Religion of Israel: From Its Beginnings to the Babylonian Exile*. Trans. and abridged M. Greenberg. New York: Schocken.

Lods, A.
  1932   *Israël: Des origines au milieu du VIIIe siècle*. Series Évolution de l'humanité 27. Paris: Renaissance du livre.

Pedersen, J.
  1926   *Israel: Its Life and Culture*. London: Oxford University Press.

Quell, G.
  1925   *Die Auffassung des Todes in Israel*. Leipzig: Deichert.

Schmidt, B.
  1994   *Israel's Beneficent Dead: Ancestor Cult and Necromancy in Ancient Israelite Religion and Tradition*. Tübingen: Mohr. Reprinted, Winona Lake, Ind.: Eisenbrauns, 1996.

Tombs and Offerings:
Archaeological Data and Comparative Methodology in the Study of Death in Israel

WAYNE T. PITARD
University of Illinois at Urbana-Champaign

The subject of Israel's responses to death and its beliefs about afterlife has attracted numerous investigators over the past century or so. Some have concentrated on the texts of the Hebrew Bible for their primary data, some on the archaeological remains of tombs and other funerary structures, while others have emphasized the importance of cultural parallels from Canaan, Mesopotamia, Egypt, and even farther afield. But the interpretation of this aspect of Israelite culture has been fraught with controversy. Occasionally, for a brief period, a fairly wide consensus among scholars has appeared to develop, but within a few years new controversies make their appearance, and the consensus breaks down.

All of this uncertainty is to be expected. The meaning and impact of death on an individual society is an exceedingly complex issue, difficult to interpret fully even in the context of modern anthropological/ethnographic research on contemporary cultures, where extensive documentation and living informants are available. Studies have shown the extraordinary range of responses to death that have developed in different cultures (cf. Ucko 1969; Humphreys 1981). It is thus impossible to predict how an individual society will deal with the various aspects of the subject. In societies far removed from us in time and space, where little documentation is preserved, the problems of interpretation can be enormous.

Some of the cultures of the ancient Near East have provided us with a fair amount of written and archaeological material from which a great deal of information can be extracted. In Egypt, where the subject was of extraordinary concern to the vast majority of the population, we have a virtual embarrassment of riches in terms of both texts and material remains. But even so, there are numerous areas of ambiguity. For ancient Mesopotamia textual evidence provides us with much insight, while less work has been done on the archaeological materials. Scholars of Syria–Palestine have produced a number of studies on the tombs discovered in this region, but they have been hampered by the relatively small amount of written material dealing with death and afterlife that has been discovered there.

Biblical Israel stands as a fascinating, special case in terms of its preserved sources. For those of us working on the subject, one of the most striking aspects about the Hebrew Bible is how little it actually talks about death and afterlife. The subject does not form a primary theme in any book of the Hebrew Bible. What we find instead are (at best) scant, rather off-hand, ambiguous and nonspecific references and allusions to the subject in a variety of contexts. These passages are not particularly harmonious in their views, with some passages seeming to presuppose that the dead carry on an active existence, while others present a very skeptical view of the afterlife, and some suggest that the afterlife does not exist at all.

While the relative lack of literary evidence for Syro-Palestinian beliefs and practices outside of Israel perhaps may be explained by the sporadic and fragmentary recovery of texts in the region, a similar explanation does not work in the case of ancient Israel. The relative silence on the part of the Hebrew Bible cannot be attributed merely to chance. The Hebrew Bible represents a carefully chosen collection of books that were understood (at least by the end of the first century C.E., but probably much earlier) to be theologically sufficient, containing what was essential for the community. Thus the absence of texts dealing in any detail with the issue of death seems to have been a deliberate choice by the post-exilic religious leadership of Judah. This apparent lack of concern for the religious dimensions of death and for speculation about the afterlife (which, after all, is a subject of enormous intrinsic interest) is intriguing and calls for explanation.

In order to piece together the Israelite understandings of death, scholars have engaged in considerable detective work, reconstructing what they can from the archaeological remains and from the biblical and inscriptional materials. They have also examined the parallel practices and beliefs of the cultures that preceded and surrounded Israel in the Near East. With regard to the latter, many scholars have made the logical assumption that Israelite funerary practices and beliefs developed from those of earlier Canaan and that insight into Canaanite thought on this subject (the Ugaritic texts being the primary source) should help in understanding Israelite developments. And in some areas, passages in the Ugaritic tablets have shown a clear relationship between second-millennium Canaanite and first-millennium Israelite practices. One thinks most notably perhaps of the parallels between the mourning practices illustrated in the Ugaritic texts and those described in the Bible (cf., for example, *KTU* 1.6.6:11–25, alongside Gen 37:34–35; Lev 19:28; 21:5; Deut 14:1). But much of the Ugaritic material has proved to be more ambiguous and impenetrable than earlier thought, and in spite of a number of important attempts by scholars to reconstruct the main lines of Ugaritic belief and practice concerning the dead (see, for example, Pope 1977: 210–229; Loretz 1978; Spronk 1986; Loretz 1990; Schmidt 1994; del Olmo Lete 1992: 109–70; 1999: 160–253), we simply do not yet have a firm grasp of what the actual situation in that culture was.[1]

Ugarit has not been the only major source of cultural parallels used by scholars. Many have approached Mesopotamia as a fertile source for comparison with Israel (particularly in regard to the nature of the netherworld and to the issue of cult of the dead, especially the *kispu* ritual; cf. Albright 1968: 203–6; Spronk 1986: 96–129; 247; 256–57; Martin-Achard 1960: 36–40; Ribar 1973: 78–80). Although it is rarely discussed in detail, scholars often assume that many Canaanite and early Israelite beliefs and practices concerning the dead were substantially identical with those of Mesopotamia, even when there is no direct evidence available from Canaanite or Israelite sources. The use of cultural comparisons does not stop here, however. Scholars have also noted similarities between Israelite notions of death and those from other parts of the eastern Mediterranean, including Anatolia and Greece (cf. Spronk 1986: 54–65 for further discussion).

All told, while we do have considerable data to work with, both in terms of archaeological and textual material from Israel itself and comparative material from its neighbors, a large percentage of it, both archaeological and textual, is ambiguous. The question of how to interpret this ambiguous material is at the crux of the problem. How much of one's reconstruction can appropriately be built upon data that can be plausibly interpreted in more than one way? Where can we draw the line between appropriate and inappropriate use of conjecture and speculation? What kind of evidence is necessary before one can argue that a belief or practice in one culture actually illuminates belief and practice in another? I believe that the study of Israelite concepts of death and afterlife has often suffered from a tendency to overinterpret one's evidence, overgeneralize from limited data, overrely on meagre and weak evidence in drawing up complex reconstructions of systems of practice and belief, and to overuse cultural parallels from neighboring or more distant societies for interpreting unattested or ambiguous aspects of Israel's thought.

In this paper I wish particularly to discuss some of the issues surrounding the interpretation of archaeological data in the reconstruction of Israelite

---

1. On the uncertainty of interpretation of some of the major elements of Ugaritic concepts of death and afterlife, see, for example, Lewis 1994: 53–71 on the interpretation of the list of filial duties in the Aqhat Epic; and pp. 80–94 on the Marzeah; Schmidt 1994: 53–59 on *Ilib* at Ugarit; and Pitard 1999 on the problem of the identity of the Rapi'uma.

beliefs and practices concerning death and the dead, emphasizing the limitations inherent in that data and the dangers in the use of comparative data for
explaining elements of culture in a specific society. I do not expect to present
any startlingly new insights here but rather wish to review several aspects of
the issue that at times seem to get lost.

Archaeological remains have provided us with a very large pool of data
concerning several aspects of Canaanite and Israelite funerary practices,
much of which is not illustrated in the surviving texts. Recent analyses of this
data in Palestine, such as Rivka Gonen's work on Late Bronze Age burial
practices in Canaan (1992) and Elizabeth Bloch-Smith's fine study of the
Iron Age tombs in Judah (1992), have been a major step in gaining a greater
understanding of these two periods. For example, we now have a much
clearer view of the range of different tomb types and burial customs in second
and first millennium contexts.[2] Excavations throughout Syria–Palestine
have indicated a fascinating variety of customs. For example, many tombs are
situated in cemeteries outside settlements, while others, such as those at
Ugarit, are found inside the settlements, either in intramural cemeteries, or
under the floors of houses or in courtyards of temples. Some groups preferred
individual burial in a single grave or tomb, while others practiced multiple
burial. Some tombs are simple graves dug into the ground, while some groups
used caves, either natural or artificially hollowed out. In other cases, vaulted-
ceiling tombs were built, sometimes with elaborate staircases into the chamber. A few examples of cremation have also been found. Very little of this
variety of practice would be known if we only had textual sources available.

The material remains have allowed scholars to examine a number of aspects of life and death in Canaan and Israel. For example, some of the variations in burial practices have been used to distinguish differences in social
class. The relative elaborateness of a tomb, the types of funerary offerings
found in it and sometimes its location may suggest a particular social standing
of its owner(s), although a simple correlation between such features and status may at times be problematic and is sometimes unsustainable.[3] Another
growing area of research is the detailed analysis of skeletal remains from the
tombs. This work has been very fruitful in investigating issues of age and life
expectancy, gender issues and ancient medical pathology (see, for example

2. Both of these authors provide careful discussions of the various types of
tombs and the characteristic contents found in each type. See Gonen 1992: 9–31 and
Bloch-Smith 1992: 25–62 (for Iron Age burial types) and 63–108 (for the contents of
the tombs). There is not as yet a comparable study of tombs in Syria for any of the
ancient periods.

3. See Ucko 1969: 266–68 for examples of societies where the elaborateness of a
burial clearly shows no relation to the social standing of the deceased and his/her
family.

Chapman, Kinnes, and Randsborg 1981; Roberts, Lee, and Bintliff 1989; Thornton 1995; Loebl 1995).

The objects buried with the dead perhaps give hints about some of a culture's beliefs concerning the dead. A significant element is pottery, much of which probably contained food and drink when deposited with the burial. Many tombs also preserve jewelry, weapons, other personal items, as well as furniture (beds, chairs, etc.). In Egypt, a wide array of items relating to magic were placed in tombs as well (Spencer 1982: 67–70, 109–11), and in Canaan and Israel some figurines and other items may also have had such a function. Written documents and inscriptions, common in some cultures such as Egypt, rarely appear in or around Levantine tombs (on Judean tomb contents, cf. Bloch-Smith 1992: 63–108). And this too, perhaps, is significant.

This kind of basic data is itself very valuable for increasing our understanding of death in Israel. However, this is far less than what most of us as historians of Israel's religion and culture want to know. What can the remains tell us about Israel's *beliefs* concerning the dead and the afterlife? What is the meaning of the different tomb types? Do the multiple types of tombs give evidence of cultural diversity within Israel, or are they related to the economic status of the occupants, or are the styles simply a matter of preference? What is the function of the burial offerings? Can one definitively determine whether offerings continued to be given to the dead after the burial? Why did the Israelites bury their dead exclusively outside their habitational boundaries? How do the archaeological remains relate to the written sources? It is in attempting to answer such questions that the complications arise.

What can material remains tell us about the belief systems of those who created them? I believe that the answer to this question is a painful one—fairly little! The problem is that material remains are susceptible to numerous potential and plausible interpretations. Without some kind of written data, it is very difficult to say with any certainty what a specific group of people meant when they did things the way they did. Numerous caveats stand before the would-be interpreter. In 1969, anthropologist Peter J. Ucko published a very influential paper in which he effectively pulled the rug out from under many of the traditional interpretive procedures used by most Near Eastern archaeologists and biblical scholars as they made use of tomb discoveries to illuminate Israelite concepts of death and afterlife. In the article, Ucko drew together example after example from contemporary ethnographic data that flies directly in the face of what we would consider common-sense interpretations of funerary remains. He emphasized the fact that while there may be some universal aspects of the way humans deal with death, there are at the same time an extraordinary variety of specific responses and beliefs that usually cannot be illuminated by examination of archaeological remains. Different populations can do similar things—including making similar types of tombs or placing similar types of objects in the tomb—for entirely different reasons. In addition, a particular funerary practice, when carried out through time, might come to have a completely different meaning from the meaning it had in an earlier period. It is clear that while many of us in Near Eastern studies are aware of Ucko's point, we have had a difficult time taking it to heart.

The extent of the difficulty in interpreting the belief system that lies behind the archaeological remains is sometimes hard to grasp. In discussing this issue, Ron Tappy (1995: 61) points out that even something as apparently straightforward as the presence in Israelite tombs of vessels with food and drink is difficult to interpret definitively, even with access to the biblical text. Is the deposited food intended for the dead, or is it the leftovers of the mourning feast of the survivors, which is mentioned several times in the Bible? Does it therefore indicate that the dead were thought to need sustenance after death, or does it actually say nothing about such matters? Even less can the presence of food help us interpret the Israelite understanding of the nature of the deceased's existence in the afterlife. Some scholars argue that the food represents an offering to the dead as a deified spirit (cf. Bloch-Smith 1992: 122–26). The food is interpreted then as having a significant cultic function. Others argue that the food and drink are provided because the dead, like the living, simply continue to have basic needs for survival. The food does not signify any belief in the deification of the dead. The dead are in fact dependent on the living for their well-being in the netherworld (cf. Schmidt 1994: 4–13; 274–81). Unfortunately, there is no explicit and unambiguous discussion of the meaning of food placed in tombs in the Hebrew Bible (or, for that matter, in Canaanite/Ugaritic texts). Thus the archaeological data remains mute on this issue.

It is my contention that in reconstructing beliefs from archaeological material, less is more. I believe that it is more helpful to the field to emphasize the ambiguity and uncertainty of our knowledge than to choose one possibility and construct an edifice of speculation upon it. This does not mean that we as scholars are precluded from making some intelligent speculations. But first we must remember that they are guesses, and second, we must be aware of the limits of appropriate deduction. For example, I believe that we may reasonably propose that cultures such as that at Ugarit, in which the dead were buried in tombs beneath houses—tombs that were fairly accessible from the living quarters—did not have major concerns about the impurity of the dead and the potential for ritual pollution from the proximity of a corpse that characterizes much of the Israelite legislation concerning the dead. On the other hand, the fact that the Late Bronze Age Canaanites in the southern Levant consistently buried their dead outside their towns and cities like the later Israelites, does not allow us to conclude that they held the same purity views concerning the dead as did the Israelites. There might be many reasons

why the Canaanites in this area did not bury their dead within their settlements. Without written documentation, we simply cannot determine what
this difference between Ugaritic and the contemporary Canaanite practice to
the south actually means.

If there are such complications in the interpretation of materials that
seem fairly straightforward, how much more careful should we be when we
deal with more complicated and uncertain elements found in excavations.
Perhaps some of the best examples of unfortunate reconstruction of Levantine funerary practice have occurred when scholars link ambiguous objects,
installations, and even buildings to hypothetical rituals thought to be performed in a complex, but also hypothetical, cult of the dead. I would like to
look at two examples, one specifically in an Israelite context and one from
Middle Bronze Age Ebla, where ambiguous materials and generalized anthropological models have been used to produce an almost entirely conjectural
reconstruction of funerary practices.

Example 1: Offerings for the Dead?

My first example of such a situation is the well-known idea that many
tombs in the Levant were supplied with tubes or holes in their ceilings which
were used by the living to introduce regular offerings into the tombs as part
of the cult of the dead. In Syria–Palestine, the primary type-site with tombs
possessing such means of providing offerings has been the Late Bronze Age
city of Ugarit and its harbor town, Minet el-Beida in northern Syria. From
1929 through the late 1930s, Claude Schaeffer excavated numerous tombs
and neighboring installations, which he interpreted as examples of just such
complex systems for feeding the dead. His basic analysis of the tombs was
worked out during the first few seasons of excavation at Minet-el-Beida, before any tombs were discovered at Ugarit. When Schaeffer began excavating
at Minet el-Beida in 1929, he was under the impression (quite logical at the
time) that he was excavating a Late Bronze Age cemetery. After all, the reason excavations were undertaken at the site was that a farmer had discovered
a well-built tomb in his field. What Schaeffer did not know was that at Minet
el-Beida and at Ugarit tombs were normally built under the floors of the
houses and that he was actually excavating Ugarit's harbor town. For the first
five seasons of excavations, Schaeffer interpreted all of his finds based on the
assumption that Minet el-Beida was a cemetery. Thus, drainage pipes and
gutters of the houses under which the tombs were built were identified as libation installations, used in conjunction with the tombs. Olive oil presses
were identified as sacrificial altars, staircases to the second floor of the house
became stepped altars, storehouse rooms filled with jars became enormous

votive offerings to the dead, etc. (for details, see Pitard 1994). Schaeffer's reconstruction of the Ugaritic concepts of death and afterlife was primarily formed during this period, and this interpretation of the supposed tomb material was never revised by him in print, as far as I know, and it has continued to influence work on Canaanite and Israelite funerary beliefs ever since. Reanalyses of this material by the new team at Ugarit have only begun to appear during the past few years (Salles 1987, 1995; Callot 1994: 168–76).

The most influential part of Schaeffer's interpretation of elements relating to the cult of the dead at Ugarit was doubtless his identification of holes in the roofs of some of the tombs at both Minet el-Beida and Ugarit as libation installations, direct entryways for dropping drink and/or food offerings into the tombs from the room or courtyard directly above. Schaeffer argued that this represented a more convenient means of fulfilling the ritual requirements than having to open the main entry of the tomb every time food was to be given to the dead (cf. 1939a: 51). But his interpretation of the holes in the ceilings has proved to be highly suspect. Where the floor levels in the rooms above the tombs have been recorded, it is clear that the roofs of the tombs were generally well below floor level. Schaeffer never indicated finding any apparatus that connected the holes to the actual floor level. But perhaps more importantly, examination of the openings in the tomb ceilings shows that they were not crafted into the structure of the tombs but are, instead, gaps where one or two of the stones that seal the apex of the corbelled vault along the length of the chamber have been removed. They are much more plausibly interpreted as holes made in the roofs by the vandals who searched for and robbed the tombs in antiquity (for more details see Pitard 1994: 30–33).

Not surprisingly, most of the features that Schaeffer identified as belonging to the post-funeral cult of the dead (i.e., the gutters, sacrificial tables, stepped altars, etc.) were never identified at any other site. But there have been a few tombs found in Israel that possess holes of one kind or another in their ceilings. With Ugarit as the primary type-site for the interpretation of these holes, scholars have often identified them as similar conduits. John Ribar, in his widely read but unpublished dissertation of 1973, gathered relevant examples of ceiling holes from Palestine. From the Middle and Late Bronze Ages, he found examples at three sites: Megiddo (1 example— Grabkammer II, see Schumacher 1908: 19–21; pl. 6); Hazor (2 examples— Cave 9038, the "Porcupine Cave," see Yadin et al. 1958: 100–106; and Cave 7013/7015, 1958: 146; 155–58); and Gezer (an unknown number, since the holes at Gezer are only mentioned in a single summary paragraph in R. A. S. Macalister's excavation report (1912: 394; there is a reference to a "crack" in the roof of Tomb 58, p. 323).

Ribar's Iron Age evidence for ceiling holes was even more sparse (Ribar 1973: 55–63). The only examples from Israel or Judah were two tombs from

Beth-Shemesh dating to the 8th–6th centuries. From outside Israel and Judah proper, he noted an Iron Age tomb from Sahab near Amman, Jordan with a ceiling hole.

But the collapse of Ugarit as the parade example of a tomb structure with libation holes suggests that we should approach the proposed examples of the same thing in Israel with caution. In fact, most of Ribar's examples are problematic. For example, the hole in the capstone of Grabkammer II at Megiddo appears to have been covered immediately and made inaccessible when the room above the tomb was completed. The excavators gave no indication that there was any evidence that the hardpacked floor of the room, slightly over 40 cm above the top of the tomb roof, was repeatedly dug up so that offerings could be poured into the hole (cf. Schumacher 1908: 19–20; pl. 6).

The caves at Hazor are even less helpful. Neither of Ribar's two examples can even be positively identified as a tomb. The "Porcupine Cave," Cave 9038, found in Area D was a well-cut cave with a vaulted entrance opening off of a prepared courtyard. It was built during the early part of MB II. Besides its main entrance, it appears that the ceiling (now collapsed) at one time had an opening in it, which Yadin suggested was used as a means of access to the cave by the inhabitants who lived above it (Yadin 1958: 100). Ribar, however, suggested that it was the means by which offerings were introduced into the tomb. Some skulls and bones were found in the cave, but Yadin stops short of identifying it as a tomb. The fact that the cave contained debris from a period after the front entrance to the cave had been sealed off suggests that the cave might have been reused with a new entrance from the top. And this reuse was certainly not as a tomb. With all of the ambiguity about the function of the cave and the date of the hole in the ceiling, it does not seem appropriate to use it as an example of a tomb with a libation installation.

The double cave 7013/7015 is even less helpful. The complex consisted of two carved-out rooms with a tunnel joining them. Cave 7013 had a standard entrance in its side, with two steps leading in. Cave 7015, however, could be entered either from 7013 or from the ceiling, which had a large hole in it (Yadin 1958: 146). Yadin believed that a small opening may have existed in the roof of 7013 as well, but no clear traces of it were found. A few MB II sherds found inside suggest that the caves were first used in that period. But most of the finds came from the Late Bronze period. During the Late Bronze Age, the regular entrance to Cave 7013 was blocked, so that the only entry into the caves was through the ceiling in 7015 (Yadin 1958: 155–56). No bones were found in the caves. This certainly compromises their identification as tombs. They thus are of no help in the discussion of apertures in tomb ceilings.

Holes in the ceilings of some Gezer tombs were given only the briefest mention by Macalister, so the character of these holes and their relationship to the tomb material found in the caves is unknown. Note should be made, however, that the LB tomb (Cave 10A) excavated by the more recent expedition to Gezer and published by Seger (1988: 47–59, and plan II, section 1) had a hole in the ceiling. But this is because the tomb was originally a cistern, and the hole was its original opening.

The two examples Ribar described from Iron Age Israel and Judah are somewhat more interesting (Ribar 1973: 57–60). Both are tombs from Beth Shemesh, Tombs 1 and 2. Tomb 1 had a large shaft ca. 1 meter in diameter and ca. 1 meter in length, cut through the ceiling of the primary chamber (MacKenzie 1912–13: 52–53; pl. IV). The excavators had suggested that this shaft was the main access into the tomb, but Ribar argued that the room was too deep for this access to be convenient. One might note, however, that many tomb openings of this period were long vertical shafts as deep or deeper than the situation here. In addition, there seems little reason to make a hole 1 meter wide for the introduction of food and drink offerings into a tomb.

Tomb 2 is quite striking. It contains a shaft some 2.5 meters long that begins on the surface and curves downward to exit in the side wall of the tomb chamber (MacKenzie 1912–13: 64–66, pl. V). Its mouth on the surface is ca. 1 meter in diameter and the hole inside the tomb chamber is ca. 65 cm. This hole could indeed be a conduit for the presentation of libations inside the tomb. But again, the size of the hole seems excessive, and the curvature of the tunnel, along with its exit location on the wall seem not entirely appropriate for that function. One can certainly not discount that interpretation, but the evidence remains ambiguous.

To these two tombs studied by Ribar, we can add an Iron Age tomb excavated by Eilat Mazar in the southern cemetery of Achzib that had a hole bored through one of the ceiling slabs. Mazar reports that the hole had been sealed with a stone. Mazar identified the hole as a means of pouring libations into the tomb, partially based on the supposed parallels from Ugarit (Stern 1993: vol. 1, 35).

To summarize, then: Ribar's widely accepted proposal that the Israelites participated in regular offerings of libations to the dead through holes in the ceilings of their tombs is actually based on the evidence of five published tombs (and the vague reference to ceiling holes in the early Gezer reports). His primary evidence for interpreting the tombs in this way is his comparative use of the Ugaritic tombs, which at the time of his writing were thought to show the widespread appearance of this practice. This has now been discredited. In addition, four of his five examples prove to be highly problematic for his interpretation on general archaeological grounds. Only Tomb 2 at Beth Shemesh actually provides a plausible example that could be interpreted in this fashion. One might accept the tomb at Achzib as a second possible example, and there are likely to be a few more of which I am not aware.

But in comparison to the hundreds of tombs found in Canaan/Israel from the Middle Bronze to the Iron Age, how can the installations found in such a tiny number of tombs be used to delineate the funerary practices of a culture? This is a significant over-reaching of the evidence.

The same problem faces those who argue that a widespread cult of the dead can be reconstructed on the basis of such evidence as the Late Bronze Tomb I at Dothan, with its "window" through which one might pour drink offerings inside (cf. Cooley 1983), or the Iron Age Tomb of the Royal Steward in Jerusalem, which seems to have a table for offerings at its entrance (Ussishkin 1993: 193–97, 293), or the Iron Age built tombs in the southern cemetery at Achzib, which are reconstructed as having offering tables over the roofs of the tombs (Prausnitz 1969). Again, each of these elements is virtually unique among the repertoire of tombs found in Israel and its surroundings. They can hardly be used as windows into the general practices of the Canaanites or Israelites.

In fact, I would argue that the archaeological remains contain no clear evidence that the Israelites provided their dead with additional offerings of food or drink after burial. Of course, this lack of evidence does not allow us then to conclude that the Israelites did not perform such offerings. That would be a very dangerous argument from silence. But it means that we need considerably more evidence before arguing that the practice existed. I have argued elsewhere (Pitard 1992)[4] that the written remains of ancient Israel also provide little evidence that post-funeral offerings were given to the dead, but that is another issue.

Example 2: Ebla Areas B and Q

The interpretive problems just described are not confined to the study of tombs and tomb furnishings. A number of other structures at various sites have been identified as locations for funerary cult. Perhaps the most famous argument for interpreting non-tomb archaeological remains as elements of a funerary cult was that proposed by W. F. Albright in support of his view that the Hebrew *bāmâ* 'high place' was primarily related to the cult of the dead (Albright 1957). In his work on this subject, Albright suggested that a number of excavated structures were involved in the cult of the dead in the second and first millennia B.C.E., including the stela shrine found at Gezer (the famous Gezer High Place; 1957: 243–44, 247), Shrine 6136 at Hazor (the shrine with the group of small stelae that centered upon one with a carving of two outstretched arms under a crescent moon; 1957:251–53) and others.

---

4. This unpublished paper is part of a monograph that will deal with several aspects of the Israelite and Canaanite concepts of death and afterlife.

Although Albright's interpretation has few supporters today (cf. Barrick 1975), similar interpretations of other structures have arisen occasionally.

A current example is Paolo Matthiae's interpretation of the Middle Bronze Age quarter of Ebla located directly west and southwest of the central citadel (Areas B, C, G, and Q), which he argues was the locus of a very active royal cult of the dead. His reconstruction is based entirely on the archaeological remains; no written sources have been found. In a number of articles published over the past quarter century, Matthiae has analyzed the three major public buildings uncovered in the quarter, called Temple B1, Sanctuary B2 and the Western Palace, along with a number of tombs scattered through the area (1974: 24–25; 1975: 69–71; 1979; 1980a; 1980d; 1981b; 1984; 1990).

Temple B1, the first to be uncovered, is a typical one-room "fortress" temple, with very thick walls and a ledge against its back wall. Before exacavations began there, a large stone basin, with carved reliefs on its sides, was discovered by chance and proved later to have been from this temple (1981a: 126–27). Because the reliefs show two rows of soldiers marching into battle, Matthiae has argued that the god of Temple B1 was probably Rasap (= Resheph), whom he has identifed as the primary netherworld deity at Ebla (1990: 349).

Just south of B1 was the structure called Sanctuary B2, a fairly large building with a plan that is quite uncharacteristic of identifiable religious structures at Ebla and elsewhere (for a description and plan, see Matthiae 1981a: 128–30). Somewhat squarish, the building has a large central room whose walls were lined with benches and which contained a rectangular mudbrick dais approximately 2.20 by 1.40 m. in size, near the southern wall. Ranged around this central room were several long, thin rooms and a few small, square ones. In a long room on the southeastern side of the building (Room 2113), the excavators found a small structure consisting of two stone slabs standing vertically and parallel to one another, perpendicular to the wall, with a single mudbrick placed between them. A similar structure was found in the small squarish room directly south of Room 2113 (Room 2140). Also in Room 2113, two very well-made basalt tables were found, sitting on a low bench in the southeast corner of the room.

It is from these finds that Matthiae identified the building as a sanctuary. He identified the two stone-slab structures as altars (by which he seems to mean cult-statue platforms rather than places for the burning of sacrifice), and the basalt tables as offering tables for blood sacrifice (1981b: 60–61; see most recently 1990). He envisioned the central room as the location of sacred community meals, with offerings placed on the mudbrick dais. Recognizing that the building has no real parallels to any other clearly identified sanctuary, Matthiae has argued that it must not have been used for the worship of a single deity but was more likely a sanctuary dedicated to the cult of dead royal ancestors. He saw the "altars" as the locations where small bronze images of the deceased kings were set up, while communal meals, related to the *kispum* of Mesopotamia, were served in the central room (1990: 352–54).

This interpretation was strengthened by the presence of a number of tombs found throughout Areas B, Q, and C. During the 1978 excavations in the Western Palace (Area Q), the third major building in the area, three tombs were discovered under the palace floors. They were located under three contiguous rooms, and, in fact, their hypogea were connected with one another. All showed evidence of having been wealthy tombs, plundered in antiquity, but substantial finds were still located in two of them, the "Tomb of the Princess" and the "Tomb of the Lord of the Goats." Each appeared to have been used for the burial of a single individual. Matthiae dated the "Tomb of the Princess," the earliest, to the last half of the 19th century B.C.E. Then came the "Tomb of the Lord of the Goats," which he dated to ca. 1750 or slightly later, and finally the badly-damaged "Tomb of the Cisterns," ca. 1700 (1984: 23–24).

With the discovery of these tombs and the evidence of other tombs in the area around the palace, Temple B1 and Sancturary B2, Matthiae began speaking of a "royal necropolis," which was the focus around which the three buildings revolved. For him the temple was dedicated to Rasap, the god of the netherworld, Sanctuary B2 was the location of the funerary rites of the cult, and the palace was probably the seat of the crown prince (cf. 1990: 353), who would have been responsible for carrying out the cult for the ancestors.[5]

But Matthiae's interpretation of this area is not very likely. Note the following points:

(1) There simply is no evidence that a "royal necropolis" exists in Areas B, C, and Q. The only excavated tombs that suggest a connection with royalty are the three located within the Western Palace. But they hardly constitute a royal cemetery. Each apparently was built for a single individual, one certainly female. The pottery dates the earliest tomb to the late 19th century, while the latest is dated ca. 1700. Only five or six other potential tombs have been noted in Areas Q, C, and B (see the plan and description of these tombs in Matthiae 1980a: 220–22), but they have provided no evidence of a royal nature. To the east of this area, in the sections of Area G called the "Southern Quarter" and the "Peripheral Section" (in grids Ea–g, IV10–8), along the southern rim of the acropolis, 27 Middle Bronze tombs were uncovered,

---

5. Further elaboration of this interpretation of the archaeological evidence has come from R. Dolce (1990: 126), who proposes that the eastern storerooms of the Western Palace, which are near the three tombs, might have served particularly to supply the functionaries who served in the funerary cult, which she sees as the primary function of this area of the town.

seven of them clearly built under the floors of houses, while the other 20 were in what appears to have been a cemetery, perhaps necessitated by the sudden deaths of many people, maybe as the result of an epidemic. All of them were simple burials, with one or two bodies per grave (D 24 has three bodies), a small number of pottery vessels, and modest personal items (Guardata 1988). Certainly none of these qualify as royal burials or even noble interments. Even if the three tombs in the Western Palace are royal tombs (and this is far from certain, it being just as likely that they belonged to high officials), three such tombs, constructed over a period of at least a century, do not constitute a royal necropolis.

It is further clear from the tombs in Area G that the practice of intramural burial was common in Middle Bronze Age Ebla, as was the practice of burial under the floors of houses. This is a cultural element found at numerous other sites in the Levant during this period.[6] But the presence of tombs in Areas Q, C, and B does not provide evidence regarding the functions of the buildings round about, any more than the presence of a tomb in a house turns that house into a cult building. Tomb B.72.A, the one located closest to Sanctuary B2, was found in the building adjoining B2 to the north and beside Temple B1. It would not be surprising if that tomb belonged to a priest related to Temple B1. But in no way does that tomb, or can that tomb, define the function of B2 or hint at the identity of the god worshiped in B1, any more than the substantial presence of tombs surrounding the Temples of Baal and Dagan at Ugarit (cf. Schaeffer 1931: 4–5; 1932: 16–20) suggests a mortuary function for those buildings.

So there is no evidence for identifying a royal necropolis, or true cemetery as such, in Areas Q, C, and B that can be used to suggest a unified function for the Western Palace, Temple B1 and Sanctuary B2.

(2) There are many reasons to doubt Matthiae's identification of B2 as a sanctuary for the cult of the dead, or as a sanctuary at all. First, as Matthiae himself has noted (1975: 68–69), there are no real parallels to a sanctuary with the type of floorplan found in B2. He has compared it tentatively with the so-called "Double Temple" in Area F of Hazor (Matthiae 1981: 63), and even more tentatively with the Square Building at the Amman Airport (1979: 567). Unfortunately, neither the character nor the function of these two buildings is well understood. The structure in Area F, Stratum 3, identified as a double temple by Yadin, the excavator, was very poorly preserved, and the editors of the recent publication of the excavations of Area F (Yadin, et al. 1989: 138–43) have pointed out that there is no evidence that either supports or disproves the identification of the building as a temple. In addi-

---

6. See, for example, Ugarit (Salles 1995: 173); Dan (Ilan 1995: 121); Megiddo (Kenyon 1970: 188–89).

tion, Yadin argued that the tomb system found below the "Double Temple" belonged to a stratum (Stratum 4) earlier than that of the "Temple" (Stratum 3).[7] Yadin believed that during the Middle Bronze IIC, the tunnels were converted for use as a drainage system (1975: 70–77). Thus there is no clear evidence to connect the building with a cult of the dead.

The enigmatic building found on the grounds of the Amman Airport also provides little help for interpreting B2 at Ebla. This large square building, with a central court flanked on all sides by rooms, only generally resembles the ground plan of B2. Its function remains uncertain, although there is evidence that it was used for some kind of mortuary rituals. A significant number of burned human bones were found in the building and around the structured rock pile nearby, bones that belonged primarily to adults. But whether one should interpret these as evidence that the building was a temple used for either human sacrifice or cult of the dead, or whether it was more specifically a storehouse for tomb furnishings beside a pyre for cremation, is impossible to say at this point (Herr 1983: 24–30; cf. Mazar 1990: 255–57). In any case, none of this resembles the situation at Ebla, where there is no hint around B2 (or anywhere else on the site) of the burning of human bodies, either as a burial custom or as a sacrifice. Nor were large numbers of human bones found in the building. In addition, the small finds in the Amman building, including the large amounts of imported Minoan and Mycenaean pottery, Egyptian vessels and scarabs, gold jewelry, etc., do not seem to compare to those found in B2. Nor are any of the furnishings of B2 (benches around central room, "altars," "sacrificial tables,") paralleled at the Amman building.

I believe that the evidence better suggests that B2 was a palatial or administrative structure rather than a sanctuary. Even the central area of the Western Palace at Ebla, while somewhat more complex than B2, has a squarish room surrounded by long, thin or squarish rooms that provide a closer parallel than any Middle Bronze temples in the Levant (cf. the plan of the palace in Dolce 1990: 141). Matthiae has noted that the northern section of B2 was clearly used for food storage and preparation (Matthiae 1990: 352). The central court with its benches and mudbrick dais provides little evidence of its function. Whether communal meals were celebrated in the room or not, there is nothing here that suggests a funerary character of such meals or even whether they had a specifically religious function at all.

Ambiguity of function is also a problem with the "altars" Matthiae identified in Rooms L. 2113 and 2140. Matthiae calls them "quite peculiar" altars

7. See the plan of Stratum 4, with the "Temple" superimposed on it in Yadin et al. 1989: 136–37; and the index of loci, pp. 159–63. Note, for example, that the entrance to Tomb 8185 appears to have been blocked by the wall of the "temple."

(1990: 352), with their two parallel, vertical slabs forming more or less a niche with a small brick podium inside, but he argues that they were designed to hold small bronze cult statues of deceased kings, which presumably played a role in the cult of the dead (1990: 352). Although such a proposal is feasible, it remains entirely speculative. No such statues have been found at Ebla (1990: 345–48), and none of the statues identified by Matthiae as depicting deified royal ancestors has been found in such a context at other sites.[8]

In addition, the location of these "altars" within the two rooms of B2 is peculiar and does not immediately suggest that they have a cultic, display function. In the long room, 2113, the structure is located in the northeast corner of the room, next to the doorway leading to Room 2115, and at the opposite end of the room from the "sacrificial offering tables." The one in Room 2140 is set up in the northeast corner of the room. The one parallel that Matthiae has cited for these "altars," in the Late Bronze Age Southern Temple at Tell Fray (Matthiae 1990: 352 n. 54; 1980c: 42–44, also Tav. V:2, VI), is found in a much more traditional temple, a longroom temple, with the pilasters ("altar") jutting out of the wall directly opposite the entrance to the room, with a podium directly in front of it. Its function is also ambiguous, but its context within the room and in relation to the podium is quite different from that of either installation in B2. This makes the Fray structure difficult to use to illuminate the function of those at Ebla.

A more striking parallel, however, comes from a Middle Bronze II patrician's house at Tell Beit Mirsim in Israel (Stratum D, see Albright 1938: 35–39; pls. 14–15; 51; 55). Room 1, a square storage room off the main courtyard, is provided with an installation quite similar to those in B2, and the room itself is similar to Room 2140. The niche here is placed in the corner of the room, like the one in Room 2140, and it appears from the photograph (Albright 1938: pl. 15a) to have had a raised floor. Although it is not clear what use was made of this niche, there can be little doubt that it had to do with storage, since the room itself was without question a storeroom. Within it were found fourteen storejars still partially in place (Albright 1938: 37). This leads us to suspect that the similar installations in B2 also had a storage function of some kind. Such a function would also make sense in terms of the installations' location in the back, downstairs rooms of the building. This seems particularly obvious for the small, isolated, square Room 2140.

The "offering tables for blood sacrifice" also merit some attention. As far as I am aware, Matthiae has not published any evidence, such as traces of blood on the tables or the bench, that would show that these tables were ac-

---

8. In fact, Matthiae's identification of these statuettes as depictions of deified dead kings (Matthiae 1990: 345–48) is far from substantiated and is heavily influenced by a number of the presuppositions that have been questioned above.

tually used for the slaughter of animals. In fact, their location in a back room of the building seems an odd place for the preparation of animals for sacrifice. I am unaware of any clear parallels for the two tables as interpreted, either in the function of animal sacrifice or in such a location within a cultic building.

Here, too, it seems worthwhile to examine other possible interpretations of the evidence, and once again, more mundane parallels suggest a much less exotic identification of these tables. In Syria–Palestine, the most common identifiable function for large shallow tables with drainage spouts is that of an olive press. Several such presses have been found in the excavations at Ugarit and elsewhere (see Callot 1987). Some of them are rectangular in shape, while others are round. None of the Ugarit examples exhibit such fine crafts-manship as those in B2, but if the latter was the house of a nobleman or a building owned by the king, such well-made presses might be in order.

The process of extracting oil from olives required three major proce-dures: crushing the olives, pressing them, then separating the water from the oil. In the first procedure, the olives were broken open to allow for the escape of the oil. Little is known of the details of this practice from Middle and Late Bronze Age sites, but it seems likely that it was done in stone mortars or on flat stones (Ben-Tor and Portugali 1987: [Qiri] 134–36). Nor is the location where the process occurred always discernible archaeologically. In some houses at Ugarit and elsewhere (see Callot 1987: 203–5, figs. 8 and 9; also Gitin 1990: 36–38) a crushing stone or basin has been found in a room or courtyard adjoining the room with the press. But many sites have produced no evidence for this part of the process in the buildings where the press was located (Hopkins 1985: 231).

In the second part of the procedure, the crushed olives were placed in baskets or sacks and taken to a press. Different types of presses are known dur-ing the Middle/Late Bronze and Iron Ages (Borowski 1987: 119–21). The kind that is relevant for our purposes consisted of a large, flattish stone, with a slightly carved-out center and a spout on one side. The baskets or sacks were put on the table and heavy stones were placed on top of them to squeeze the oil from the olives. The basket or sack acted as a strainer, and the relatively pure oil then drained through it, down the spout and into a jar that could be taken and poured into larger storejars elsewhere at regular intervals (Callot 1987: 207; Borowski 1987: 120–22). Two presses beside one another are at-tested at Tel Dan from the 10th century B.C.E. (Stager and Wolff 1981). The beam press, which allowed extra pressure to be placed on the weights pressing the olives, is not known until the Late Bronze Age (Callot 1987: 206).[9] Some of the press tables are round (Callot 1987: 206), but several rectangular ones

---

9. The beam press apparently was not introduced in Palestine until the Iron II period. See Borowski 1987: 122–23; Hopkins 1985: 231–32.

have been discovered from the Late Bronze and Iron Ages (cf. particularly the one published by Callot [1987: 198, fig. 1 and the other examples on p. 206]). The two tables in Building B2 may quite plausibly be identified as olive oil pressing tables. The presence of oil manufacturing facilities in B2 fits in well with the overall context of the building and may explain the function of the storeroom filled with pithoi in the northern section, which could have been the repository for the oil.

If one accepts the identification of the tables as belonging to oil processing, then a tantilizing parallel can be noted between the tables and niches in Rooms 2113 and 2140 and installations at Iron Age Tell Miqne in Israel. Excavators there have found an extensive area of olive oil production dating to the 7th century B.C.E., occupied by a number of shops with crushing and pressing installations (Gitin 1989, 1990). Each of these shops also had at least one incense altar, usually located in the anterooms of the buildings (Gitin 1989: 60*; 1990: 39). One of these altars was located in a stone niche, ca. 25 inches high, which protruded out from the wall in the same manner as the two "altar" installations in B2 (see the photo in 1990: 39). Might this have been the function for these installations at Ebla? Gitin has suggested that the incense altars at Ekron may have had a dual purpose, first to provide propitiation to the gods, and second, to deodorize the air in the shops (1990: 40; see also Gitin 1992 for a defense of the identification of these altars as incense altars). Such a dual function, while not attested archaeologically at any other site, is certainly something that might be used in different locales and cultures. However, I am reluctant to press this parallel, since some 1000 years separate the buildings at Ebla and Miqne, and the cultural differences between the Semitic Eblaites and the Philistine Ekronites must be taken into account. In any event, no such altars were found in B2.

We may conclude from all this that the interpretations drawn by Matthiae have gone well beyond the evidence in identifying B2 as a sanctuary for the worship of deified royal ancestors. None of the evidence adduced by Matthiae really points toward such a function. The building may be more plausibly interpreted as part of the royal complex around the Western Palace, functioning perhaps in the production and storage of various foodstuffs.[10] Because this identification is a foundational element in Matthiae's reconstruction of the function of a large part of Areas B, C, and Q at Ebla, recognition of the weakness of his identification of B2 throws his entire interpretation into question.

---

10. V. Fritz (1980: 60–61) also viewed B2 as a palatial structure rather than a temple, but he did not discuss the reasons for his conclusions.

Conclusion

All of this reinforces my primary theme that we as scholars need to be more careful than we often are in how we interpret archaeological evidence. It is deceptively easy to move from a small, unfounded speculation to the construction of an entire theoretical edifice that is based on little or no firm evidence. Such moves have created great confusion in various areas of the study of Israel's religion and history. This is not a call for us to be overly skeptical about everything (I would not place myself in the camp of the so-called biblical minimalists), nor is it a call to banish speculation from the floor of scholarly discourse. But it is a call to make sure that we build our reconstructions of Israelite thought more soundly by judiciously and seriously considering exactly what the evidence can tell us and by labeling speculation clearly and carefully when moving beyond the evidence.

Bibliography

Albright, William F.
　　1938　　*The Excavation of Tell Beit Mirsim, Volume II: The Bronze Age.* AASOR 17. New Haven: ASOR.
　　1957　　The High Place in Ancient Palestine. Pp. 242–58 in *Volume du Congrés: Strasbourg 1956.* VTSup 4. Leiden: Brill.
　　1968　　*Yahweh and the Gods of Canaan.* Garden City, N.Y.: Doubleday. Reprinted, Winona Lake, Ind.: Eisenbrauns. 1979.
Barrick, W. Boyd
　　1975　　The Funerary Character of "High-Places" in Ancient Palestine: A Reassessment. *VT* 25: 565–595.
Ben-Tor, Amnon, and Portugali, Y.
　　1987　　*Tell Qiri: A Village in the Jezreel Valley.* Qedem 24. Jerusalem: Institute of Archaeology, Hebrew University.
Bloch-Smith, Elizabeth
　　1992　　*Judahite Burial Practices and Beliefs About the Dead.* JSOT Supplement Series 123. Sheffield: JSOT Press.
Borowski, Oded
　　1987　　*Agriculture in Iron Age Israel.* Winona Lake, Ind.: Eisenbrauns.
Callot, Olivier
　　1987　　Les huileries du Bronze Récent à Ugarit. Pp. 197–212 in Marguerite Yon (ed.), *Le Centre de la ville, 38ᵉ–44ᵉ campagnes (1978–1984).* Ras Shamra-Ougarit 3. Paris: Éditions Recherche sur les Civilisations.
　　1994　　*La tranchée "Ville Sud": Études d'architecture domestique.* RSO X. Paris: Éditions Recherche sur les Civilisations.
Chapman, Robert; Kinnes, Ian; and Randsborg, Klavs, eds.
　　1981　　*The Archaeology of Death.* Cambridge: Cambridge University.

Cooley, Robert E.
    1983   Gathered to His People: A Study of a Dothan Family Tomb. Pp. 47–58
            in Morris Inch and Ronald Youngblood (eds.), *The Living and Active*
            Word of God: Studies in Honor of Samuel J. Schultz. Winona Lake, Ind.:
            Eisenbrauns.

Dolce, Rita
    1990   Les Magasins et les lieux de traitement des denrées alimentaires à Ebla au
            IIIème et au IIème millénaires. *AAAS* 40: 122–45.

Gitin, Seymour
    1989   Incense Altars from Ekron, Israel, and Judah: Context and Typology.
            ErIsr 20: 52*–67*.
    1990   Ekron of the Philistines, Part II: Olive-Oil Suppliers to the World.
            BARev 16/2: 32–42.
    1992   New Incense Altars from Ekron: Context, Typology, and Function. *ErIsr*
            23: 43–49.

Gonen, R.
    1992   *Burial Patterns and Cultural Diversity in Late Bronze Age Canaan*. ASOR
            Dissertation Series 7. Winona Lake, Ind.: Eisenbrauns.

Guardata, Francesca B.
    1988   Les Sépultures d'Ebla à l'Age du Bronze Moyen. Pp. 3–20 in *Wirtschaft*
            und Gesellschaft von Ebla. Heidelberger Studien zum Alten Orient 2.
            Heidelberg: Heidelberger Orientverlag.

Herr, Larry G. (ed.)
    1983   *The Amman Airport Excavations, 1976*. AASOR 48. Winona Lake, Ind.:
            ASOR/Eisenbrauns.

Hopkins, David C.
    1985   *The Highlands of Canaan*. Social World of Biblical Antiquity Series 3.
            Sheffield: Almond.

Humphreys, S. C.
    1981   Introduction: Comparative Perspectives on Death. Pp. 1–13 in S. C.
            Humphreys and Helen King (eds.), *Mortality and Immortality: The An-*
            thropology and Archaeology of Death. London: Academic Press.

Ilan, David
    1995   Mortuary Practices at Tel Dan in the Middle Bronze Age: A Reflection
            of Canaanite Society and Ideology. Pp. 117–139 in Stuart Campbell and
            Anthony Green (eds.), *The Archaeology of Death in the Ancient Near East*.
            Oxford: Oxbow.

Kenyon, Kathleen
    1970   *Archaeology in the Holy Land*. Third Edition. New York: Praeger.

Loebl, Walter Y.
    1995   A Case of Symmers' Fibrosis of the Liver during the 18th Dynasty?
            Pp. 185–187 in Stuart Campbell and Anthony Green (eds.), *The Ar-*
            chaeology of Death in the Ancient Near East. Oxford: Oxbow.

Loretz, Oswald
    1978   Vom kanaanäischen Totenkult zur jüdischen Patriarchen- und Elter-
            nehrung: Historische und tiefenpsychologische Grundprobleme der Ent-

stehung des biblischen Geschichtsbildes und der jüdischen Ethik. *Jahrbuch für Anthropologie und Religionsgeschichte* 3: 149–204.

1990   *Ugarit und die Bibel: Kanaanäische Götter und Religion im Alten Testament.* Darmstadt: Wissenschaftliche Buchgesellschaft.

Macalister, R. A. S.

1912   *The Excavation of Gezer: 1902–1905 and 1907–1909.* Two Volumes. London: John Murray.

MacKenzie, Duncan

1912–13   *Excavations at Ain Shems (Beth Shemesh).* Annual of the Palestine Exploration Fund 1912–1913. London: Palestine Exploration Fund.

Martin-Achard, Robert

1960   *From Death to Life.* Trans. from the French by John P. Smith. Edinburgh/London: Oliver & Boyd.

Matthiae, Paolo

1974   Tell Mardikh. *Archéologia* 69: 17–31.

1975   Unité et développement du temple dans la Syrie du Bronze Moyen. Pp. 43–72 in *Le temple et le culte.* Istanbul: Nederlands Historisch-Archeologisch Instituut.

1979   Princely Cemetery and Ancestors Cult at Ebla During Middle Bronze II: A Proposal of Interpretation. *UF* 11: 563–69.

1980a   L'Area cemeteriale principesca nella citta bassa di Ebla amorrea. *La Parola del Passato* 192: 212–31.

1980b   Campagne de fouilles à Ebla en 1979: Les tombes princières et le palais de la ville basse à l'époque amorrhéenne. *CRAIBL*: 94–118.

1980c   Ittiti ed assiri a Tell Fray: lo scavo de una città medio-Siriana sull'Eufrate, *Studi micenei ed egeo-anatolici* 22: 35–51.

1980d   Two Princely Tombs at Tell Mardikh-Ebla. *Archaeology* 33: 9–17.

1981a   *Ebla: An Empire Rediscovered.* Garden City: Doubleday.

1981b   A Hypothesis on the Princely Burial Area of Middle Bronze II at Ebla. *Archiv Orientalní* 49: 55–65.

1984   New Discoveries at Ebla: The Excavation of the Western Palace and the Royal Necropolis of the Amorite Period. *Biblical Archaeologist* 47: 18–32.

1990   A Class of Old Syrian Bronze Statuettes and the Sanctuary B2 at Ebla. Pp. 345–60 in P. Matthiae, M. van Loon and H. Weiss (eds.), *Resurrecting the Past: A Joint Tribute to Adnan Bounni.* Istanbul: Nederlands Historisch-Archaeologisch Instituut.

Mazar, Amihai

1990   *Archaeology of the Land of the Bible 10,000–586 B.C.E.* New York: Doubleday.

Olmo Lete, Gregorio del

1992   *La Religión Cananea según la liturgia de Ugarit.* Aula Orientalis Supplementa 3. Barcelona. Editorial AUSA.

1999   *Canaanite Religion according to the Liturgical Text of Ugarit.* Bethesda, Md.: CDL.

Pitard, Wayne T.
1992   The Practice and Function of Feeding the Dead in Canaan, Egypt and Israel. Paper read at the National Meeting of the Society of Biblical Literature. San Francisco, California.

1994   The "Libation Installations" of the Tombs at Ugarit. *Biblical Archaeologist.* 57: 20–37.

1999   The *Rpum* Texts. Pp. 259–269 in W. G. E. Watson and N. Wyatt (eds.), *Handbook of Ugaritic Studies.* Handbuch der Orientalistik 39. Leiden: Brill.

Pope, Marvin
1977   *The Song of Songs.* Anchor Bible 7C. Garden City, N.Y.: Doubleday.

Prausnitz, M. W.
1969   Israelite and Sidonian Burial Rites at Akhziv. Pp. 85–89 in Pinchas Peli (ed.), *Proceedings of the Fifth World Congress of Jewish Studies.* Jerusalem: R. H. Hacohen.

Ribar, J. W.
1973   *Death Cult Practices in Ancient Palestine.* Ph.D. Diss. University of Michigan.

Roberts, Charlotte A.; Lee, Frances; and Bintliff, John
1989   *Burial Archaeology: Current Research, Methods and Developments.* British Archaeological Reports, British Series 211. Oxford: BAR.

Salles, J.-F.
1987   Deux nouvelles tombes de Ras Shamra. Pp. 157–95 in M. Yon (ed.), *Le centre de la ville: 38ᵉ-44ᵉ campagnes (1978–1984).* Ras Shamra-Ougarit 3. Paris: Éditions Recherche sur les Civilisations.

1995   Rituel Mortuaire et Rituel Social à Ras Shamra/Ougarit. Pp. 171–84 in Stuart Campbell and Anthony Green (eds.), *The Archaeology of Death in the Ancient Near East.* Oxford: Oxbow.

Schaeffer, C. F.-A.
1931   Les fouilles de Minet-el-Beida et de Ras Shamra: Deuxième campagne (Printemps 1930): Rapport sommaire. *Syria* 12: 1–14.

1932   Les fouilles de Minet-el-Beida et de Ras-Shamra: Troisième campagne (Printemps 1931): Rapport sommaire. *Syria* 13: 1–27.

1939a   *The Cuneiform Texts of Ras Shamra-Ugarit.* Schweich Lectures 1936. London: Oxford University.

Schmidt, Brian
1994   *Israel's Beneficent Dead: Ancestor Cult and Necromancy in Ancient Israelite Religion and Tradition.* Tübingen: J. C. B. Mohr. Reprinted, Winona Lake, Ind.: 1996.

Schumacher, G.
1908   *Tell el-Mutesellim I.* Leipzig: Rudolf Haupt.

Seger, Joe D.
1988   *Gezer V: The Field I Caves.* Jerusalem: Hebrew Union College/Nelson Glueck School of Biblical Archaeology.

Spencer, A. J.
1982   *Death in Ancient Egypt.* London: Penguin.

Spronk, Klaas
  1986   *Beatific Afterlife in Ancient Israel and in the Ancient Near East.* AOAT 219.
            Kevelaer: Butzon and Bercker.
Stager, Lawrence E., and Wolff, Samuel R.
  1981   Production and Commerce in Temple Courtyards: An Olive Press in the
            Sacred Precinct at Tel Dan. BASOR 243: 95–102.
Stern, Ephraim (ed.)
  1993   *The New Encyclopedia of Archaeological Excavations in the Holy Land.* Four
            volumes. New York: Simon and Schuster.
Tappy, Ron
  1995   Did the Dead Ever Die in Biblical Judah? BASOR 298: 59–68.
Thornton, Francis
  1995   Change in Oral Pathology through Time of Nile Valley Populations, Pre-
            dynastic to Roman. Pp. 41–44 in Stuart Campbell and Anthony Green
            (eds.), *The Archaeology of Death in the Ancient Near East.* Oxford: Oxbow.
Ucko, Peter J.
  1969   Ethnography and Archaeological Interpretation of Funerary Remains,
            World Archaeology 1: 262–80.
Ussishkin, David
  1993   *The Village of Silwan: The Necropolis from the Period of the Judean Kingdom.*
            Jerusalem: Israel Exploration Society.
Yadin, Yigael, et al.
  1958   *Hazor I: An Account of the First Season of Excavations, 1955.* Jerusalem:
            Magnes.
  1975   *Hazor: The Rediscovery of a Great Citadel of the Bible.* New York: Random
            House.
  1989   *Hazor III–IV: An Account of the Third and Fourth Seasons of Excavation,
            1957–58: Text.* Edited by Amnon Ben-Tor. Jerusalem: Israel Exploration
            Society / Hebrew University.

How Far Can Texts Take Us?
Evaluating Textual Sources for Reconstructing Ancient Israelite Beliefs about the Dead

THEODORE J. LEWIS
The Johns Hopkins University

Introduction

An Opportune Time

Reexamining ancient Israelite notions about the dead is important for our time. On the academic side, new research challenging a long-held consensus regarding the presence of death cults in ancient Israel as well as new hermeneutical models that diminish the historical worth of the biblical text have forced us to reevaluate the accuracy with which we can say anything about ancient Israel's mortuary cults. On the practical side, the raging debate in Israel regarding the excavations of tombs[1] begs for a greater dialogue to underscore the worth of the archaeological enterprise as well as the preservation and respect of ancestral remains.

I am pleased that ASOR saw fit to explore further the interface of archaeology and textual studies and the contributions and limitations of each for reconstructing the religion of ancient Israel as it pertains to death.[2] The triad will be complete when these two fields are combined with a systematic

---

Author's note: This essay was completed in 1997 during a research fellowship at the Center for Advanced Judaic Studies of the University of Pennsylvania. I am very grateful to the center for its superb staff and resources; to the University of Georgia, which provided a leave of absence for research; and to the University of Georgia Office of the Vice-President for Research for travel support.

1. See Shanks 1996 and Shiloh 1997. On the Hesed Shel Emet burial society, see Halevi 1997.

2. For a recent attempt at correlating the archaeology of burial practices and textual material in Mesopotamia (Nippur), see Postgate 1990.

treatment of the iconography of death.[3] For ancient Israel, the latter needs to be gleaned primarily from the archaeological record, word-pictures, and comparative material. Artistic representation of death coming from the ancient Semitic world is sparse when compared to that of the illustrated mortuary texts from Egypt (such as the Book of the Dead, which inherited traditions from the Coffin Texts of the Middle Kingdom, which in turn were the heir of the Pyramid Texts of the Old Kingdom), as well as pictorial representations on tomb walls, coffins, and the *ꜣḫ iḳr n Rꜥ*-stelae.[4]

The focus of my remarks will be textual, both biblical and extrabiblical. In addition to the material found in the Hebrew Bible, it is essential to treat the inscriptional material,[5] fragmentary though it may be, as well as comparative material coming from elsewhere in the ancient Near East. This latter corpus is extremely relevant, for it has been used extensively by scholars to reconstruct ancient Israelite beliefs about the dead. In fact, in some cases, scholars have treated the comparative sources from ancient Egypt, Mesopotamia, and Ugarit as more influential than the biblical texts themselves. I will be treating the texts that have a bearing on reconstructing ancient Israelite religion of the Iron Age. I will leave for other specialists the treatment of Jewish funerary inscriptions and other literary material written in Hebrew, Aramaic, and Greek coming from Hellenistic and Roman times.[6]

A Complex Endeavor

Anthropologists, sociologists, poets, and artists have each in a unique way documented the human fascination with the mysteries of death. Topics range from pragmatic concerns of burial and mourning rites to musings on the nature and disposition of the dead and on the images of the netherworld in which they live. A historian of Israelite religion is at a decided disadvantage in understanding ancient conceptions of death because he/she is so far removed both chronologically and culturally. Even though we can rely on both archaeological and textual sources to fine-tune our reconstructions, the com-

---

3. Keel (1997: 62–73) has already written an initial treatment. Like most disciplines, iconographic study is not an exact science. Thus compare Keel's treatment of tomb headrests (1987) with Barkay's reevaluation (1988).

4. For introductions to the iconography of death elsewhere in the ancient Near East, see ANEP ##630–43; Hornung 1995: 1718–23; Demarée 1983; Schulman 1986; Niwinski 1988; Porada 1980; Hawkins 1980. Porada (1980: 259) attributes the "relative paucity of images" of death in Mesopotamia to their fear of death.

5. For a convenient collection of Palestinian funerary inscriptions, see Puech 1992 with bibliography.

6. See Puech 1992: 130–34 and his bibliography, to which now may be added Healey 1993; Rahmani 1994.

plexity of the task and our inability to arrive at a full and accurate synthesis needs to be underscored. Because we are so far removed from the Iron Age, we must resist homogenizing the relatively little data we do possess into a monolithic society that never existed. There is no catholic response to death, be it inter- or intracultural. Societies are rarely so monolithic or simplistic. The best we can do is approximate the situation.

Advantage: Archaeology

That the nature of burial practice is a complex endeavor has been a truism underscored by social archaeologists ever since Ucko's ethnographic study almost thirty years ago. As a student of texts, I value the tremendous potential of archaeology for uncovering such diversity. This potential has yet to be fully realized, but we may hope that the near future will showcase the finesse of modern archaeology with its interdisciplinary sophistication (physical anthropology, social archaeology, and so forth), its ability to utilize the best of modern technology (medical imaging, DNA analysis, and so on), and its embrace of various though complementary theoretical approaches.[7]

Physical Death

When it comes to describing physical death, archaeology can be far more precise than texts. Like a text, the patterns in burial practice must be "interpreted" to flesh out cultural values and questions concerning rank and social status. But when it comes to bones, the physical anthropologist can measure them empirically without any worry about sifting through the layers of editorial activity that I must face as a text scholar.

Often my texts are mute. The Bible does not always tell the age of a person at death and all too often we must be satisfied with formulaic generalities about a person dying at 'a ripe old age' (*śēbâ tôbâ*) being 'full of days' (*mĕlē' yāmîm*) or, if one's life is cut short, being 'short of days' (*qĕṣar yāmîm*).[8] In contrast, my archaeological colleagues, after "reading" their evidence, can come up with a close approximation of an individual's actual biological age. Even when my textual sources are more specific about the age of one's death,

---

7. For a recent attempt to combine various theoretical approaches for the funerary practices at MB Tel Dan, see Ilan 1995. For various papers devoted to mortuary practices and social organization in the Levant, see two forthcoming issues of *Near Eastern Archaeology*, with papers by A. Berlin, E. Bloch-Smith, G. Gilmour, R. Hallote, D. Ilan, A. Joffe, A. Porter, and S. Wolff.

8. For the various Hebrew expressions for longevity and ancient Near Eastern cognate expressions, see Malamat 1982. The extrabiblical inscriptional material is of little help. See the blessing for old age in a Khirbet el-Qôm tomb inscription (McCarter 1996).

one may doubt the reference is to actual biological age because, as noted already by Malamat (1982: 218), "biblical literature (and ancient Near Eastern literature generally) treats life span as an expression of moral and religious evaluation, long life a divine reward, and short life a punishment."

In the Bible, bones only come to life when Ezekiel speaks divine breath into them (Ezek 37:1–14) or when Elisha's bones perform healing miracles in death much as the prophet did in life (2 Kgs 13:20–21). Even though I read that Jeremiah's and Job's bones "are all shook up" (Jer 23:9; Job 4:14) and the psalmist's bones are "out of joint" (Ps 22:15), the text tells me precious little about how an ancient Israelite writer viewed and handled skeletons. Granted, I can read of occasional references to the treatment of bones, including their burial (1 Sam 31:13, 2 Sam 21:12–14),[9] their protection if the individual was righteous (2 Kgs 23:17–18), their desecration and/or use in defiling non-Yahwistic altars (Amos 2:1, 1 Kgs 13:2, 2 Kgs 23:14–16, 2 Chr 34:5, Ezek 6:5), and their use in imprecations (Jer 8:1, Ps 141:7). And while I can also read of an assortment of sickness and disease, I quickly agree with the palaeopathologist Zias (1991: 147; cf. 1997) that "the Bible . . . was not intended to serve as a medical text."

In contrast, physical anthropologists and archaeologists (if they reach their full potential) can resurrect information from skeletal remains to chart, not only an individual's age, but also his/her gender, diet, and physiological history. From skeletal remains, palaeopathologists can trace an assortment of illnesses (for example, parasitic infections, infectious diseases, leprosy, venereal disease, tuberculosis, trauma, and mutilation) and perhaps even determine which was the cause of death.[10]

Burial Practice

It is difficult to envision an actual burial from my meager textual evidence. Unless an individual is a prominent biblical personage, I have no record of the location of his/her tomb. Common graves go virtually unmentioned; only important graves such as the Abrahamic cave of Machpelah (Gen 49:29–31) or David's and Solomon's tombs in the City of David (1 Kgs 2:10, 11:43; 2 Chr 9:31) or those of people of higher social status deserved mention (Bloch-Smith 1992a: 114–21). From time to time I read of communal ("lay my bones beside his bones," 1 Kgs 13:31) and even mass burials (2 Sam 21:2–4). Once I read of a type of cremation.[11] Sometimes the text

9. Although the text is broken, bones of a husband and his slave-wife are mentioned as residing together in the royal steward's tomb in Avigad 1953: 143.

10. See Zias 1991, 1997; P. Smith 1997.

11. 1 Sam 31:12 describes the burning of the bodies of Saul and his sons, yet their bones are then buried.

might tell me of a burial under a tree (1 Sam 31:13, 1 Chr 10:12, Gen 35:8; cf. Bloch-Smith 1992a: 114–15), in a hewn-rock cliff (Shebna's tomb in Isa 22:16; cf. 2 Kgs 23:16, Isa 57:7), or even in a commoner's burial plot (*qeber/ qibrê běnê hā'ām*) such as the one in the Kidron Valley (2 Kgs 23:6; cf. Jer 26:23). I can even read of the exhumation of bones and the lack of burial being used in imprecations by Jeremiah (8:1). Yet in the end, words such as *qeber* or *qěburâ* on a page of text do not allow me to picture the size and quality of a tomb or the actual interment of a corpse. Likewise, the terms *maṣṣēbâ* (Gen 35:20), *ṣîyyûn* (1 Kgs 13:30, 2 Kgs 23:15–18), and *yad* (2 Sam 18:18; cf. Isa 56:5, 57:8)[12] leave me guessing about the shape and size of burial markers. And only rarely can one read of the spices or perfumes used in the actual interment process (Jer 34:5, 2 Chr 16:14).

In contrast, an archaeologist can paint a marvelous portrait of the types and quality of tombs, *maṣṣēbôt* beyond numbering, various stages of burial rites, and sometimes even repeated actions that might constitute a cult of the dead. To be sure, some aspects of an archaeologist's reconstruction of these matters are necessarily impressionistic, yet from the text alone one could never generate the diversity of Iron Age burials that, as marvelously catalogued by Bloch-Smith, include: (a) simple graves, (b) cist graves, (c) jar burials, (d) anthropoid, wooden, and stone-coffin burials, (e) bathtub coffin burials, (f) cave, shaft, and chamber tombs, (g) bench and arcosolia tombs, (h) above-ground monolithic tombs, (i) cemeteries, and (j) cremation burials.[13]

The texts speak to me in idioms such as the characteristic P phraseology of the dead being 'gathered to his kin' *way-yē'āsēp 'el 'ammāyw* (Gen 25:8, 17; 35:29; 49:29, 33; Num 20:24, 26; 27:13; 31:2; Deut 32:50) or the Deuteronomist's 'lying with one's ancestors' *šākab 'im 'ǎbôtāyw*.[14] Expressions like these help me to appreciate the familial and clan solidarity that was seen to transcend life,[15] yet they do not tell me of physical death or interment. In contrast,

---

12. On 2 Sam 18:18 and Isa 57:8, see Lewis 1989: 118–20, 149–50. On Isa 56:5, see Van Winkle 1997.

13. See Bloch-Smith's well-documented appendix and series of figures (1992a: 152–271).

14. See also now the expression *wyškb 'by yhk 'l ['bhw]h* 'my father lay down, he went to his [ancestors]', in the Tel Dan Aramaic inscription as reconstructed by Biran and Naveh (1995: 12–14). The Deir 'Alla texts also contain the expression *tškb mškby 'lmyk lhlq* 'you will lie down on your eternal bed (= the funerary bench) to die' (*Deir 'Allā* II 11). See Hoftijzer and Jongeling 1995, s.v. *škb* and *mškb*. On the biblical phraseology, see the in-depth study by A. Alfrink (1948). See also G. R. Driver 1962; Wächter 1967: 71ff.; and Tromp 1969: 168–71; Illman 1979: 43–45; and van Keulen 1996.

15. The solidarity felt with one's ancestors is also reflected in the use of kinship terms as theophoric elements. See van der Toorn 1996b.

archaeologists can not only point to the physical gathering of the deceased to his kin in secondary burials, but they can also chart patterns concerning "the orientation and position of the interred; the number of interments per tomb and per burial type; and the age/sex distribution of interments per burial or tomb type" (Ilan 1995: 119).

Grave Goods

Never do the canonical texts give me an inventory of what was placed in the tomb at the time of interment.[16] I cannot read of the adornment of the dead or the enclosure of items that were thought to aid the deceased in the afterlife. In striking contrast, in a tomb one can study the quantity and quality of burials goods and correlate the value of each to the gender and age of the deceased.[17] Moreover, archaeology can help us make an intimate connection with the ancient dead: in a tomb one can hold the very jewelry considered dear enough to accompany a beloved deceased. Once again, Bloch-Smith's catalogue of grave goods from Iron Age burials could never have been itemized by use of the text alone. I would never have known that items placed with the deceased would include: (a) pottery of all shapes and sizes including bowls, lamps, juglets, and assorted vessels for food preparation, (b) jewelry ranging from rings, bracelets, and earrings to amulets and pendants, (c) personal items including clothing and grooming articles, seals and stamps, game pieces, and so on, (d) tools befitting a wide variety of trades, and (e) the famous terra-cotta "pillar" figurines.[18]

Social Phenomena

It is therefore quite clear that tombs and their contents allow archaeologists to draw inferences about rank and social persona that go beyond inferences drawn from the Hebrew Bible. The biblical texts are limited in nature, having been written and edited by presumably elite, educated persons. Consequently, they are not reflective of society at large.

This is not to say that archaeology, especially social archaeology, is an assumption-free, empirical science that works solely with the *bruta facta*. As

16. Compare, however, the rare description of funerary furnishings preserved in a pre-Sargonic Sumerian text, perhaps from Adab (UCLM 9-1798 in Foxvog 1980). Compare also the use of *taklimtu* to designate grave goods rather than the deceased lying in state (Scurlock 1991: #3; 1995b: 100ff.).

17. See Bloch-Smith (1992a: 68, 140), who notes that quantity and quality of grave goods increase with age.

18. Once again, I am indebted to the splendid catalogue prepared by Bloch-Smith (1992a: 72–103). For bibliography on the pillar figurines, see Lewis 1998; to which add Kletter 1996 and Gilbert-Peretz 1996.

Brandfon has correctly stated, "material evidence, although exceptionally valuable, is no more intrinsically accurate or objective than any other kind of evidence."[19] Indeed, when it comes to the interpretation of funerary material, the assumptions are readily admitted, as can be seen in the works of Saxe, Binford, Ucko, Levy and Alon, and others. For example, Levy and Alon assume, along with Binford, that "deceased individuals of higher rank will be entitled to a larger amount of corporate involvement in the act of interment and to a greater degree of disruption or normal community activities for the mortuary rite." Following Tainter and Gordy, they assume that "both corporate involvement and disruption of activity will correspond to the amount of human energy expended in the mortuary act." Finally, they assume "that energy expenditure, as reflected in mortuary remains, is an adequate measure of differences among ranks" (Levy and Alon 1982: 42).

Summary Statement about Archaeology

In sum, archaeology has great potential for exploring our topic of death in ancient Israel. Archaeologists need to explore the limitations of their material and decide whether we have a large enough statistical sampling coming from well-dated sites (cf. Holladay 1987: 282).

Archaeologists should be the final arbiters on the degree to which archaeology should be a purely descriptive science articulating burial practice[20] or a science that includes an inferential component where the artifactual record is used to make statements regarding social organization, cultural values, and ultimately religious beliefs. (Do amulets imply warding off ghosts? [see Bloch-Smith 1992a: 83–86]; do tools mean the dead engaged in "daily chores to meet their physical needs after death"? [see Bloch-Smith 1992a: 90]; are ostrich eggshells in tombs symbolic of "the principle of life, the continuity of generations"? [see Moscati 1988: 456]; do candles in tombs light the way to the underworld? [so Greenhut 1995: 32]; does death have a fertility function? [Ilan 1995: 135–36]; and so on). I am drawn toward studies such as Brody's (forthcoming) that combine the archaeology of death within ethnohistorical and ethnographic frameworks in order to produce "aspects of funeral ceremonies and beliefs about the dead . . . which go beyond just the presentation of the archaeology of the burials." When it comes to the hermeneutics of archaeology, I would side with Ilan that "ceremonial behavior,

---

19. Brandfon 1987: 43. See also his remarks on p. 7, where he criticizes claims such as those of S. Piggott that archaeology is "*absolutely free* from the bias and ignorance which so frequently distort the statements of the historian" (emphasis mine).

20. Cf. Davis 1988: 180: "It is far easier to adopt a purely descriptive approach to burial practice while ignoring an analysis of the ritual of religious acts which accompanied the whole practice."

religious beliefs and social systems are clearly interrelated and should not be disassociated" (Ilan 1995: 132).[21] As always (and especially for dealing with the realm of Mot), the devil is in the details.

The Use of Texts

In light of the poverty of textual information that I have described above and the great potential for information coming from the archaeological record, it would be easy to minimize the contributions of the text. Add to this the skepticism of new hermeneutical approaches, and one may be tempted to cease using the text altogether. I would counter that if one is moderate in judgment and not prone to making overstatements, the text can still yield a wealth of information.

Indeed, just as M. Miller has concluded that it is "theoretically possible"—although not advisable—to write a history of ancient Israel without the Hebrew Bible, a similar conclusion applies to writing ancient Israel's *religious* history. I would argue that, while it is theoretically possible to chart ancient Israel's religious beliefs regarding the dead apart from the text, the final product would be so incomplete and so minimalist that it would warp our perception greater than any damage that could be done by having an incomplete picture of a text's redactional history. Miller's comment is astute: "The important question is not *whether* we should use the Hebrew Bible . . . but *how* we should use it" (Miller 1991: 101). Hallo (1990), in correctly challenging the limits of our skepticism, argues for a critical sifting of each fragmentary bit of the limited evidence we have so that we can make valid inferences from the text. And here the details may be far more devilish.

Advantage: Texts

Texts are uniquely suited for unpacking religious belief. There are a myriad of questions for which the material culture has no answers. What words did the ancients use to describe the dead and their state/condition? What did the ancients think happened to the life force that once inhabited the flesh?

---

21. For a more complete synthesis, see Ilan 1995: 119; Ilan suggests the following line of questioning: "What do patterns in burial practice indicate on the social and ideological plane? Do particular burials or tomb types, burial goods, interment methods, etc., indicate ecological circumstances, social status, wealth, or a belief system? What do deviations from recognised patterns mean? Which patterns at [a particular site] occur elsewhere and which do not, and why? Where do burial practices originate? How much cultural homogeneity and continuity exists in the Near East . . . and what does this homogeneity and continuity, or lack of it, reveal about the diffusion of ideas and/or movement of peoples."

Did they hold to a belief in an afterlife? Where were the dead thought to re-side, and were they thought to have a patron deity? Was their state one of weakness or vitality? Did the ancients attribute to the dead any knowledge and/or abilities beyond those of the living? Did they petition their deceased relatives for favors? Or did they view the dead as malevolent creatures who had to be accorded the proper funerary cult lest they harm the living with all sorts of diseases?

Laying aside skeptical hermeneutics for the moment (see below), we will find it instructive to document what texts can tell us about death in ancient Israel that would be hard or impossible to glean from the archaeological record.

Words Used to Describe the Dead

At the outset, we should note that texts (biblical and extrabiblical tomb inscriptions) give names to the dead.[22] A skeleton can be used to chart a per-son's physiological history, yet only a text can identify the individual's name. And considering the degree to which our identity is wrapped up in our names (*nomen est persona*),[23] texts can personalize the individual similar to grave goods left in a tomb.

Were it not for the text, we would not know that the dead were called *mēt/mētîm* and *rĕpā'îm*.[24] The meaning of *mēt/mētîm* is not in doubt and was used to refer to the dead, regardless of the manner of death. Thus it can refer to a person who dies by the sword or famine (Jer 11:22) or even to a stillborn (Num 12:12).[25]

In contrast to *mēt/mētîm*, the exact connotations of *rĕpā'îm* remain in doubt and cannot detain us here.[26] In brief, it should be noted that the term *rĕpā'îm* is used to represent the dead (Ps 88:11; Prov 2:18, 21:16; Isa 26:14; Job 26:5) as well as an ancient people, sometimes referred to as giants (Gen 14:5; cf. Deut 2:10, Num 13:33). Scholars have debated for some time the degree to which these two classifications are related. Perhaps the oldest sub-stratum of the term referred to an ancient people, especially the royal heroes

22. For the inscriptional material, note the names on the Khirbet el-Qôm tombs inscriptions (Ophay and Uriyahu).

23. So Lambert's treatment of Gilgamesh Tablet X, column VI 10: 'Mankind, which is like a reed in the cane-brake, is snapped off' (*a-me-lu-tum šá kīma qanî a-pi ha-ṣi-PI+IP šùm-šú*). See Lambert 1980: 54–56.

24. These two terms occur parallel to each other in Ps 88:11 ("Do you work wonders for the dead, do the shades rise to praise you?") and Isa 26:14 ("The dead do not live, the shades do not rise"; cf. 26:19).

25. When *mēt* refers to the corpse, the masculine form may be used for both genders (Gen 23:3–4).

26. See discussion and bibliography in Lewis 1996: 117–19, 142.

of old (see Isa 14:9 and the Ugaritic cognate [*rapi'ūma*] referring to the royal dead). As time went on perhaps the term became democratized to refer to the dead in general.

Biological death was thought by some ancient Israelites to be the departure of the life-force (*nĕšāmâ* or a *rûaḥ*)[27] thought to animate a person. This life-force was thought to come from God and, upon death, was thought to return back to God (Job 34:14, Qoh 12:7). Upon animation, an *'ādām* became a living creature (*nepeš ḥayyâ*; cf. Gen 2:7). Once this life-force departs, one was a *nepeš mēt* ('dead person'), an expression that referred to the corpse itself,[28] as does *nepeš 'ādām* (Num 9:6, 7; Ezek 44:25). Sometimes *nepeš* alone is used to designate the dead (for example, the characteristic usage by H and P: Lev 19:28, 21:1; Num 5:2, 6:11, 9:10).

Both *peger* and *gĕwiyyâ* can refer to either a living or a dead body (a carcass or corpse).[29] On two occasions *peger* is modified by the word *mētîm* (2 Kgs 19:35, Isa 37:36). *Peger* refers to the human corpse exclusively, except for Gen 15:11. *Gĕwiyyâ* (compare *gûpâ* 1 Chr 10:12 // 1 Sam 31:12) can refer to a human corpse (Saul in 1 Sam 31:10, 12) or an animal corpse (Judg 14:8–9). *Nĕbēlâ* can also refer to the corpse of either an animal or a person, yet it is never used for a living body.

As mentioned above, in the Hebrew Bible bones are known for their defiling nature (see Num 19:16, 18; 2 Kgs 23:20). 2 Kgs 13:20–21 shows that bones (at least Elisha's) were not viewed merely as skeletal remains but could have healing powers.

Burial and Mourning Customs

As stated above, the text tells me very little about actual burial procedure. The closest I come in the text is the funeral of Abner in 2 Sam 3:31–36, which describes mourning rituals, the carrying of his body on a bier (*miṭṭâ*), and a procession of some sort. Compare, too, the description of Asa's funeral, which is brief yet elaborate. It included burial in a hewn tomb on a funerary 'bed' (*miškab*)[30] in conjunction with precious aromatic spices deftly prepared

---

27. Compare *nišmat ḥayyîm* in Gen 2:7, *rûaḥ ḥayyîm* in Gen 6:17, and *nišmat rûaḥ ḥayyîm* in Gen 7:22. The "going out" of the *nepeš* or *rûaḥ* is pictured in Gen 35:18 and Ps 146:4.

28. Lev 21:11; Num 6:6; cf. Seligson 1951.

29. Compare also *ḥālāl* 'slain' and *nāpal* 'to fall (= to die)'; note the *nĕpîlîm* (= fallen heroic dead?), which are equated with the Rephaim in Deut 2:11; compare *mappēlâ* 'carcass' only in Judg 14:8.

30. The use of the word *miškab* for 'tomb' is attested in biblical texts and extrabiblical inscriptions. In addition to the present passage, see Isa 57:2, 7 (on the double

(*bĕśāmîm ûznîm mĕruqqāḥîm bĕmirqaḥat maʿăśeh*) and an elaborate fire ritual (*wayyiśrĕpû lô śĕrēpâ gĕdôlâ ʿad lim'ōd*).[31]

Burial markers are another matter. Standing stones are well attested in every archaeological age, dating as early as the eleventh millennium in the Uvda Valley and continuing through the MB, LB, and Iron Ages. Thanks to Mettinger (1995), we now have this material assembled in a convenient collection (compare Lewis 1998). Stones such as these were used in a variety of contexts, with primary usage being one of commemoration. Yet it is often hard to tell from the archaeological context which type of commemoration underlies their usage. Textual sources have shown that at least one of the commemorative uses of standing stones was *funerary* in nature (Gen 35:19–20, 2 Sam 18:18, 1 Kgs 13:30, 2 Kgs 23:15–18).[32]

Regarding mourning customs the texts are more forthcoming. In fact, the biblical texts yield a great deal of information that would be difficult to extract from the archaeological record.[33] Texts do not merely tell us about beliefs. Occasionally they can unpack ritual practice of the type that cannot be easily traced through quantifiable artifacts.

The generalities of the text describe a seven-day mourning ritual (see Gen 50:10) that included ritual laments (2 Sam 1:17–27, 3:33–34; 1 Kgs 13:30; Jer 22:18; Amos 5:16). The survivors followed specific dress codes that could include the tearing of one's garments (Gen 37:34, 2 Sam 3:31), the removal of sandals (2 Sam 15:30, Mic 1:8), and the wearing of sackcloth (Gen 37:34; 2 Sam 3:31; Isa 15:2–3, 22:12). In addition, we read of the abstinence from certain hygienic acts (stop washing and anointing one's body, 2 Sam 14:2) and the symbolic manipulation of one's hair, be it of the head or beard (Lev 10:6; Isa 15:2; 22:2, 12; Jer 16:6; 41:5; Job 1:20; Ezra 9:3). Even though articles of dress and grooming have been found in the archaeological record (Bloch-Smith 1992a: 86–88, 140–41), future anthropological studies of tonsure and mourning rituals will be forced to rely primarily on the text (Olyan 1998).

---

entendre, see Lewis 1989: 149–58), Ezek 32:25, and Hoftijzer and Jongeling 1995, s.v. *mškb*.

31. For a complete discussion of biblical descriptions of burials, see Bloch-Smith 1992a: 114–21.

32. Such usage is frequently attested in Phoenician and Punic texts. See Hoftijzer and Jongeling 1995, s.v. *mṣbḥ, nṣb³, zkr, skr*. Cf. KTU 1.17.1.27; 6.13; 6.14 (Lewis 1989: 53–79); KAI no. 215.1, 60, 67, 72–73; the use of *sikkānu* at Emar?; and the *³ḥ iḳr n Rʿ*-stelae from Egypt (Demarée 1983; Schulman 1986).

33. The bibliography on mourning in the biblical period is immense. See the treatments and additional bibliography in de Ward 1972; Spronk 1986: 244–47; Anderson 1991:59–97; Levine 1993b. See also the use of mourning in international relations (Artzi 1980).

Other mourning procedures include dietary acts such as fasting (1 Sam 31:13, 2 Sam 1:12) and funeral meals (Jer 16:7; Ezek 24:17, 22),[34] sitting (and even rolling) in dirt and ashes (2 Sam 13:31, Jer 6:26, Ezek 27:30, Mic 1:10) or putting such on one's head (Josh 7:6, 1 Sam 4:12), beating one's breast (Isa 32:12), and self-inflicted wounds (Lev 19:28; Deut 14:1; Jer 16:6, 41:5).[35]

We must again keep in mind that the texts might not be representative of the entire populace and are limited to the degree to which they describe practices that were localized spatially and temporally and thus perhaps not indicative of more widespread ritual. In addition, we need to be sensitive to the art of literary expression and the metaphorical use of language, as well as an editor's creativity with his material.

Fear of Desecration and the Dead Speaking beyond the Grave

We can see quite easily through archaeology how tombs were robbed in antiquity, showing tomb-robbers' lack of respect for the dead as well as their lack of fear, despite curses invoked against them. Texts, however, give us a better window into the psychology of fear over the desecration of one's tomb. Here the contribution of the inscriptional material supersedes the biblical narratives. Compare one of the inscriptions from the Tomb of the Royal Steward (dated palaeographically to the end of the 8th century B.C.E.), which reads:

> This is [the tomb of . . .]-yahu, steward of the house. There is neither silver nor gold here, only [his bones] and the bones of his maidservant with him. Cursed be the person who opens this (tomb). (Avigad 1953)

A parallel to this text is found in one of the early-7th-century B.C.E. Aramaic Nerab inscriptions, which mentions the lack of silver or bronze placed in the tomb to discourage would-be violators, followed by a curse on any such activity. The fear of desecration of one's tomb was widespread throughout the ancient Near East.[36]

---

34. On the widespread marzeaḥ banquets sometime associated with the dead, see Bryan 1973; Barstad 1984: 127–42; Lewis 1989: 80–94; McLaughlin 1991; Loretz 1993; Schmidt 1994: 22–23; 62–66; M. S. Smith 1994: 140–44; and their additional bibliographies.

35. See Anderson (1991: 59–97) who argues that mourning rituals may be symbolic in nature for purposes of identification with the dead.

36. For one of the longest curses against desecration, see the 5th-century B.C.E. Phoenician Eshmunazor inscription (KAI no. 14; ANET 662). For other such texts, see Avigad 1953: 147–49. In the Bible we have a grave malediction in Isa 14:19.

While the tomb of the Royal Steward inscription speaks in the third person, other West Semitic funerary inscriptions sometimes have the dead speaking from beyond the grave (KAI nos. 11, 13, 14, 35, 226). The priest Siʾ-gabbar, mentioned in the Nerab inscription, speaks in the first person about the day he died, how he was still able to converse, and how he saw his children mourning over him. The Phoenician Eshmunazor ponders his death: "Surely I am to be pitied. I am snatched away before my time, as a son of a few days I am swept away."

That the Israelites also saw the dead as being able to speak from beyond the grave (and with it some notion of a recognizable afterlife existence)[37] is clearly seen in the dead Samuel's speech in the first person in 1 Samuel 28. In fact, the vocabulary that the dead Samuel uses for Saul's 'disturbing' him (*rgz*; 1 Sam 28:15) is the same vocabulary found for the violation of tombs (KAI no. 13:4, 6, 7; McCarter 1980: 421; Lewis 1989: 116). Compare also the first-person narration by the dead found in a late Kition funerary inscription which sounds like the types of words that Absalom could have said after his death (compare KAI no. 35 with 2 Sam 18:18).

Depending on how one understands the Ketef Hinnom amulet and its accompanying inscription (an abridged version of the priestly benediction of Num 6:24–26 from the late 7th–early 6th century B.C.E.), this too may have been placed in the tomb, not only for the deceased person's well-being in the afterlife, but also for the protection of his corpse from desecration (see Puech

---

37. That the dead continued to exist in the afterworld is clear, and Samuel is recognized by his customary attire. The question of the resurrection of the dead is far more complex (see Greenspoon 1981; Collins 1993: 394–98). Some scholars see metaphorical reflexes in the Song of Hannah (1 Sam 2:6: "Yahweh brings death, and brings to life; he brings down to Sheol and he raises up"), Hos 6:2, 13:14 (compare Pryce 1989), Ezek 37:1–14, and Isa 26:19. The earliest uncontested passage of physical resurrection is Dan 12:2 (compare 2 Maccabees 7), which accords with the well-known notion of resurrection in the Hellenistic period. See Lieberman 1965; Meyers 1971–72; Nickelsburg 1972; Bauckham 1990; and Sysling 1996. The related question of immortality is equally complex and will have to await another time. According to tradition, two of the dead, Enoch and Elijah, never die, but they are exceptional. Though the dead continue to exist in the afterworld and could even be referred to as *ʾĕlōhîm*, they do not have the type of immortality that would be described as *ḥay lĕʿōlām* (Gen 3:22). Perhaps they are best described as the 'eternal dead' *mēt lĕʿōlām* (compare *mētê ʿôlām* in Ps 143:3 // Lam 3:6 and *ʿam ʿôlām* in Ezek 26:20 describing those who "descend to the Pit" and "dwell in the netherworld among the primeval ruins." See also *rpim qdmym* in KTU 1.161.8). They exist, in Qoheleth's words, in an 'eternal home' (*bêt ʿôlām*; see Qoh 12:5; *byt ʿlmn* at Deir ʿAllā, and *bʿlm* in the Ahiram inscription. See further Hoftijzer and Jongeling 1995, s.v. *byt* 2 (1.160); Negev 1971: 50–51.

1992: 127). Compare also the Khirbet el-Qôm tomb inscription from the late 8th century B.C.E. The mention of "Yahweh and his asherah" in this text has blinded most scholars from seeing its *funerary* connections. A notable exception is Puech, who notes that the inscribed hand has the force of an amulet. He concludes that the inscription is

> a conjuration-imprecation of an apotropaic character in which the benediction of the deceased Uriyahu before Yahweh and his asherah assures him of salvation, and serves at the same time as a malediction against encounter with his adversaries or enemies, perhaps violators of the tomb and dark forces of the netherworld. (Puech 1992: 128)

Purity Codes

The text also gives us a glimpse at purity codes regarding those who came in contact with or in close proximity to a corpse or a grave. Such codes and the seriousness with which they were viewed by their promulgators (especially regarding the sanctuary; see Num 19:13, 20; Ezek 43:7–9)[38] would be impossible to extract from the material record. We read of elaborate purification rituals thought to last for seven days. The rites included cleansing with water on the third and seventh days, washing clothes, bathing, and the sprinkling of anything unclean (people, tent, and furnishing) with a mixture of water and ashes from the red cow (Num 19:11–22).[39] The studies that have examined pollution and purification resulting from coming in contact with the dead and what they teach us about life/death boundaries (for example, Frymer-Kensky 1983; Wright 1985; Levine 1991) have been and will continue to be primarily text-based.[40]

Burial and Inheritance

Textual perspectives also give us insight into how death and burial are intimately connected to inheritance rights. The interconnected relationship between kin, land, and death has been articulately described in Brichto's famous treatment (1973; see also Stager 1985: 23). One of the primary reasons

38. Levine (1993a: 476) suggests that Ezekiel's restoration plan, which places the royal palace away from the Temple precincts (in contrast to former practice), was motivated by a desire to avoid the pollution of the Temple that occurred at the death of the monarch.

39. See Levine 1993a: 457–79; Milgrom 1990: 157–63, 437–47.

40. For pollution rites as they relate to a cult of the dead in ancient Israel, see Levine 1993a: 468–79. Contrast Ugarit (see Pitard, in this volume, who notes that the location of tombs underneath Ugaritic houses implies that the Ugaritians "did not have major concerns about the impurity of the dead and the potential for ritual pollution from the proximity of a corpse"; p. 150 above).

that the ancestral *naḥălâ* was deemed so important was because it contained the family tomb. Thus we find references to Joshua's grave being located in the ancestral estate (*naḥălātô;* Josh 24:30, 32). Similarly, Judg 2:9 describes Joshua's burial within the borders of his *naḥălâ* (compare 1 Sam 25:1; 1 Kgs 2:34; Gen 23:9, 20). The tomb could also be used by the family as evidence to support their claim to property rights. Bloch-Smith, following L. Stager, has commented on how "sometimes burials functioned as territorial boundary markers as in the cases of Rachel, *bigbûl binyāmin* ('on the border of Benjamin') (1 Sam 10.2), and Joshua, *bigbûl naḥalātô* ('on the border of his inheritance') (Josh. 24.30)."[41]

How Was the Underworld Described/Envisioned?

Sheol was intimately connected to the grave, and thus our textual characterizations include darkness, dust, and silence.[42] Archaeology is very important for helping us to visualize how tomb images underlie such verbal expressions of the netherworld. At the same time, the text is far more detailed in its poetic description of Sheol and thus helps us understand the psyche of death to a better degree.

The texts paint the picture of Sheol as a place of descent, a place to which one "goes down,"[43] and, in the thinking of some authors, it is imagined to be far lower than the grave was dug. It represents the lowest place imaginable (Deut 32:22, Isa 7:11), often used in contrast with the highest heavens (Amos 9:2, Ps 139:8, Job 11:8).[44] In addition to the dirt images drawn by visualizing tombs, Sheol is often associated with various water images, with our best example being found in Jonah 2:3–6, where the author couples *šĕ'ôl* with numerous terms for the chaotic waters, including Sea (*yām/yammîm*), River

41. Bloch-Smith 1992a: 111, 115; Stager 1985: 23. See Lewis (1991) on *naḥălat 'ĕlōhîm* as the ancestral estate and the inheritance rights of widows (see also a new inscription mentioning *naḥălâ* in connection with a widow's plea for inheritance rights in Shanks 1997: 30–32). Now see Bordreuil, Israel, and Pardee 1996, 1998, and Eph'al and Naveh 1998.

42. On additional terminology for the abode of the dead (for example, *'ereṣ, šaḥat, bôr, māwet, 'ăbaddôn*), as well as the way in which Sheol is equated with the grave and darkness, see Tromp 1969: 23–128; Lewis 1992. For various understandings in the later rabbinic literature, see n. 37 above (p. 181).

43. For example, Num 16:30, Job 7:9, Isa 57:9; cf. Isa 29:4, Ps 88:3–4; KTU 1.161.21–22; 1.5.6.24–25; CAD A/2 216, s.v. *arādu*). To further emphasize the depth of Sheol we also find *šĕ'ôl*, as well as *'ereṣ* and *bôr*, modified by *taḥtît/taḥtiyyôt* (for example, Deut 32:32, Ps 86:13, Ezek 31:14–18) usually translated 'the lowest parts of the underworld'.

44. On A. Lods's notion that there are levels in the netherworld, see Greenberg 1997: 539, 662–64.

(nāhār), breakers (mišbārîm), waves (gallîm), waters (mayîm), and the deep (tĕhôm).[45]

The gates of Sheol are mentioned several times in the Hebrew Bible (Isa 38:10; Ps 9:14[13], 107:18; Job 38:17; cf. Jer 15:7) in accord with the gates and guardian gatekeepers prominent in the Egyptian, Mesopotamian, and Anatolian conceptions of the netherworld.[46] Similarly Jonah 2:7[6] describes the 'bars' (bĕrîḥîm) of the underworld.[47] Both of these images have to do with the imprisoning power of Sheol and its impassable nature, which prevents escape.[48]

Although there are allusions to providing foodstuffs for the dead in the Bible that coincide with jars and bowls found in Iron Age burials (see Bloch-Smith 1992a: 106–8, 119–26, 141), the biblical texts do not preserve any description of a banquet in Sheol. Yet the dismal cuisine described in Rabshakeh's speech in 2 Kgs 18:27 // Isa 36:12 may, according to Xella (1980), show that ancient Israel knew of the notion that the dead could be forced to eat their own excrement and drink their own urine, concepts amply attested in Mesopotamia, Egypt, and Anatolia.

The authors of our texts also personified both šĕ'ôl and māwet.[49] Sheol, like Death, is described in the Hebrew Bible as having an insatiable appetite (Isa 5:14; Hab 2:5; Prov 27:20, 30:15b–16), which is remarkably reminiscent of Ugaritic Mot's voracious appetite (KTU 1.5.1.19–20; 5.2.2–4).[50] Twice in

45. See Tromp 1969: 59–66; Lewis 1992a; and Rosenberg (1980: 102–69), who builds on the earlier work of McCarter and Frymer-Kensky for understanding the forensic context of Sheol. Compare ḫubur in Akkadian (CAD Ḫ 219), which is a designation for both the place of the river ordeal and the netherworld.

46. The same concept continues in later Jewish (Wis 16:13; 3 Macc 5:51) and Christian (Matt 16:18; cf. Rev 1:18) literature.

47. See Job 38:10; the common translation 'bars of Sheol' in Job 17:16 (see RSV) is doubtful.

48. Compare Job 7:9, yôrēd šĕ'ôl lō' ya'aleh 'he who goes down to Sheol does not come up', and the Akkadian description of the netherworld as māt la târi 'the land of no return'. Compare also the ropes and snares of Sheol/Death (2 Sam 22:6 = Ps 18:5–6[4–5]). Yet in the minds of many Mesopotamians, the ghostly dead could indeed return to call upon the living, as evidenced by the large number of texts on how to deal with ghosts (Scurlock 1988).

49. Zimmerli (1983: 152) comments that "the lack of the article in all the occurrences [of Sheol] in the OT would certainly suggest that the word still had something of the ring of a proper name about it." There seems to have been a fluidity between Sheol/Death as a person and a locality. We might mention a similar notion in Mesopotamia, where ḫubur and irkallu are used as both a term for the netherworld and a name of a deity (CAD Ḫ 219; I 178; see also the Greek abode and deity Hades).

50. Compare also the swallowing imagery used of Sheol (Prov 1:12; cf. Ps 141:7). Isa 25:8 plays on this imagery and turns the tables by having Yahweh swallow up Death forever.

Hos 13:14 Yahweh is described as ransoming Ephraim from the grasp of personified Sheol and Death (Andersen and Freedman 1980: 639). In Isa 14:9, Sheol seems to be the personified monarch of the kingdom of the dead who rouses the shades of the dead to greet the tyrant of Babylon.[51]

In light of these personifications, scholars have asked whether the ancient Israelites believed in a deity of death called Mot similar to their Ugaritic counterparts. It seems best to conclude that there is a fluidity in the biblical texts between Mot (and Sheol for that matter) as both a person and a locality. The personification of Death in the Hebrew Bible is too prevalent and enduring to be regarded merely as a poetic metaphor or literary device (Lewis 1992b).[52]

Molech?

The textual material also yields a fascinating debate about whether child sacrifice and/or the god Molech were present in ancient Israel. This material has been thoroughly reworked recently with scholars either updating O. Eissfeldt's view, which takes Hebrew *mōlek* as a technical term for child sacrifice (cognate to Phoenician/Punic *mulk*), or asserting that there existed a chthonic deity named Molek to whom children were sacrificed.[53] The archaeology of "tophets" throughout the Mediterranean world as well as at Tyre and Achzib has also been reexamined with an eye toward reconstructing Jerusalem practice (Dearman 1996). If cremation was an integral part of such rituals, then it could only have been practiced in a limited fashion in Iron Age Israel, to judge from the burial patterns we possess to date.[54] Suffice it to say that the existence of the deity Molek will continue to be debated, with the last word being written only after archaeologists find more epigraphic evidence. At this point I would side with those who see *mōlek* referring to the name or epithet of a god.

51. Compare also Isa 28:15, 18, where the leaders are accused of making covenants with Sheol//Death (see van der Toorn 1988).

52. Scholars also debate whether the expression *bĕkôr māwet* in Job 18:13 refers to a child of Mot, an idiom for deadly disease, or a reference to Mot as El's firstborn. See Lewis 1995; 2d ed. 1999.

53. For discussion of scholars arguing for the technical term (for example: Mosca, Ackerman, Muller) versus the chthonic deity (for example: Heider, Day, Levenson, Cogan and Tadmor), see Heider 1985; Day 1989; Smelik 1995; and Dearman 1996.

54. Bloch-Smith 1992a: 52–55, 178–79, 210–14, 244; cf. Bienkowski 1982; Haas 1995: 2023–27. Dever (1995: 42) has noted that the potential relevance of the archaeological material from Carthage has yet to be fully explored.

Cults of the Dead in Ancient Israel?

Finally we come to the question of the existence of cults of the dead in ancient Israel. From the texts we learn that several terms are used to refer to the shades of the dead (*rĕpā'îm*, *mētîm*, and *'iṭṭîm*, a hapax legomenon in Hebrew clearly cognate with the Akkadian *eṭemmu* 'spirit of the dead') and the powers surrounding them (*'ôb/'ōbôt* and *yiddĕ'ōnî/yiddĕ'ōnîm*). As seen above, the dead were also known to speak from beyond the grave. A great deal of literature has been written in the past two decades by textual scholars and archaeologists alike that has emphasized the existence of a cult of the dead in ancient Israel characterized by an active existence of the shades, the quasi-deification of the dead, the practice of necromancy, and the postinterment feeding of the dead.[55] According to what has been a broad consensus, texts (both biblical and extrabiblical) and archaeology complement one another and speak with a unified voice that indeed there were cults of the dead in West Semitic religious practice (Israel included),[56] which mirrored similar (although not identical) death cults in Egypt and Mesopotamia.[57] Rather than rehearsing this vast literature, I have chosen to address recent work on the topic that has radically challenged the consensus.

Evaluating Textual Sources for Reconstructing Ancient Israelite Beliefs about the Dead

W. W. Hallo has remarked that "in the perennial tug-of-war between credulity and skepsis, between maximalism and minimalism, all of us would no doubt like to stake out a place on the middle-ground of sweet reasonableness" (Hallo 1990: 187).

Considering myself to be a reasonable person, I entered the debate regarding cults of the dead over a decade ago with what at that time was a

---

55. See the following incomplete list of works and their bibliographies: Brichto 1973; Ribar 1973; Dietrich, Loretz, and Sanmartín 1976; de Moor 1976, 1995; Burns 1978; Pope 1981; Heider 1985; Spronk 1986; Rouillard and Tropper 1987a, 1987b; Smith and Bloch-Smith 1988; Lewis 1989; Day 1989; Tropper 1989; Bloch-Smith 1992a, 1992c; M. S. Smith 1993; Cooper and Goldstein 1993; van der Toorn 1988, 1991, 1993, 1994, 1996a, 1996b; Barkay 1994; Xella 1995; de Tarragon 1995; Blenkinsopp 1995.

56. There also developed a strong reaction *against* cults of the dead coming from priestly and Deuteronomistic hands, not to mention prophetic diatribes and the wisdom school's notion that the dead know nothing. Such reaction against cults of the dead is further evidence of their existence. See further Lewis 1989. Scurlock (1997: 77, 96) points out that, "although ancient Mesopotamian ghosts were capable of wreaking havoc," they could also be characterized "as stupid, weak, and helpless."

57. An exception would be Cooley 1968, written prior to the discovery of KTU 1.161, which was not published until 1975.

moderate position. On the one hand, I argued against the minimalist views of scholars such as Wright, Kaufmann, and de Vaux, who argued that ancient Israel never had ancestor cults merely because the Deuteronomist said so. On the other hand, I argued against the maximalist tendencies of Pope and Albright, who saw references to death cults that went beyond what I felt the text could support (for example, the *marzeaḥ*, KTU 1.17, and the *bāmôt* material; Lewis 1989: 53–71, 80–94, 140–41).

Continuing in this vein, I have argued against the maximalist views of de Moor and Spronk, who reconstruct, without textual warrant, the revivification and resurrection of the dead and the restoration of Aqhat to Danel in the Rapiuma texts (Lewis 1996: 119–23). I have also argued against Cooper's and Goldstein's (1993) associations of death cults with the *maṣṣēbôt* and *'ĕlōhîm* in the Pentateuchal narratives. I also would argue, following the lead of Pitard (1994), against maximalist archaeology, such as the identification of the so-called libation pipes at Ugarit (about which I was duped earlier, due to Schaeffer's cemetery theory).

In the space that remains, I would like to address the other side of the coin: recent minimalist views that (in Hallo's words) elevate skepsis beyond reasonableness.

Minimalist Voices

Everybody loves a skeptic. The shake-up of a widely held consensus can liberate us to see things anew. Yet skepsis can also result in an overly negative and skewed portrait.

Philip Johnston, *The Underworld and the Dead in the Old Testament*

Philip Johnston's work reacts strongly against the consensus. Johnston's thesis is that "there is little reference to the ancestor cult" in ancient Israel (Johnston 1993: ii), and "the evidence for veneration of the ancestors remains meagre" (1993: 2). Yet, as much as he charges that scholars have gone out of their way to see a death cult where there is none, the reverse seems to be true. For example, Johnston spends an entire chapter trying unsuccessfully to debunk the notion that *'ereṣ* can refer to the underworld. He defeats his own efforts with his conclusion (Johnston 1993: 43) that there are indeed some texts after all "in which ארץ on its own could mean underworld" (however, he is quick to add that "there is no [text] which demands and therefore proves this interpretation"). It is hard to understand how Johnston can so easily dismiss the relevancy of cognate languages and cultures (compare *erṣetu* in Akkadian and *'arṣ* in Ugaritic with the clear meaning of 'underworld').[58]

---

58. The word *'rṣt* is even used to designate the sarcophagus in both of the Aramaic Nerab inscriptions (KAI nos. 225: 4, 7, 12; 226: 8).

Have scholars gone overboard in seeing 'underworld' behind many occurrences of *'ereṣ*? Yes. But Johnston is guilty of throwing the baby out with the bath water. Just because some have gone too far (for example, Tromp [1969: 23–46], following Dahood) does not mean that *'ereṣ* never means 'underworld'.

The same can be said about the use of *'ĕlōhîm* to designate spirits. Have some scholars gone too far in seeing *'ĕlōhîm* as designating spirits everywhere? Yes.[59] But scholarly abuse does not eliminate the usage in Hebrew (which is strengthened once again by cognate usage in Ugaritic and Akkadian). Johnston admits as much when he says several times that this usage in Hebrew "is possible."[60]

Throughout his work, Johnston acts as if we have a complete corpus of literature from ancient Israel on which he can do meaningful statistical analysis, yielding firm conclusions. For example, consider his treatment of Sheol. Because Sheol is used more often to describe the wicked, Johnston concludes that Sheol was perceived by all Israelites as a place for the wicked ("not a term for the underworld which awaits all"). Where did the righteous go after death if not to Sheol? We do not have a complete data set. The marginal statistics that we do have regarding what happens to some of the righteous (they went to Sheol) implies (as most scholars have recognized) that Sheol was a place for all of the dead. Johnston is correct when he follows Pedersen in seeing the underground location of Sheol as "an obvious extension from burial practice" (Pedersen 1993: 15). He should investigate the ramifications of this metaphorical extension (all people are buried; all people go to Sheol).

Yet the major flaw of Johnston's work is his monolithic understanding of ancient Israelite society. At several points he speaks of "the Israelite" or "the Yahwistic" point of view, which he says runs counter to ancestor cults—as if everyone in society had uniform perspective. Johnston's projection of a completed canon back onto the formative stages of Israelite religion is also reflected in his lack of interest in redactional history, which he jettisons at the outset.

59. Examples include Levi (1975), unknown to Johnston, and the work of Cooper and Goldstein (1993).

60. Johnston's analysis of 1 Samuel 28 (1993: 111–12) strains credulity. Rather than seeing Johnston's putative conjurational formula, it is far easier to see *'ĕlōhîm* in 1 Sam 28:13 as referring to the dead Samuel. The antecedent of *to'ŏrô* in v. 14, "what is his (i.e., the *'ĕlōhîm*'s) appearance," is Samuel, who is then immediately described as an old man. Johnston's conclusion on pp. 114–15 (that the use of *'ĕlōhîm* by the medium is a non-Yahwistic usage "clearly" not used by "biblical authors") is forced. Who is writing this material?

Johnston's thinking is close to the thinking of a generation ago: if the Deuteronomist outlawed a practice, then it never occurred. Yet one can infer that laws against certain acts are promulgated precisely because they are going on in society at large! Johnston seems to think that everyone was in agreement with the Yahwistic prophets or the Deuteronomist rather than seeing that ancient Israelite society was a very complex and pluralistic entity spanning hundreds of years. Did everyone think that Yahweh was without a consort? The Kuntillet ʿAjrûd and Khirbet el-Qôm Asherah material would indicate otherwise.

In short, Johnston's minimalist claim that there were no ancestral cults in ancient Israel is a rush to conclusion based on an insufficient understanding of the nature of editorial activity and the complexity of ancient Israelite society.

Brian Schmidt, Israel's Beneficent Dead

A far more credible and astute challenge appears in Brian Schmidt's *Israel's Beneficent Dead*. Schmidt holds that "the ancestor cult was non-existent in early Israelite, or for that matter, West Asiatic societies." In contrast to the passing evaluations of the likes of Kaufmann, Wright, and de Vaux, Schmidt presents a much more thoughtful and thorough treatment on the subject.

The aim of Schmidt's work is, in his words,

> to illustrate how the interface of text, artifact, and theory can significantly inform the modern interpretation of ancient cultures, how the comparative method can serve as a corrective to long revered paradigms based on antiquated versions of that same method and how the application of current anthropological data and theory . . . can inform the analysis of the mortuary data that have played so central a role in the *re-imaging* of that history. (1994: 293, italics mine)

For Schmidt, the operative word in the above quotation is "re-imaging," because in his opinion Dtr's rhetoric and ideology has produced "its own inventive creation" (Schmidt 1994: 293), an exilic or postexilic production that, regarding "a wide range of mortuary rites . . . can tell us little or nothing about pre-Assyrian beliefs in Israel or Judah" (Schmidt 1994: 282). In particular, "necromancy was introduced late." "The dtr writers reconfigured Mesopotamian necromancy as an ancient 'Canaanite' ritual" (1994: 281, 293).

Such a bold thesis is a direct challenge to the consensus of scholars who have used biblical and extrabiblical texts to reconstruct death cults in West Semitic societies, notably Ugarit, Emar, and Israel. If Schmidt is correct, three decades of scholarship must be set aside. What were thought by many to be ancient death cults, are, according to Schmidt, the products of overzealous scholarly reconstruction and imagination. Rather than promoting a greater appreciation for a segment of ancient Israelite religious culture, scholarly consensus has been duped by Dtr's fictitious rhetoric. In this essay I argue that, while scholars have in certain cases stretched meager evidence too far, the general thrust of the consensus is indeed on the right track.

Schmidt begins his work with a descriptive glossary of the terminology associated with mortuary rites because "the history of interpretation has suffered from terminological inaccuracy and methodological isolationism" (1994: 2). Schmidt seeks to correct our terminology and isolationism, as well as to correct our comparative method, by turning to anthropological theory.

Schmidt's Descriptive Glossary for Determining Ancestor Worship	Schmidt's Reasoning for Assignment to a Category
Funerary Rites Burial Mourning	Rites occur between death and arrival in afterworld (≠ cult of the dead)
Cult of the Dead/Ancestor Worship Veneration of the Dead Worship of the Dead	Dead can act positively (through gods, no direct assistance) Dead can act positively (direct assistance to living)
Mortuary Cult (≠Cult of the Dead) Care of the Dead Feeding of the Dead Commemoration of the Dead	 Dead are weak and powerless/inactive Dead are weak and powerless/inactive Perpetuate memory of the dead *only* (≠ persistence of person after death)
Magical Mortuary Rites Necromancy Exorcism	 Positive in nature Negative in nature [not treated]

Admittedly, our field has a lot to learn from the insights of anthropologists, yet there is the danger of importing definitions and comparisons from cultures that are too far afield, both in proximity and chronology, to be applicable to the ancient Near East.

Feeding the Dead Implies Weakness and Powerlessness? While comparing Hultkrantz's work on the cult of the dead among North American Indians, Schmidt "underscores" that feeding the dead is to be "excluded . . . from the category of the death and ancestor cult." According to Schmidt's definition, care for or feeding of the dead typically carries with it the implicit notion that the dead are weak; they have no power to affect the living in a beneficial way. . . . Care for and feeding . . . keeps the ancestors alive. Nevertheless, . . . they lack power . . . such care does not necessitate the belief that the dead supernaturally bestow some benefit upon their devotees. . . . (Schmidt 1994: 10)

Schmidt is also dependent on M. Fortes (known for his work on African ancestor worship), who describes the dead as dependent infants in need of food.

With this definition in hand, Schmidt analyzes the ancient Near Eastern material. It is not a coincidence that he concludes that

a. wherever the dead are associated with offerings (KTU 1.20–22, 1.161; GHD; KAI no. 214, Emar), the texts must be read as other than related to ancestor cult rituals (despite, I would argue, clear death cult vocabulary [see below]);
b. scholars are wrong in defining certain terms as denoting the dead (*rpum, ilm*) if the terms imply any activity or active state on the part of the referents. These entities must be "living warriors" or "living elites."

It seems that Schmidt's conclusion is derived from his definition. This is fine if his definition is correct. But does his definition square with ancient Near Eastern practice? Does feeding the dead imply weakness and lack of beneficent power in ancient Near Eastern cultures, as it does in the cultures of the North American Indian? Consider the following examples from ancient Egyptian letters to deceased relatives, many of which were written on offering bowls.[61] A husband writes to his deceased wife:

How are you? Is the West taking care of you [according to] your desire? Now since I am your beloved upon the earth, fight on my behalf, and intercede on behalf of my name . . . Remove the infirmity of my body! Please become a spirit [before] my eyes so that I may see you in a dream fighting on my behalf. I will then deposit offerings for you. . . . I have not withdrawn offerings from you . . . Fight on my behalf, and fight on behalf of my (new) wife and children. (Wente 1990: 215)

On the Hû-bowl we find the inscription: "One makes invocation offerings (*prt-ḫrw*) to an *ʒḫ* in return for (*ḥr*) interceding for (*sbi ḥr*) the sake of the survivor!" (Demarée 1983: 214). The Chicago Jar Stand, which most likely held an offering bowl (Keller 1989: 144), requests fit children from the intercessor's deceased father: "Cause now that there be born to me a healthy male

---

61. The relevance of the letters to the dead has also been treated by Tropper (1989: 32–46). For general works on death in Egypt, see now Hornung 1999 and Taylor 2001.

child. (For) you are an *3ḫ iḳr*" (Demarée 1983: 215). Another man writes to
a deceased relative about an ill maidservant: "Fight on her behalf anew this
day that her household may be maintained and water be poured out for you"
(Wente 1990: 216). Clearly the people presenting offerings to the dead in
these texts do not think they are weak and without power. Precisely the opposite is true. The dead here are envisioned as having the power to fight on
one's behalf.[62] Elsewhere we read of the dead who promise favors in exchange
for libations: "The dead is a father to him who acts for him, He forgets not
him who libates for him."[63]

The situation is similar in Mesopotamia. Jo Ann Scurlock has shown
that the dead indeed have power in her collection of ghost expulsion texts.
Schmidt omits this material because he defines death cults only as having to
do with the *beneficent* power of the deceased. But the exorcistic texts are extremely relevant for determining the overall state (active or inactive) and
ability (powerful or weak) of the dead. In short, if the dead were thought to
be so powerful in a negative sense, why would one then imagine that they
were weak and powerless when it came to acting positively on behalf of the
living? Indeed, Scurlock includes "ghost assistance prescriptions" in her collection (Scurlock 1988: ##85–88; cf. #68), which document friendly ghosts.
One petition reads as follows:

> You are the ghosts of my relatives. . . . I have made for you a funerary of-
> fering; I have poured you (a libation of) water. I have honored you; I
> have made you proud; I have shown you respect. . . . before Shamash
> (and) Gilgamesh stand forth and judge my case, make a decision about
> me . . . seize it (bodily infirmity?) and take it down to the 'land of no re-
> turn.' May I, your servant, live; may I get well. . . . Let me give (you)
> cold water to drink via your water pipe. Keep me alive so that I may
> praise you. (Scurlock 1988: #85; 1997: 92; cf. Skaist 1980)

Another ghost text, known to Schmidt (1994: 207, 283), is used in legit-
imating kingship. It contains the phrase "the ghost blesses him [in this case
the crown prince] in the same degree as he has revered [*palāḫu*] the ghost."
K. van der Toorn is correct that the verb used here, *palāḫu*, refers to "honour-
ing the dead," which "implies their provision with victuals."[64] Van der Toorn

62. Schmidt (1994: 156; 1995: 116) acknowledges the Chicago Jar Stand but
minimizes it, saying that the dead have to be hostile in nature; their beneficent acts
are merely "side effects."

63. Lichtheim 1976: 20; cf. Foster 1995: 131; Baines 1991: 150–61; Demarée
1983; Schulman 1986. Schmidt (1994: 155–57) acknowledges but minimizes some
Egyptian material. He may be right that the letters to the dead are not necromantic
per se (as defined by Schmidt), but we still have offerings and beneficent power.

64. Cf. too Sigrist's (1982: 245) opinion that Itur-DA and Iphur-Dagan 'honor'
(*kunnû*) "the gods and the dead," a hendiadys referring to deceased ancestors according

concludes that "the 'blessing' was mutual: the living were to bless the dead by invoking their name and presenting them with food and drink, and the dead would bless the living with peace" (van der Toorn 1996a: 56, 65).

The common giving of offerings to malevolent ghosts (the well-known *kispu* material) underscores our basic premise that the ghosts were seen to have power, more often for the bad than good (judging from the greater number of malevolent texts preserved). But even in exorcistic texts, offerings can be made to family ghosts asking them to be beneficial by assisting in the exorcism.[65] In one ghost expulsion text, the offerings to the family ghosts are so extensive that they put the ghosts, according to Scurlock, "almost on a par with Šamaš."

> You make funerary offerings to the ghosts of (his) relatives. You give them gifts. [You] exalt them; you honor them. [To] the other [gho]st(s) of relatives, hot broth you lay out. You give them a gift. [You ex]alt them; you honor them. . . . You pour out a libation of [water] for them. . . . You bring the [shoulder], caul fat (and) roasted meat near (to the offering table). You pour out a libation of [first quality beer]. You pu[t] aside a rib section for the ghost of his relatives."

> The ghosts had seats next to his, were given presents as well as funerary offerings, and were praised and honored. The other ghosts got a libation of water, and the family ghosts even got a portion of the meat sacrifice— the rib section. (Scurlock 1988: 114; 1997: 91–92)

Once again, giving food and drink to the dead does *not* imply their weak state. Rather, they are given offerings, as one would to a god, precisely because the petitioner thought the dead were able to exercise power on his behalf (cf. Scurlock 1997: 83).

The above texts underscore the opposite of Schmidt's conclusions. In the past, Skaist (1980: 125–27) criticized Bayliss for relying too much on foreign anthropological models, especially models from Africa, when she articulated Mesopotamian ancestor worship (primarily regarding the notion that all Mesopotamian ghosts are malevolent in nature). Similarly, Schmidt's dependence on non-ancient Near Eastern anthropological and comparative material leads him to separate the care and feeding of the dead from the veneration and worship of the dead (see glossary chart). Schmidt would have us believe that malevolent ghosts have power, but cared-for ghosts are powerless

---

to van der Toorn (1994: 47), by establishing regular offerings. See Pitard 1996: 127 n. 15: "As long as X his father lives, Y his son shall honor him (*li-ip-lah̬-šu*). As he honors him (*i-pal-lah̬-šu*), after his destiny takes him, he may have my house and all my belongings." Honoring one's father continues after death (cf. Brichto 1973: 30–32).

65. Scurlock 1988: 46; text #63 line 5, #68 lines 12–15, #77 line 10, #55 lines 12–14.

because giving food and drink implies a weak state. In contrast, it seems that food and drink can be offered either to ward off ghosts or to have the dead exercise their power on behalf of the living. Thus Schmidt dismisses too easily many of the texts (for example, KTU 1.20–22, 1.161; GHD; KAI no. 214; Emar VI #452, #463), which are in fact related to cults of the dead. As for the Hebrew Bible, the protestation that the rephaim are stripped of energy (see Isa 26:14, Ps 88:11) is the polemic that proves the point. The biblical mandates outlawing seeking the dead (Deut 18:9ff.; Lev 19:31; 20:6, 27) were delivered precisely because the dead were thought to have power.

Commemoration Rather than Ancestor Worship? Equally important for understanding Schmidt's tendency not to see death cults where others have is his decision to define *commemoration* of the dead as distinct from ancestor worship. Again Schmidt seems to be influenced by a lack of the dead's postmortem existence in African ancestor cults (citing the works of Good and Fortes) and secular modern parallels. Schmidt comments that among the Ashanti "the constituent of personality is not imagined to survive in a supernatural realm after death" (Schmidt 1994: 7) and that secular modern rites of commemoration of the dead need not "necessitate a belief that the dead obtain an afterlife" (Schmidt 1994: 11). Is it correct to project these so-called "parallels" onto ancient Near Eastern commemoration of the dead? Elsewhere Schmidt writes: "regularly observed mortuary rites might *merely* constitute the perpetuation of the dead in the mind of the living in which case commemorative rites would be in view rather than ancestor worship or veneration" (Schmidt 1996b: 144; italics mine).

At issue is the meaning of the words *šuma zakāru* and similar cognate expressions. The consensus of scholars is that these words refer to the *invocation* of the dead as a part of an ancestor cult (documented in Mesopotamian *kispu* rituals, KAI no. 214, Emar, 2 Sam 18:18, and so on). Schmidt prefers to translate these expressions, not as the invocation of the name of the dead, but as "speaking" or "reciting" the name of the dead, "*merely* . . . to memorialize"[66] (Schmidt 1994: 127, 133; italics mine). Thus Schmidt writes:

> "speaking the name" as observed on behalf of the ancestors in Mesopotamia (*šuma zakāru*) might point to a commemorative act and not to ancestor veneration or worship. A straightforward reading of the Assyrian text often cited in support demonstrates that it expresses *merely* the concern to memorialize the recent dead along with the olden dead: *šumka itti eṭemmē azkur*, "I have recited your name along with the ghosts of the dead (*eṭemmū*)," *šumka itti kispi azkur*, "I have recited your name while (offering) the *kispū*." (Schmidt 1994: 127; 1996b: 150; italics mine)

---

66. At one point Schmidt writes with more caution: "this rite [*šuma zakāru*, etc.] *probably* points to a commemorative act and *not* to an act *necessarily* expressive of ancestor veneration or worship" (Schmidt 1994: 133; my italics).

How are philologians to interpret an idiom such as *šuma zakāru*, which can literally refer to either the mentioning of a name (implying memorializing) or the invocation of the name (implying a ritual)? Clearly this expression at a minimum can refer to memorializing the dead, but are there clear examples of the use of *šuma zakāru* that go beyond merely mentioning one's name and constitute the ritual invocation of the dead? Yes. But they are the negative texts that Schmidt eliminated from his survey because he defines ancestor worship as involving only an active and powerful dead providing *blessings* for the living. Again, I would argue that the negative texts regarding ghosts and their power to affect the living must be part of any treatment of a cult of the dead. Consider the following incantation:

> Whether you be the ghost of one unburied, or whether you be the ghost who has none to take care of him (*pāqidu*), or whether you be a ghost who has none to make him a funerary offering (*kispu*), or whether you be a ghost who has none to pour out water for him (*mê naqû*), or whether you be a ghost who has none to call his name (*šuma zakāru*).
> . . . (Bayliss 1973: 116; Scurlock 1997: 79–80)

Clearly, *šuma zakāru* is used here in a ritual context having to do with warding off the effects of the powerful dead. If the name of the dead was invoked to ward off their ill effects, then isn't it logical to interpret the same idiom (*šuma zakāru*) in a similar fashion (in texts such as KAI no. 214, Emar, 2 Sam 18:18) as invoking the dead to act beneficently (as opposed to the mere mentioning of their name)?

Thus when we turn to texts such as KAI no. 214.21 that involve both the invocation of the name (*zkr 'šm*) of Panammu and the petition,

> May the 'soul' (*nbš*) of Panammu [eat] with you, and may the 'soul' (*nbš*) of Panammu drink with you. Let him always invoke the 'soul' (*yzkr nbš*) of Panammu with Hadad (KAI no. 214.16–17),

it makes much more sense to follow Greenfield's lead in seeing the dead ghost of Panammu being invoked than Schmidt's "commemorative act" done for a living Panammu as king emeritus.[67] Furthermore, if the recent interpretations

---

67. Greenfield 1973; 1987: 70–71; Schmidt 1994: 133. Note again the connection between the dead and feeding which, according to Schmidt's definition, cannot constitute a cult of the dead. Thus Schmidt must opt for a "royal banquet following (the living *Pannamū's*) coronation" (1994: 134) rather than a banquet with the dead Pannamu (so most commentators) so as not to violate his definitions. Note also the closely related text, KAI no. 215.18, which, unfortunately, is broken. It tells of the death of Panammu, massive weeping on his behalf, and memorials (including the stone on which KAI no. 215 is carved) erected for him. In this context, scholars have reconstructed [*t'kl wtšt*]*y nbšh* '[may] his "soul" [eat and drin]k' in line 18, but

of Tropper and van der Toorn are correct that the first line refers to the statue that was erected by Pannamu *at his grave* (*bᶜlm*), Schmidt's interpretation would have to be ruled out.[68]

A close parallel to the expression *zakāru* is the use of *qr'* that can also refer to mentioning one's name or invoking one's presence. In KTU 1.161 the verb *qr'* is used repeatedly to summon the *rpu*, which most scholars see as referring to dead ancestors (see *qr'* in 1 Sam 28:15 for Saul's invoking the ghost of Samuel). Thus, in contrast to Schmidt's analysis (1994: 100–120), here we have the *invocation* of the dead—this time in a beneficent context. M. S. Smith (1993) has argued for a similar use of *qr'* in Ps 49:12 (compare Schmidt 1994: 265).

Schmidt's "commemoration hypothesis" is key to his entire work. It is one of the primary hermeneutic guides by which he denies ancestor cults where others have seen them. But why do we have to say that commemoration is *merely* to memorialize? Would the ancients have split such hairs? Analogously, what is one doing when one "invokes/mentions the name of" a deity? Is one just calling a name to memory or invoking the power of the deity behind the name? Thus, whereas Schmidt argues for a commemorative ritual *as opposed to* an ancestor cult, would it not be preferable to assert a commemorative ritual *as a part of* an ancestor cult?

Commemorating the dead is one of the ways of binding the living with their departed ancestors. I have argued in the past that such clan solidarity is at the heart of cults of the dead (Lewis 1989: 165). In a recent work on family religion, van der Toorn has underscored that "the dead were included in the community of the living." Commemoration (*šumam zakāru*), which van der Toorn calls "the central rite of the cult of ancestors," is not *merely* mentioning someone's name but invoking the names of one's ancestors so as to preserve their identity and thereby endow "the living with a family identity that is anchored in the past. In addition to fostering cohesion, then, the cult of ancestors reinforces a sense of identity in those participating" (van der Toorn 1996a: 48, 52).[69]

---

this cannot be confirmed. Finally, see Greenfield (1985: 51–53; 1987: 71), who finds a parallel in lines 16–18 of the Aramaic section of the Tell Fekheriyah bilingual inscription.

68. Tropper 1993: 60–61; van der Toorn 1996a: 166. On *ᶜlm*, see n. 37 (p. 181).

69. Note also the conclusion of Bayliss: "the invocation of the name (*šumu*) of the deceased appears to have been an important part of the regular cult. . . . The recurring use of *šumu* in expressions of the hopes invested in offspring, especially in personal names, omens, curses and blessings, suggests that the need for a *pāqidu* to keep the name of the individual alive after his death may have been an important element in the desire for offspring. References in omens and curses to potential offspring as *nāq mê* and *zākir šumi* confirm this suggestion" (Bayliss 1973: 117).

Summation. In short, I do not see how Schmidt's reliance on anthropological models—which suggest (a) the lack of a postmortem existence for the dead and (b) that feeding the dead implies their weakness[70]—leads to an advancement in our reconstructions of ancient Israel and its neighboring cultures. Rather, those anthropological models seem foreign to the ancient Near East and are apt to hinder a clear reading of the few texts at our disposal.

The "Deification" of the Dead. The deification of the dead has been a topic of recent debate.[71] What is at issue is whether the common Semitic term for deity (*ilu/ilāni/ilūma/ʾĕlōhîm*, and so on) can also refer to the dead.

70. Combining both aspects, Schmidt (1996b: 163) can acknowledge that there was "the *feeding* and *commemoration* of the family dead" (my italics) at Emar and at the same time conclude that a domestic ancestor cult (which he defines as "rites expressive of a corresponding belief in the supernatural beneficence of the dead or their deification") is *not* attested. Because Schmidt argues (incorrectly) that feeding and commemorating the dead do not constitute ancestor worship, he concludes that cults of the dead are not in any West Semitic literature. Some of the texts that Schmidt eliminates include the following:

a. The dead *rapiʾūma* in KTU 1.161 are not *invoked* in a *funerary* ritual to bless the new king (= the scholarly consensus); rather they are "weak shades lacking the powers of the dead" (Schmidt 1994: 114) who are "*called*" to a *coronation* ceremony. Why are they present at the opening of this ritual? What is the function of lines 2–5 in this sacred celebration? According to Schmidt, "the call or summons merely alerted the dead to prepare to receive the soon-to-descend throne" (Schmidt 1994: 106, 120).

b. The Genealogy of the Hammurapi Dynasty (GHD) has been universally interpreted as describing the dead who are invited to "come, eat this, drink this and bless Ammisaduqa." But for Schmidt, the dead can not be so beneficent; thus, rather than deceased ancestors, he reads active military personnel who merely "commemorate the dead." Should we ignore the fact that GHD invokes the ancestral dead and uses the characteristic death cult vocabulary of *pāqidu*, vocabulary that has led the likes of all previous scholars (Finkelstein, Malamat, Lambert, Wilson, Röllig, Tsukimoto, Charpin, and Durand; see Schmidt 1994: 73 n. 143 for bibliography) to identify the GHD as a *kispum* ancestor cult feast?

c. Similarly, KAI no. 214 (see above), which has been universally described as referring to food and drink offerings to the ghost of Panammuwa, is reread by Schmidt to be a royal banquet following the coronation of a living Pannamuwa. Once again, should we ignore the clear death-cult vocabulary of invocation (*šuma zakāru*) and the description of the *nbš* (ghost) of Panammuwa, which has led almost all scholars to recognize plain references to a death cult (for bibliography, see Schmidt 1994: 134 n. 5)?

71. See, for a sampling, the works of Tropper, Lewis, Loretz, van der Toorn, Johnston, Schmidt, and Pitard.

The texts that some scholars have presented as evidence of this usage include a wide array of Akkadian texts (including Nuzi and Emar) as well as cognate usage in the Ugaritic texts (KTU 1.6.6.45ff.; 1.20–22, 1.113, 1.124; the *ilib* material), perhaps the Pyrgi inscription (Knoppers 1992), and the Bible (1 Sam 28:13, 2 Sam 14:16, Isa 8:19; compare Ps 106:28 with Num 25:2).[72] Especially relevant is the collocation of the terms *ilāni* and *eṭemmū* (or *mētū*) in many of these texts. Scholars differ over whether the collocation of the term for the divine and the term for an ancestral ghost (or the deceased) is a hendiadys (implying the deification of the dead; so Tsukimoto, Rouillard and Tropper, Lewis, Loretz, van der Toorn, and others) or whether the two terms are not to be taken as a hendiadys. In the latter case, the two terms are not to be related to each other (the gods in question are regular family gods), and thus there is no deification of the dead (so Schmidt, Pitard).

Many scholars have used the phrase *deification of the dead* without comment. Elsewhere I have argued that terming the dead *ilu/ʾĕlōhîm* reflects the poverty of ancient Near Eastern vocabulary. In my view, the term is a description of their *preternatural* nature rather than an attempt to deify the dead fully (in the sense of making them equal to the high gods of the pantheon; Lewis 1989: 49–50). See, in particular, D. Pardee's recent article, which notes with respect to the Ugaritic ritual texts that "the ancestors occupied a very minor position in [the] ritual pantheon" (Pardee 1996: 285).

Space does not allow me to address each of the numerous passages and to counter the arguments put forward by Johnston, Schmidt, and Pitard that the dead were not referred to as *ilu/ʾĕlōhîm*. Certainly some scholars have gone too far in seeing ancestors behind many references to the word *ʾĕlōhîm*.[73] The strongest passage documenting the fact that the dead in ancient Israel were indeed called *ʾĕlōhîm* is 1 Sam 28:13 (see Lewis 1989: 104–17). Both Johnston's and Schmidt's interpretations of this passage are strained.[74] Schmidt's rejection is related to his notion that necromancy is not indigenous to ancient Israel but, rather, a false projection of Mesopotamian origin. A straightforward reading of the text yields the long-held and widely-held view that the necromancer, when asked after conjuring the spirit "what does the dead Samuel look like?" (*mâ rāʾît; mah-toʿŏrô*) replies by calling him an *ʾĕlōhîm* coming up from the underworld.

---

72. McCarter (1980: 421) suggests that we may also have this kind of usage in Job 12:6.

73. See n. 59 above (p. 188) and compare van der Toorn 1993: 382 n. 25.

74. See n. 60 above (p. 188). Schmidt's treatment (1994: 219) "leaves the gods unidentified," but the reference probably refers to chthonic gods, due to the allusion to Shamash.

I have chosen to address Schmidt's handling of KTU 1.6.6.45ff because it is telling. I have presented a typical translation in the chart below. Although scholars may debate whether we have a verb (*taḥattikī*) meaning 'to judge, preside over, watch over' or a preposition (*taḥt*) meaning 'under', they speak with one accord that this passage describes four synonymously parallel terms for the dead (the A couplet pairing *rapiʾūma*//*ʾilāniyūma* and the B couplet *ilūma*//*mitūma*).[75] In contrast, Schmidt translates the quatrain, not synonymously, but chiastically. Thus the two inner terms for deities are parallel (*ʾilāniyūma*//*ilūma*), as are the two outer terms (*rapiʾūma*//*mitūma*). Elsewhere in his book, Schmidt argues that "the *rpʾum* of the mythological texts are nowhere portrayed as the shades of the dead" but are, rather, human warriors (Schmidt 1994: 88).[76] He then interprets the word *mitūma* not as 'the dead' but as 'humans', thus ending up with his outer pair (see chart, p. 200).

But a closer look at the passage at hand shows, as already noted by M. S. Smith,[77] that the text is clearly not chiastic. *Each* term in *each* cola is fully synonymous (most often identical) with the term in its paired cola. *Šapšu* in line A is parallel to *šapšu* in A′; *taḥattiki* in line A is parallel to *taḥattiki* in A′; *ʿiduki* in line B is parallel to *ʿiduki* in line B′. Thus it is apparent, as most translators have recognized, that *rapiʾūma* parallels *ʾilāniyūma* and *ilūma* parallels *mitūma*. In short, like its ancient Near Eastern cognates, Ugaritic does indeed refer to the dead as *ilūma*. If there were any doubt, one need only turn to the Ugaritic Rapiuma texts (KTU 1.20–22), which have the commonly repeating

---

75. For a discussion of the terms *tḥtk* and *ʿd* in this text, see Lewis 1989: 36.

76. In Schmidt's "alternative paradigm" (1994: 90), all references to the Ugaritic word *rpum* (standing alone) are a "military contingent" of living warriors (also called "living elites" 1994: 269). Everywhere that the majority of scholars have seen shades of the dead, Schmidt reads living warriors. The clear meaning of *rpʾm* as 'shades' in both Hebrew and Phoenician is of no relevance for Schmidt because it is "much later and should not take precedent over the internal evidence from Ugarit" (Schmidt 1994: 84). Complicating his interpretation is KTU 1.161.6–8, where he is forced to recognized a group of *rpum* as dead (they end up in the netherworld in 1.161.23–24). But this is the only place, and he says this is why these are called the *rpum qdmym*. Only the *rpum qdmym* are dead. The biblical writers due to "conscious compression or unwitting confusion" replaced this term with *rĕpāʾîm* alone. As a result, "the term used to denote living elites at Ugarit, *rpʾum* . . . was now applied to those inhabiting the underworld" (1994: 269). But rather than suggesting that the biblical authors are unwittingly confused, why not just see *rpʾm* as able to refer to the dead in both Ugaritic and biblical literature (coinciding w/Phoenician)? The fact that the Bible also uses the term for giants is easily fit into this scenario (see the entries on "Rephaim" by M. S. Smith 1992 and Rouillard 1995; 2d ed. 1999).

77. M. S. Smith 1996: 724–25.

KTU 1.6.6.45ff.

špš rp'im ṯḥtk
špš ṯḥtk 'ilnym
'dk 'ilm
hn mtm 'dk

Typical translation by scholars seeing four parallel terms for the dead:

A   O Shapshu, may you preside over the *shades*,
A'   O Shapshu, may you preside over the *divinities*,

B   The *divine ones* are your company,
B'   Behold, the *dead* are your company.

Synonymous parallelism of all elements:

A		A'			
špš	//	*špš*			
ṯḥtk	//	*ṯḥtk*			
rp'im	//	*'ilnym*		*rp'im* // *'ilnym*	
				'ilm // *mtm*	

B		B'
'dk	//	*'dk*
'ilm	//	*mtm*

Schmidt 1994: 88; 1995: 125:

A   Shapash, the *rp'u*-warriors are under you,
B   Shapash, the *'ilnym* divinities are under you;
B'   Your witnesses are the gods,
A'   Behold, humans are your witnesses.

Chiasm: *rp'im* // *mtm*   =   warriors//humans
              'ilnym //'ilm   =   divinities//gods

Schmidt's conclusion: "the *rp'um* of the mythological texts are nowhere portrayed as the shades of the dead. This is crucial to understanding the mention of *rp'um* in 1.161" (1994: 88). KTU 1.161 = a "coronation ritual . . . commemorative rite . . . a royal ancestor cult rite is nowhere in view" (1994: 120).

---

pairs of *rapi'ūma*//*'ilāniyūma* and *rapi'ūma*//*'ilūma* (KTU 1.20.1.1–2, 1.20.2.1–2, 1.20.2.6, 1.20.2.8–9, 1.21.2.3–4, 1.21.2.11–12, 1.22.2.5–6, and so on).[78]

78. For a critical edition of the text and discussion of restorations, see Pitard 1992; Lewis 1996.

Evaluating the Worth of Biblical Sources. The above analysis brings us directly to the question of the worth of the biblical sources. Our texts are meager and have undergone layers of editorial activity that can obscure our ability to reconstruct the precise timeline of ancient Israelite religious practice. One can either (a) adopt Hallo's view that we need not "limit the inferences we extract from the evidence," but we should be all that more careful in critically sifting and analyzing the limited evidence that we do have;[79] or (b) take refuge in skepsis and present such an incomplete view of Israelite religion that it in itself warps reality with its minimalism.

Of course, one scholar's critical eye is different from another's. Schmidt's led him to dismiss death cults in *all* of the West Semitic material (Ugarit, Emar, Zinjirli, Israel). Having done so, his conclusion is not surprising. Once he deems the comparative Late Bronze and Iron Age West Semitic backdrop irrelevant, he turns to an approach *au courant* with pan-Deuteronomistic hermeneutics. Schmidt concludes his work by saying that "the Canaanite origins tradition for Israelite necromancy is the product of a rhetorical strategy intended to enhance the authority of dtr ideology" (Schmidt 1994: 142).[80] As much as Schmidt aims to interface "text, artifact and [anthropological] theory" (1994: 293), in the end his new thesis is primarily a literary one[81] that argues that the biblical text is a fictitious construct that reflects

---

79. Hallo argued "not to limit the inferences we extract from the evidence, but to treat the evidence, precisely because it is limited, as a precious resource—none of it to be ignored, or squandered, but every fragmentary bit of it critically sifted . . . — much as the archaeologist must use every surviving potsherd to reconstruct and restore a fragmentary vessel" (Hallo 1990: 199). With respect to death in ancient Israel, M. S. Smith asserts a methodology that sounds much like Hallo's:

> The near absence of textual and archaeological evidence is not tantamount to evidence for the absence of many after-death rituals and beliefs. Given the lack of evidence, scholars may have to be satisfied, at least for now, with the tidbits which point to a more widespread situation for the dead and their roles in Israelite religion (M. S. Smith 1996: 725).

A recent example of sifting the type of minute data that are often overlooked is van der Toorn's work on anthroponyms (1996b).

80. The priority for Deuteronomism is evident in Schmidt's handling of the H material (for example, Leviticus 19–20), which he ignores for the most part as "dtr related" (Schmidt 1994: 148, 150, 154, 167). It is curious, in light of Leviticus 19–20, for Schmidt to write that "no trace of that [ancestor] cult made it into the priestly tradition either by allusion or polemic" (1994: 280). Schmidt is also silent on the wisdom school's argument against the dead's having knowledge (Qoh 9:4–6, 10; compare Job 14:21).

81. Elsewhere, Schmidt describes his as a "traditio-historical reconstruction" (Schmidt 1994: 286).

Dtr's reimaging of Israelite religion out of whole cloth. Dtr's "own creative invention" reconfigures late Mesopotamian necromancy into a Canaanite practice. In short, Schmidt tries to make the case for the "highly rhetorical character" of the biblical presentation of ancestor cults and necromancy (1994: 138), but this only succeeds the degree to which he has been successful in showing that these practices were absent in West Semitic religious practice.

It is precisely here (when one privileges literary theory) that we should turn to the judgment of archaeologists and anthropologists. I will not speak on their behalf, yet it is hard to imagine an ancient Near Eastern anthropologist who can document the widespread use of divination throughout the ancient Near East (including Israel where we have found liver omens) concluding that Iron Age Israel never considered the divinatory practice of necromancy until Dtr introduced the concept in his literary fiction. It is hard to imagine the epigrapher poring over the second-millennium lú professional lists that document an array of necromancers (*mušēlû eṭemmi, mušēlit eṭemmi, mušēlû, mušē-litu,* and *ša eṭemme*)[82] concluding, as does Schmidt, that necromancy is also introduced late in Mesopotamia (see also Enkidu and the Netherworld lines 238–43 and TCL 4.1–5).[83] It is hard to imagine the archaeologist who has found hoards of amulets in excavated tombs concluding that no West Semitic person ever considered that the dead might have powers bad or good. (Even though Schmidt is aware of the discovery of amulets found in Iron Age Judean tombs, as well as apotropaic inscriptions, he concludes that "this does not establish an underlying fear of the dead, for such fear, even in a mortuary context such as a tomb, might be caused by malicious demons other than the dead"[84] [Schmidt 1994: 288].) Last, it is hard to imagine the archaeologist who has climbed through all of the burial vaults located directly under numerous Ugaritic houses concluding that at the family and clan level no Ugaritian ever practiced death cults.

---

82. For a convenient collection of these and other terms for necromancers and witches, see Henshaw 1994: 152–53. Schmidt's analysis of some of this material (for example, *mušēlû eṭemmi* is an exorcist, not a necromancer) seems forced (Schmidt 1994: 215).

83. Schmidt 1994: 215; 1995: 118. Schmidt minimizes the Gilgamesh reference by calling it "an exceptional phenomenon, not a known mantic practice." He does, however, acknowledge that the nineteenth-century B.C.E. Kültepe material is "the strongest evidence for necromancy in the earlier periods."

84. Elsewhere Schmidt states that the archaeology of mortuary ritual supports "the weak and marginal role of the dead" (1994: 282). Archaeologists specializing in Judean burial practices (for example, Bloch-Smith 1992a, 1992c) have concluded the opposite.

Dennis Pardee: A Minimalism One Can Live With

The last of the minimalist perspectives treated here is Dennis Pardee's recently published article (1996), which is more moderate than minimalist, despite its title. Though dealing with the Ugaritic material, it is directly relevant for ancient Israel. Pardee argues against a widespread on-going mortuary cult at Ugarit, based on his study of the Ugaritic ritual texts.[85] He also concludes, as I had earlier, that "none of the data from Ugarit justifies a connection between the *marziḥu* and the mortuary cult" (Pardee 1996: 277; cf. Lewis 1989: 94).

At the same time, Pardee is very clear to say that he is not arguing against the presence of a funerary cult. Pardee argues for a funerary interpretation of KTU 1.161 in which "the departed ancestors participated" (Pardee 1996: 275) and against scholars who would see a coronation ceremony (Malamat, Levine, and Schmidt). In addition, he "states explicitly" (Pardee 1996: 284) that "the *Rapa'ūma* and the *Malakūma*" are "clear terms for the dead" at Ugarit[86] and that KTU 1.113 in its use of *ilu* "describes the deceased kings as deified" (Pardee 1996: 276; see also Pardee 1983: 127–40; 1988: 179–82 on KTU 1.124).[87] Moreover, though Pardee thinks that the Ugaritic *pagru*-rite may be "vestigial at Ugarit and practiced episodically rather than regularly," he still is of the opinion that "it is not unlikely that the Ugaritic *pagru*-rite was itself mortuary" (1996: 281–82).

While Pardee does not see KTU 1.161 as a *kispu* ritual, he remains cautiously moderate that "some of the (para-mythological) texts may, however, refer obliquely to such a *kispu*-type ritual" (Pardee 1996: 276). Though he is of the opinion that "the ancestors occupied a very minor role in (the) ritual pantheon" (see my remarks on deification above), he concludes judiciously that death-cult practices "may have flourished outside the realm of the state-sponsored cult . . . probably on the family and clan level" (Pardee 1996: 284–85). Here it is important to introduce the presence of the DN *ilib*, which occurs frequently in Ugaritic in epic texts, pantheon lists, and sacrificial and

---

85. See Pardee's definitions (1996: 273–74) and compare with Schmidt's (1994: 4–13). In particular, Pardee argues against del Olmo Lete's classification of the ritual texts as mortuary (Pardee 1996: 281–85). The full exposition of Pardee's view (written after the manuscript of this article went to press) can now be found in Pardee 2000, 2001. See especially his treatments of KTU 1.108, 1.113, 6.13, and 6.14.

86. Pardee argues (1996: 274) in consensus with most scholars and against the position of Schmidt (1994: 100–120) that *rpum* and *rpum qdmym* in KTU 1.161 are "two categories of the deceased . . . rather than a living group and *their* ancestors."

87. On KTU 1.124's referring to deified ancestors, see also Spronk 1986: 193–95; Tropper 1989: 151–56. Contrast Schmidt 1994: 79.

offering lists.[88] See K. van der Toorn's recent treatment, which underscores that *ilib* refers to the spirit of the divine ancestor.[89]

New Material from Emar

I should note the most recent comparative material that is relevant to the topic, the Late Bronze tablets from the Syrian site of Meskene, identified as ancient Emar. Although this material was published by D. Arnaud in 1986, much of it is still in the initial stage of investigation.[90] Nonetheless, several works have appeared on its funerary character, including studies by Fleming (1992, 1997, 2000), van der Toorn (1994), Pitard (1996), and Schmidt (1994, 1996b). Of special interest is whether the texts refer to the deified dead (see above).

Emar texts #452 and #463, which describe rituals associated with the month of Abi, are just now being brought into the discussion.[91] Key to understanding the ritual are the events associated with the 25th–27th days that include sacrifices and offerings 'at the gate of the grave' (*ina bāb kimāḫi*) and the 'barring of the doors of the gate'. Fleming (2000: 184–89) associates the timing of the ritual with the disappearance of the lunar crescent and suggests a concern for the underworld. In contrast to Pitard, he goes on to suggest that *abū* refers to ancestors and that "it is simplest to understand [the offerings to the realm of the *ilu*] as offerings to the dead." Dagan, who is the primary deity honored in the ritual, has underworld connections elsewhere (Lewis 1989: 72–79). Compare especially the references on days 26 and 27 to "the *abu* of Dagan's temple" and "the *abu* of Alal's temple," Alal being an underworld deity.

The question of the deification of the dead at Emar will continue to be debated. Even though Pitard is of the opinion that "these tablets cannot be used as independent evidence for a cult of the deified dead at Emar," he concludes that the texts "do suggest, however, that the dead were conceived as

88. For a list of occurrences and discussion of etymology, see Lewis 1989: 56–59; van der Toorn 1993.

89. While Pardee does discuss KTU 1.17 and "the proper care of the family or clan deity" (1996: 279), he curiously omits a discussion of the *ilib* material from this treatment. See van der Toorn 1993; 1996a: 155–60. But now see Pardee's comments on *'Ilu-ibī* and *'Ināšu-'Ilīma*, "perhaps men (who have become) divine (after death)" in Pardee 2000, 2001.

90. An inventory of the Emar texts can be found in Beckman 1996; van der Toorn 1994: 39 n. 4.

91. See Fleming's initial understanding (1992: 295–301). Readers are directed to Fleming's fuller treatment (2000: 173–95, 280–93), which arrived too late to be incorporated fully. See also the extensive treatments by Pitard (1996) and van der Toorn (1994; 1996a: 55–56, 222–23). On the month of Abu in Mesopotamia, see Scurlock 1995a: 1889; 1995b: 93, 104–7; 1997: 90–91.

continuing to have basic needs in the afterlife, needs that could only be filled by living descendants . . . the dead were provided with food and drink offerings and were invoked by their descendants" (Pitard 1996: 129–30). Thus their relevance for discussing the cult of the dead elsewhere in ancient Syria (that is, Ugarit) and ancient Israel is patent.

Conclusion: Archaeology and/or Texts?

What then shall we conclude about the interface of archaeology and textual studies? The tremendous potential of archaeology that I have documented at the outset of my remarks could argue for archaeologists working alone. Indeed, Bill Dever has often commented orally (somewhat in jest) that, if current skeptical hermeneutics makes textual scholars gun-shy of writing a history of Israelite religion, then they should "move over and let us archaeologists write one." Consider also John Holladay's article describing Israelite religion from "an explicitly archaeological approach" (Holladay 1987).

Or, reflecting on the unique role that language plays in uncovering cultural belief systems, philologians could go it alone. Consider Watkins's hubris in stating that ". . . a reconstructed protolanguage is 'a glorious artifact, one which is far more precious than anything an archaeologist can ever hope to unearth'" (Watkins 1992: xxv). His apology for the primacy of language reads:

> Though by no means a perfect mirror, the lexicon of a language remains the single most effective way of approaching and understanding the culture of its speakers. . . . The evidence that archaeology can provide is limited to material remains. But human culture is not confined to material artifacts alone. The reconstruction of vocabulary can offer a fuller, more interesting view of the culture of a prehistoric people than archaeology precisely because it includes nonmaterial culture. (Watkins 1992: 2084)

Each of our disciplines has legitimate bragging rights that, if held so passionately that we ignore one another, can lead to equally incomplete treatments of death in ancient Israel. Common sense leads to the obvious conclusion: why choose? We need both disciplines working critically and independently yet informing each other. Sadly, all too often, textual scholars refrain from wrestling with the archaeology due to its complex nature in an age of specialization and sophistication. Likewise, archaeologists more and more bypass the text, perhaps out of fear that the skills of philologians have become equally specialized or perhaps out of a fear that even considering the text may lead to a charge of Albrightian bibliolatry.[92]

---

92. Dever (1995: 51) writes: "what actually constitutes our 'primary' data. Texts alone? Artifacts and artistic representations? Both? And if so, in what sort of balance?

Archaeology: W. G. Dever, Religion in Two Dimensions

For archaeology, a model is found in the works of W. G. Dever. Ironically, as much as Dever has been labeled "He Who Killed Biblical Archaeology," it is he, more than any other archaeologist alive today, who has argued for the integration of both disciplines. In a series of programmatic essays dating back at least to 1983, Dever has set the stage for a method of integrating, including treating the Bible as a "curated artifact," studying how religious belief can be revealed through iconography, and his most recent contribution, which argues for analyzing "religion in two dimensions" (1995: 52). As far as death in ancient Israel is concerned, Dever (underscoring the work of Bloch-Smith) asserts both the value of archaeology for uncovering "popular" and familial expressions of religious practice, such as cults of the dead, and the value of the textual studies that are sophisticated enough to "read against the grain" of our texts edited from a normative perspective.

Texts: No Magic Wand

In textual study, there is no magic wand for evaluating the historical veracity of textual traditions regarding religious belief. All that we have at our disposal is the tedious work of textual criticism, dating through linguistic and orthographic considerations, redaction criticism, traditiohistorical criticism, and the other well-known methodologies that constitute our discipline. In addition, ancient Israel must be understood against its ancient Near Eastern backdrop. We must cease referring to the Bible *and* the ancient Near East, as if the former were not a part of the latter. This necessitates a properly cautious use of comparative texts from the ancient Near East (not the parallelomania of old) that is sensitive to interpreting each text in its respective culture.

The Plurality of Israelite Religious Expressions

My last remark is methodological, having to do with the nature of societies. Ancient Israelite society (like societies in general, including those of the ancient Near East) was probably more pluralistic than we tend to imagine. Only recently have scholars begun to argue for the *polyvalent*[93] nature of an-

---

Above all, how is the critical historian to sift and evaluate any of the pertinent data? Again, these questions are too infrequently raised in our discussions, perhaps because each discipline considers itself autonomous, its aims and methods beyond criticism. Moreover, there is no serious commitment to dialogue, so no necessity to lay down common methodological ground rules."

93. The term *valence* (a term borrowed from chemistry having to do with the combining property of an atom, determined by the number of electrons that it will

cient Israel. Differing degrees of conservatism versus liberalism in religion are not unique to our modern society. Thus our final reconstructions—be they archaeological or textual—need to avoid homogenizing the data and make room for the strong possibility that there were numerous viewpoints (many of which were at odds with each other) that may have differed from one locale to the next. As for death, a polyvalent approach would square with what anthropologists since Ucko have been telling us about the complex and varied nature of the human response to death.

The various cultures of the ancient Near East came up with different answers to the mystery of death. Since these civilizations were not monolithic or static through time, we should underscore our inability to succeed in giving anything more than a thumbnail sketch of ancient Near Eastern thanatology in general and ancient Israelite in particular, thus demonstrating once again the need for archaeologist and philologian to work together in handling the relatively few broken pots and broken texts at our disposal.

---

lose, add, or share when it reacts with other atoms) is well suited to describe the capacity of something (here, developing Israelite religion) to unite, react, or interact with something else. The term *polyvalent* is also used by E. Nicholson (1986: 28). Compare Albertz's (1994: 83) "poly-Yahwism," following Donner. See also my remarks on pluralistic views with respect to Asherah worship (1998: 47).

Bibliography

Albertz, R.
1994   *A History of Israelite Religion in the Old Testament Period.* OTL. Louisville: Westminster/John Knox Press. [German original, 1992]
Alfrink, A.
1948   L'expression *šākab ʿim ʿăbôtāyw. OTS* 5: 118–31.
Alster, B.
1980   *Death in Mesopotamia: XXVIᵉ Rencontre assyriologique internationale.* Mesopotamia: Copenhagen Studies in Assyriology 8. Copenhagen: Akademisk.
Andersen, F. I., and Freedman, D. N.
1980   *Hosea.* AB 24. Garden City: Doubleday.
Anderson, G. A.
1991   *A Time to Mourn, A Time to Dance: The Expression of Grief and Joy in Israelite Religion.* University Park: Pennsylvania State University Press.
Artzi, P.
1980   Mourning in International Relations. Pp. 161–70 in Alster (1980).
Avigad, N.
1953   The Epitaph of a Royal Steward from Siloam Village. *IEJ* 3: 137–52.

Baines, J.
1991 Society, Morality, and Religious Practice. Pp. 123–200 in *Religion in Ancient Egypt: Gods, Myths, and Personal Practice*, ed. B. E. Shafer. Ithaca: Cornell University Press.

Barkay, G.
1988 Burial Headrests as a Return to the Womb: A Reevaluation. *BARev* 14/2: 48–50.
1994 Burial Caves and Burial Practices in Judah in the Iron Age. Pp. 96–164 in Singer (1994). [Hebrew].

Barstad, H. M.
1984 *The Religious Polemics of Amos*. VTSup 34. Leiden: Brill.

Bauckham, R. J.
1990 Early Jewish Visions of Hell. *JTS* 41: 355–85.

Bayliss, M.
1973 The Cult of Dead Kin in Assyria and Babylonia. *Iraq* 35: 115–25.

Beckman, G.
1996 Emar and Its Archives. Pp. 1–23 in Chavalas (1996).

Biénkowski, P. A.
1982 Some Remarks on the Practice of Cremation in the Levant. *Levant* 14: 80–89.

Biran, A., and Naveh, J.
1995. The Tel Dan Inscription: A New Fragment. *IEJ* 45: 1–18.

Blenkinsopp, J.
1995 Deuteronomy and the Politics of Post-mortem Existence. *VT* 45: 1–16.

Bloch-Smith, E.
1992a *Judahite Burial Practices and Beliefs about the Dead*. JSOTSup 123. Sheffield: JSOT Press.
1992b Burials—Israelite. Pp. 785–89 in vol. 1 of *ABD*, ed. D. N. Freedman. New York: Doubleday.
1992c The Cult of the Dead in Judah: Interpreting the Material Remains. *JBL* 111: 213–24.

Brandfon, G.
1987 The Limits of Evidence: Archaeology and Objectivity. *Maarav* 4/1: 5–43.

Bordreuil, P.; Israel, F.; and Pardee, D.
1996 Deux ostraca paléo-hébreux de la collection Sh. Moussaïeff. *Sem* 46: 49–76, esp. pp. 61–76, plates 7–8.
1998 King's Command and Widow's Plea: Two New Hebrew Ostraca of the Biblical Period. *NEA* 61/1: 2–13.

Brichto, H. C.
1973 Kin, Cult, Land and Afterlife: A Biblical Complex. *HUCA* 44: 1–54.

Brody, A. J.
Forth- Late Bronze Age Canaanite Mortuary Practices. In *Ashkelon I*. SAHL.
coming Winona Lake, Ind.: Eisenbrauns.

Bryan, D. B.
1973 *Texts Relating to the Marzeaḥ: A Study of an Ancient Semitic Institution*. Ph.D. Dissertation, The Johns Hopkins University.

Burns, J. B.
    1978   Necromancy and the Spirits of the Dead in the Old Testament. *Transactions of the Glasgow University Oriental Society* 26: 1–14.

Chavalas, M. W. (ed.)
    1996   *Emar: The History, Religion, and Culture of a Syrian Town in the Late Bronze Age.* Bethesda, Md.: CDL.

Collins, J. J.
    1993   On Resurrection. Pp. 394–98 in *Daniel*. Hermeneia. Minneapolis: Fortress.

Cooley, R. E.
    1968   *The Canaanite Burial Pattern in the Light of the Material Remains*. Ph.D. Dissertation, New York University.

Cooper, A., and Goldstein, B. R.
    1993   The Cult of the Dead and the Theme of Entry into the Land. *Biblical Interpretation* 1: 285–303.

Davis, J. J.
    1988   Excavation of Burials. Pp. 179–208 in *Benchmarks in Time and Culture: An Introduction to Palestinian Archaeology Dedicated to Joseph A. Callaway*, ed. J. F. Drinkard et al. Atlanta: Scholars Press.

Day, J.
    1989   *Molech: A God of Human Sacrifice in the Old Testament.* Cambridge: Cambridge University Press.

Dearman, J. A.
    1996   The Tophet in Jerusalem: Archaeology and Cultural Profile. *JNWSL* 22: 59–71.

Demarée, R. J.
    1983   *The Ȝḫ iḳr n Rᶜ-Stelae: On Ancestor Worship in Ancient Egypt.* Leiden: Nederlands Instituut voor het Nabije Oosten.

Dever, W. G.
    1995   "Will the Real Israel Please Stand Up?" Part II: Archaeology and the Religions of Ancient Israel. *BASOR* 298: 37–58.

Dietrich, M.; Loretz, O.; and Sanmartín, J.
    1976   Die ugaritischen Totengeister *rpu(m)* und die biblischen Rephaim. *UF* 8: 45–52.

Driver, G. R.
    1962   Plurima Mortis Imago. Pp. 137–43 in *Studies and Essays in Honor of Abraham A. Neuman*, ed. M. Ben-Horin et al. Leiden: Brill.

Ephᶜal, I., and Naveh, J.
    1998   Remarks on the Recently Published Moussaieff Ostraca. *IEJ* 48: 269–73.

Fleming, D.
    1992   *The Installation of Baal's High Priestess at Emar.* HSS 42. Atlanta: Scholars Press.

    1997   Two Months Joined by the Underworld with Barring and Opening of Doors. Pp. 439–42 in *The Context of Scripture, Vol. 1: Canonical Compositions from the Biblical World*, ed. W. W. Hallo and K. L. Younger. Leiden: Brill.

2000   *Time at Emar: The Cultic Calendar and the Rituals from the Diviner's Archive.* Mesopotamian Civlizations 11. Winona Lake, Ind.: Eisenbrauns.

Foster, J. L.
    1995   *Hymns, Prayers, and Songs: An Anthology of Ancient Egyptian Lyric Poetry.* Atlanta: Scholars Press.

Foxvog, D. A.
    1980   Funerary Furnishings in an Early Sumerian Text from Adab. Pp. 67–75 in Alster (1980).

Frymer-Kensky, T.
    1983   Pollution, Purification, and Purgation in Biblical Israel. Pp. 399–414 in *The Word of the Lord Shall Go Forth: Essays in Honor of David Noel Freedman in Celebration of His Sixtieth Birthday,* ed. C. L. Meyers and M. O'Connor. Winona Lake, Ind.: Eisenbrauns.

Gilbert-Peretz, D.
    1996   Ceramic Figurines. *Qedem* 35: 29–41, figs. 12–19, plates 1–10.

Gonen, R.
    1991   *Burial Patterns and Cultural Diversity in Late Bronze Age Canaan.* ASOR Dissertation Series 7. Winona Lake, Ind.: Eisenbrauns.
    1994   Burial Practices and Cultural Distinctiveness in Late Bronze Age Canaan. Pp. 77–90 in Singer (1994). [Hebrew].

Greenberg, M.
    1997   *Ezekiel 21–37.* AB 22A. New York: Doubleday.

Greenfield, J. C.
    1973   Un rite religieux araméen et ses parallèles. *RB* 80: 46–52.
    1985   Notes on the Curse Formulae of the Tell Fekherye Inscription. *RB* 92: 47–59.
    1987   Aspects of Aramean Religion. Pp. 67–78 in *Ancient Israelite Religion: Essays in Honor of Frank Moore Cross,* ed. P. D. Miller, P. D. Hanson, and S. D. McBride. Philadelphia: Fortress.

Greenhut, Z.
    1995   EB IV Tombs and Burials in Palestine. *Tel Aviv* 22: 31–46.

Greenspoon, L. J.
    1981   The Origin of the Idea of Resurrection. Pp. 247–321 in *Traditions in Transformation: Turning Points in Biblical Faith,* ed. B. Halpern and J. D. Levenson. Winona Lake, Ind.: Eisenbrauns.

Haas, V.
    1995   Death and the Afterlife in Hittite Thought. Pp. 2021–30 in Sasson et al. (1995).

Halevi, Y. K.
    1997   Militant Mercy. *The Jerusalem Report,* September 1: 18–19.

Hallo, W. W.
    1990   The Limits of Skepticism. *JAOS* 110: 187–99.

Hawkins, J. D.
    1980   Late Hittite Funerary Monuments. Pp. 213–25, plates 3–9 in Alster (1980).

Healey, J. F.
  1993   The Nabataean Tomb Inscriptions of Mada'in Salih. Oxford: Oxford University Press.
Heider, G. C.
  1985   The Cult of Molek: A Reassessment. JSOTSup 43. Sheffield: JSOT Press.
Henshaw, R. A.
  1994   Female and Male—The Cultic Personnel: The Bible and the Rest of the Ancient Near East. PTMS 31. Allison Park, Pa.: Pickwick.
Hoftijzer, J., and Jongeling, K.
  1995   Dictionary of the North-West Semitic Inscriptions. Leiden: Brill.
Holladay, J. S.
  1987   Religion in Israel and Judah under the Monarchy: An Explicitly Archaeological Approach. Pp. 249–99 in Ancient Israelite Religion: Essays in Honor of Frank Moore Cross. P. D. Miller, P. D. Hanson, and S. D. McBride. Philadelphia: Fortress.
Hornung, E.
  1995   Ancient Egyptian Religious Iconography. Pp. 1711–30 in Sasson et al. (1995).
  1999   The Ancient Egyptian Books of the Afterlife. Ithaca: Cornell University Press.
Ilan, D.
  1995   Mortuary Practices at Tel Dan in the Middle Bronze Age: A Reflection of Canaanite Society and Ideology. Pp. 117–39 in The Archaeology of Death in the Ancient Near East, ed. S. Campbell and A. Green. Oxbow Monograph 51. Oxford: Oxbow.
Illman, K. J.
  1979   Old Testament Formulas about Death. Abo, Sweden: Abo Akademi.
Johnston, P. J.
  1993   The Underworld and the Dead in the Old Testament. Ph.D. Dissertation, University of Cambridge.
  1994   The Underworld and the Dead in the Old Testament. TynBul 45/2: 415–19.
Keel, O.
  1987   The Peculiar Headrests for the Dead in First Temple Times. BARev 13/4: 50–53.
  1997   The Symbolism of the Biblical World: Ancient Near Eastern Iconography and the Book of Psalms. Reprinted, Winona Lake, Ind.: Eisenbrauns. [German original, 1972]
Keller, S. R.
  1989   Egyptian Letters to the Dead in Relation to the Old Testament and Other Near Eastern Sources. Ph.D. Dissertation, New York University.
van Keulen, P. S. F.
  1996   The Meaning of the Phrase wn'spt 'l-qbrtyk bšlwm in 2 Kings XXII 20. VT 46: 256–60.

Kletter, R.
  1996   *The Judean Pillar-Figurines and the Archaeology of Asherah.* British Archaeological Reports International Series 636. Oxford: Tempus Reparatum.
Knoppers, G.
  1992   The "God in His Temple": The Phoenician Text from Pyrgi as a Funerary Inscription. *JNES* 51: 105–20.
Lambert, W. G.
  1980   The Theology of Death. Pp. 53–66 in Alster (1980).
Levi, B.
  1975   Additional Notes on Ancestor Worship. *Beth Mikra* 21: 101–17, 171–72. [Hebrew with English summary]
Levine, B. A.
  1991   The Impure Dead and the Cult of the Dead: Polarization and Opposition in Israelite Religion. *Bitzaron* Jubilee Issue: 80–89. [Hebrew]
  1993a   *Numbers 1–20.* AB 4. New York: Doubleday.
  1993b   Silence, Sound, and the Phenomenology of Mourning in Biblical Israel. *JANES(CU)* 22: 89–105.
Levy, T. E., and Alon, D.
  1982   The Chalcolithic Mortuary Site near Meẓad Aluf, Northern Negev Desert: A Preliminary Study. *BASOR* 248: 37–59.
Lewis, T. J.
  1989   *Cults of the Dead in Ancient Israel and Ugarit.* HSM 39. Atlanta: Scholars Press.
  1991   The Ancestral Estate (*naḥălat ʾĕlōhîm*) in 2 Samuel 14:16. *JBL* 110: 597–612.
  1992a   Dead, Abode of the. Pp. 101–5 in vol. 2 of *ABD*, ed. D. N. Freedman. New York: Doubleday.
  1992b   Mot. Pp. 922–24 in vol. 4 of *ABD*, ed. D. N. Freedman. New York: Doubleday.
  1995   First Born of Death. Pp. 627–34 in *Dictionary of Deities and Demons in the Bible*, ed. K. van der Toorn, B. Becking, and P. van der Horst. Leiden: Brill.
  1996   Toward a Literary Translation of the Rapiuma Texts. Pp. 115–49 in Wyatt, Watson, and Lloyd, eds. (1996).
  1998   Divine Images and Aniconism in Ancient Israel. *JAOS* 118: 36–53.
  1999   First Born of Death. Pp. 332–35 in *Dictionary of Deities and Demons in the Bible*, ed. K. van der Toorn, B. Becking, and P. van der Horst. 2d ed. Leiden: Brill.
Lichtheim, M.
  1976   *Ancient Egyptian Literature, Vol. 2: The New Kingdom.* Berkeley: University of California Press.
Lieberman, S.
  1965   Some Aspects of After Life in Early Rabbinic Literature. Pp. 495–532 in vol. 2 of *Harry Austryn Wolfson Jubilee Volume.* Jerusalem: American Academy for Jewish Research.

Loretz, O.
1993   *Marziḥu* im ugaritischen und biblischen Ahnenkult: Zu Ps 23; 133; Am
        6,1–7 und Jer 16, 5.8. Pp. 93–144 in *Mesopotamica—Ugaritica—Biblica*,
        ed. M. Dietrich and O. Loretz. Neukirchen-Vluyn: Neukirchener Verlag.
Malamat, A.
1982   Longevity: Biblical Concepts and Some Ancient Near Eastern Parallels.
        AfO Beiheft 19: 215–23.
McCarter, P. K.
1980   *I Samuel.* AB 8. Garden City: Doubleday.
1996   Pieces of the Puzzle. *BARev* 22/2: 42–43.
McLaughlin, J. L.
1991   The *marzeaḥ* at Ugarit: A Textual and Contextual Study. *UF* 23: 265–81.
Mettinger, T. N. D.
1995   *No Graven Image? Israelite Aniconism in Its Ancient Near Eastern Context.*
        Stockholm: Almqvist & Wiksell.
Meyers, E. M.
1971–72 The Theological Implications of an Ancient Jewish Burial Custom. *JQR*
        62: 95–119.
Meyers, E. M. (ed.)
1997   *The Oxford Encyclopedia of Archaeology in the Near East.* 5 vols. New York:
        Oxford University Press.
Milgrom, J.
1990   *The JPS Torah Commentary: Numbers.* Philadelphia: Jewish Publication
        Society.
Miller, J. M.
1991   Is It Possible to Write a History of Israel without Relying on the Hebrew
        Bible? Pp. 93–102 in *The Fabric of History: Text, Artifact and Israel's Past*,
        ed. D. Edelman. JSOTSup 127. Sheffield: JSOT Press.
Moor, J. C. de
1976   Rāpiʾūma—Rephaim. *ZAW* 88: 323–45.
1995   Standing Stones and Ancestor Worship. *UF* 27: 1–20.
Moscati, S.
1988   Ostrich Eggs. Pp. 456–63 in *The Phoenicians*, ed. S. Moscati. Milan: Bom-
        piani.
Negev, A.
1971   A Nabatean Epitaph from Trans-Jordan. *IEJ* 21: 50–52.
Nicholson, E.
1986   Israelite Religion in the Pre-exilic Period: A Debate Renewed. Pp. 3–34
        in *A Word in Season: Essays in Honour of William McKane*, ed. J. D. Martin
        and P. R. Davies. JSOTSup 42. Sheffield: JSOT Press.
Nickelsburg, G. W. E.
1972   *Resurrection, Immortality, and Eternal Life in Intertestamental Judaism.*
        Cambridge: Harvard University Press.
Niwinski, A.
1988   Relativity in Iconography: Changes in the Shape and Value of Some
        Egyptian Funerary Symbols Dependent on Their Date and Authorship.

Pp. 96–104 in *Funerary Symbols and Religion*, ed. J. H. Kamstra et al. Kampen: Kok.

Olyan, S.
  1998   What Do Shaving Rites Accomplish and What Do They Signal in Biblical Ritual Contexts? *JBL* 117: 611–22.

Pardee, D.
  1988   *Les textes para-mythologiques de la 24ᵉ campagne (1961)*. Paris: Éditions Recherche sur les Civilisations.
  1983   Visiting Ditanu: The Text of RS 24.272. *UF* 15: 127–40.
  1996   Marziḥu, Kispu, and the Ugaritic Funerary Cult: A Minimalist View. Pp. 273–87 in Wyatt, Watson, and Lloyd, eds. (1996).
  2000   *Les textes rituels*. Ras Shamra–Ougarit 12. 2 volumes. Paris: Éditions Recherche sur les Civilisations.
  2001   *The Ugaritic Ritual Texts*. Writings from the Ancient World. Atlanta: Society of Biblical Literature.

Pitard, W. T.
  1992   A New Edition of the "Rāpiʾūma" Texts: KTU 1.20–22. *BASOR* 285: 33–77.
  1994   The "Libation Installations" of the Tombs at Ugarit. *BA* 57/1: 20–37.
  1996   Care for the Dead at Emar. Pp. 130–40 in Chavalas (1996).

Pope, M. H.
  1981   The Cult of the Dead at Ugarit. Pp. 159–79 in *Ugarit in Retrospect*, ed. G. D. Young. Winona Lake, Ind.: Eisenbrauns.

Porada, E.
  1980   The Iconography of Death in Mesopotamia in the Early Second Millennium B.C. Pp. 259–70 in Alster (1980).

Postgate, J. N.
  1990   Archaeology and the Texts: Bridging the Gap. *ZA* 80: 228–40.

Pryce, B. C.
  1989   *The Resurrection Motif in Hosea 5:8–6:6: An Exegetical Study*. Ph.D. Dissertation, Andrews University.

Puech, É.
  1992   Palestinian Funerary Inscriptions. Pp. 126–35 in vol. 5 of *ABD*, ed. D. N. Freedman. New York: Doubleday.

Rahmani, L. Y.
  1994   *A Catalogue of Jewish Ossuaries in the Collections of the State of Israel*. Jerusalem: Israel Antiquities Authority.

Ribar, J. W.
  1973   *Death Cult Practices in Ancient Palestine*. Ph.D. Dissertation, University of Michigan.

Rosenberg, R.
  1980   *The Concept of Biblical Sheol within the Context of Ancient Near Eastern Beliefs*. Ph.D. Dissertation, Harvard University.

Rouillard, H.
  1995   Rephaim. Cols. 1307–24 in *Dictionary of Deities and Demons in the Bible*, ed. K. van der Toorn, B. Becking, and P. van der Horst. Leiden: Brill.

1999   Rephaim. Cols. 692–700 in *Dictionary of Deities and Demons in the Bible*, ed. K. van der Toorn, B. Becking, and P. van der Horst. 2d ed. Leiden: Brill.

Rouillard, H., and Tropper, J.

1987a   *Trpym*, rituels de guérison et culte des ancêtres d'après 1 Samuel XIX 11–17 et les textes parallèles d'Assur et de Nuzi. *VT* 37: 340–61.

1987b   Vom kanaanäischen Ahnenkult zur Zauberei: Eine Auslegungsgeschichte zu den hebräischen Begriffen *ʾwb* und *ydʿny*. *UF* 19: 235–54.

Sasson, J. M., et al.

1995   *Civilizations of the Ancient Near East*. 5 vols. New York: Scribner's.

Schmidt, B. B.

1994   *Israel's Beneficent Dead: Ancestor Cult and Necromancy in Ancient Israelite Religion and Tradition*. Forschungen zum Alten Testament 11. Tübingen: Mohr. [North American edition, Winona Lake, Ind.: Eisenbrauns, 1996]

1995   The "Witch" of En-Dor, 1 Samuel 28, and Ancient Near Eastern Necromancy. Pp. 111–29 in *Ancient Magic and Ritual Power*, ed. M. Meyer and P. Mirecki. Leiden: Brill.

1996a   A Re-evaluation of the Ugaritic King List (KTU 1.113). Pp. 289–304 in Wyatt, Watson, and Lloyd, editors (1996).

1996b   The Gods and the Dead of the Domestic Cult at Emar: A Reassessment. Pp. 141–63 in Chavalas, ed. (1996).

Schulman, A. R.

1986   Some Observations on the *ꜣḫ iḳr n Rʿ*-Stelae. *BiOr* 43: 302–48.

Scurlock, J.

1988   *Magical Means of Dealing with Ghosts in Ancient Mesopotamia*. Ph.D. Dissertation, University of Chicago.

1991   *Taklimtu*: A Display of Grave Goods? *NABU* (nº1—Mars): #3.

1995a   Death and the Afterlife in Ancient Mesopotamian Thought. Pp. 1883–93 in Sasson et al. (1995).

1995b   Magical Uses of Ancient Mesopotamian Festivals of the Dead. Pp. 93–107 in *Ancient Magic and Ritual Power*, ed. M. Meyer and P. Mirecki. Leiden: Brill.

1997   Ghosts in the Ancient Near East: Weak or Powerful? *HUCA* 68: 77–96.

Seligson, M.

1951   *The Meaning of nepeš mēt in the Old Testament*. Helsinki: Societas Orientalis Fennica.

Shanks, H.

1996   Death Knell for Israel Archaeology? Why Ultra-Orthodox Jews Should Favor Archaeological Excavations of Graves. *BARev* 22/5: 48–53.

1997   Three Shekels for the Lord. *BARev* 23/6: 28–32.

Shiloh, D.

1997   Fierce Protest over Bones Threatens to Halt Archaeology in Israel. *BARev* 23/6: 54–55, 76–77.

Sigrist, M.

1982   Miscellanea. *JCS* 34: 242–52.

Singer, I.
1994   *Graves and Burial Practices in Israel in the Ancient Period.* Jerusalem: Israel Exploration Society. [Hebrew]

Skaist, A.
1980   The Ancestor Cult and Succession in Mesopotamia. Pp. 123–28 in Alster (1980).

Smelik, K. A. D.
1995   Moloch, Molech or Molk-Sacrifice? A Reassessment of the Evidence Concerning the Hebrew Term Molekh. *SJOT* 9: 133–42.

Smith, M. S.
1992   Rephaim. Pp. 674–76 in vol. 5 of *ABD*, ed. D. N. Freedman. New York: Doubleday.
1993   The Invocation of Deceased Ancestors in Psalm 49:12c. *JBL* 112: 105–7.
1994   *The Ugaritic Baal Cycle.* VTSup 55. Leiden: Brill.
1996   Review of Schmidt, *Israel's Beneficent Dead. CBQ* 58: 724–25.

Smith, M. S., and Bloch-Smith, E.
1988   Death and Afterlife in Ugarit and Israel. *JAOS* 108: 277–84.

Smith, P.
1997   Skeletal Remains. Pp. 51–56 in vol. 5 of Meyers (1997).

Spronk, K.
1986   *Beatific Afterlife in Ancient Israel and in the Ancient Near East.* AOAT 219. Neukirchen-Vluyn: Neukirchener Verlag.

Stager, L.
1985   The Archaeology of the Family in Ancient Israel. *BASOR* 260: 1–35.

Sysling, H.
1996   *Teḥiyyat ha-Metim: The Resurrection of the Dead in the Palestinian Targums of the Pentateuch and Parallel Traditions in Classical Rabbinic Literature.* Tübingen: Mohr.

Tarragon, J.-M. de
1995   Witchcraft, Magic, and Divination in Canaan and Ancient Israel. Pp. 2071–80 in Sasson et al. (1995).

Taylor, J. H.
2001   *Death and the Afterlife in Ancient Egypt.* Chicago: University of Chicago Press.

Toorn, K. van der
1988   Echoes of Judaean Necromancy in Isaiah 28,7–22. *ZAW* 100: 199–217.
1991   Funerary Rituals and Beatific Afterlife in Ugaritic Texts and in the Bible. *BiOr* 48: 39–66.
1993   Ilib and the "God of the Father." *UF* 25: 379–87.
1994   Gods and Ancestors in Emar and Nuzi. *ZA* 84: 38–59.
1996a   *Family Religion in Babylonia, Syria and Israel.* Leiden: Brill.
1996b   Ancestors and Anthroponyms: Kinship Terms as Theophoric Elements in Hebrew Names. *ZAW* 108: 1–11.

Tromp, N. J.
1969   *Primitive Conceptions of Death and the Nether World in the Old Testament.* Rome: Pontifical Biblical Institute.

Tropper, J.
    1989   *Nekromantie: Totenbefragung im Alten Orient und im Alten Testament.* AOAT 223. Neukirchen-Vluyn: Neukirchener Verlag.
    1993   *Die Inschriften von Zincirli: Neue Edition und vergleichende Grammatik des phönizischen, sam'alischen und aramäischen Textkorpus.* ALASP 6. Münster: Ugarit-Verlag.

Ucko, P. J.
    1969   Ethnography and Archaeological Interpretation of Funerary Remains. *World Archaeology* 1: 262–80.

Van Winkle, D. W.
    1997   The Meaning of *yād wāšēm* in Isaiah LVI 5. *VT* 47: 378–85.

Wächter, L.
    1967   *Der Tod im Alten Testament.* Stuttgart: Calwer.

Ward, E. F. de
    1992   Mourning Customs in 1, 2 Samuel. *JJS* 23: 1–27, 145–66.

Watkins, C.
    1992   The Indo-European Origin of English; and Indo-European and the Indo-Europeans. Pp. xxiv–xxv and 2081–89 in *The American Heritage Dictionary of the English Languages.* 3d ed. Boston: Houghton Mifflin.

Wente, E.
    1990   *Letters from Ancient Egypt.* Atlanta: Scholars Press.

Wright, D. P.
    1985   Purification from Corpse-Contamination in Numbers XXXI 19–24. *VT* 35: 213–23.

Wyatt, N.; Watson, W. G. E.; and Lloyd, J. B. (eds.)
    1996   *Ugarit: Religion and Culture. Proceedings of the International Colloquium on Ugarit, Religion and Culture, Edinburgh, July 1994—Essays Presented in Honour of John C. L. Gibson.* UBL 12. Münster: Ugarit-Verlag.

Xella, P.
    199   Death and the Afterlife in Canaanite and Hebrew Thought. Pp. 2059–70 in Sasson et al. (1995).
    1980   Sur la nourriture des morts: Un aspect de l'eschatologie mésopotamienne. Pp. 151–60 in Alster (1980).

Zias, J.
    1991   Death and Disease in Ancient Israel. *BA* 54/3: 146–59.
    1997   Diseases and Their Treatment in Ancient Israel from a Palaeopathological Perspective. *Qadmoniot* 30/1: 54–59. [Hebrew]

Zimmerli, W.
    1983   *Ezekiel 2.* Hermeneia. Philadelphia: Fortress.

Index of Authors

Index of Scripture

Hebrew Bible

Deuterocanonical Literature

New Testament